READERS' GUIDES TO ESSENTIAL CRITICISM

CONSULTANT EDITOR: NICOLAS TREDELL

Published

Thomas P. Adler	Tennessee Wi on a Hot Tir
Pascale Aebischer	Jacobean Drama
Lucie Armitt	George Eliot: *Adam Bede/The Mill on the Floss/ Middlemarch*
Simon Avery	Thomas Hardy: *The Mayor of Casterbridge/Jude the Obscure*
Paul Baines	Daniel Defoe: *Robinson Crusoe/Moll Flanders*
Brian Baker	Science Fiction
Annika Bautz	Jane Austen: *Sense and Sensibility/Pride and Prejudice/Emma*
Matthew Beedham	The Novels of Kazuo Ishiguro
Richard Beynon	D. H. Lawrence: *The Rainbow/Women in Love*
Peter Boxall	Samuel Beckett: *Waiting for Godot/Endgame*
Claire Brennan	The Poetry of Sylvia Plath
Susan Bruce	Shakespeare: *King Lear*
Sandie Byrne	Jane Austen: *Mansfield Park*
Sandie Byrne	The Poetry of Ted Hughes
Alison Chapman	Elizabeth Gaskell: *Mary Barton/North and South*
Peter Childs	The Fiction of Ian McEwan
Christine Clegg	Vladimir Nabokov: *Lolita*
John Coyle	James Joyce: *Ulysses/A Portrait of the Artist as a Young Man*
Martin Coyle	Shakespeare: *Richard II*
Sarah Davison	Modernist Literatures
Sarah Dewar-Watson	Tragedy
Justin D. Edwards	Postcolonial Literature
Michael Faherty	The Poetry of W. B. Yeats
Sarah Gamble	The Fiction of Angela Carter
Jodi-Anne George	*Beowulf*
Jodi-Anne George	Chaucer: The General Prologue to *The Canterbury Tales*
Jane Goldman	Virginia Woolf: *To the Lighthouse/The Waves*
Huw Griffiths	Shakespeare: *Hamlet*
Vanessa Guignery	The Fiction of Julian Barnes
Louisa Hadley	The Fiction of A. S. Byatt
Sarah Haggarty and Jon Mee	William Blake: *Songs of Innocence and Experience*
Geoffrey Harvey	Thomas Hardy: *Tess of the d'Urbervilles*
Paul Hendon	The Poetry of W. H. Auden
Terry Hodgson	The Plays of Tom Stoppard for Stage, Radio, TV and Film
William Hughes	Bram Stoker: *Dracula*
Stuart Hutchinson	Mark Twain: *Tom Sawyer/Huckleberry Finn*
Stuart Hutchinson	Edith Wharton: *The House of Mirth/The Custom of the Country*
Betty Jay	E. M. Forster: *A Passage to India*
Aaron Kelly	Twentieth-Century Irish Literature
Elmer Kennedy-Andrews	Nathaniel Hawthorne: *The Scarlet Letter*
Elmer Kennedy-Andrews	The Poetry of Seamus Heaney
Daniel Lea	George Orwell: *Animal Farm/Nineteen Eighty-Four*
Rachel Lister	Alice Walker: *The Color Purple*
Sara Lodge	Charlotte Brontë: *Jane Eyre*
Philippa Lyon	Twentieth-Century War Poetry

Merja Makinen	The Novels of Jeanette Winterson
Stephen Marino	Arthur Miller: *Death of a Salesman/The Crucible*
Matt McGuire	Contemporary Scottish Literature
Timothy Milnes	Wordsworth: *The Prelude*
Jago Morrison	The Fiction of Chinua Achebe
Merritt Moseley	The Fiction of Pat Barker
Carl Plasa	Toni Morrison: *Beloved*
Carl Plasa	Jean Rhys: *Wide Sargasso Sea*
Nicholas Potter	Shakespeare: *Antony and Cleopatra*
Nicholas Potter	Shakespeare: *Othello*
Nicholas Potter	Shakespeare's Late Plays: *Pericles/Cymbeline/The Winter's Tale/The Tempest*
Steven Price	The Plays, Screenplays and Films of David Mamet
Berthold Schoene-Harwood	Mary Shelley: *Frankenstein*
Nicholas Seager	The Rise of the Novel
Nick Selby	T. S. Eliot: *The Waste Land*
Nick Selby	Herman Melville: *Moby Dick*
Nick Selby	The Poetry of Walt Whitman
David Smale	Salman Rushdie: *Midnight's Children/The Satanic Verses*
Patsy Stoneman	Emily Brontë: *Wuthering Heights*
Susie Thomas	Hanif Kureishi
Nicolas Tredell	Joseph Conrad: *Heart of Darkness*
Nicolas Tredell	Charles Dickens: *Great Expectations*
Nicolas Tredell	William Faulkner: *The Sound and the Fury/As I Lay Dying*
Nicolas Tredell	F. Scott Fitzgerald: *The Great Gatsby*
Nicolas Tredell	Shakespeare: *A Midsummer Night's Dream*
Nicolas Tredell	Shakespeare: *Macbeth*
Nicolas Tredell	Shakespeare: The Tragedies
Nicolas Tredell	The Fiction of Martin Amis
David Wheatley	Contemporary British Poetry
Martin Willis	Literature and Science
Matthew Woodcock	Shakespeare: *Henry V*
Gillian Woods	Shakespeare: *Romeo and Juliet*
Angela Wright	Gothic Fiction
Michael H. Whitworth	Virginia Woolf: *Mrs Dalloway*

Forthcoming

Pat Pinsent and Clare Walsh	Children's Literature
Enit Steiner	Jane Austen: *Northanger Abbey/Persuasion*
Britta Martens	The Poetry of Robert Browning
Nick Bentley	Contemporary British Fiction
Kate Watson	Crime and Detective Fiction
Andrew Wylie and Catherine Rees	The Plays of Harold Pinter

Readers' Guides to Essential Criticism
Series Standing Order ISBN 978–1–4039–0108–8
(outside North America only)

You can receive future titles in this series as they are published by placing a standing order. Please contact your bookseller or, in the case of difficulty, write to us at the address below with your name and address, the title of the series and the ISBN quoted above.

Customer Services Department, Macmillan Distribution Ltd, Houndmills, Basingstoke, Hampshire, RG21 6XS, UK

Virginia Woolf: *Mrs Dalloway*

MICHAEL H. WHITWORTH

Consultant Editor: NICOLAS TREDELL

macmillan education palgrave

© Michael H. Whitworth 2015

All rights reserved. No reproduction, copy or transmission of this publication may be made without written permission.

No portion of this publication may be reproduced, copied or transmitted save with written permission or in accordance with the provisions of the Copyright, Designs and Patents Act 1988, or under the terms of any licence permitting limited copying issued by the Copyright Licensing Agency, Saffron House, 6–10 Kirby Street, London EC1N 8TS.

Any person who does any unauthorized act in relation to this publication may be liable to criminal prosecution and civil claims for damages.

The author has asserted his right to be identified as the author of this work in accordance with the Copyright, Designs and Patents Act 1988.

First published 2015 by
PALGRAVE

Palgrave in the UK is an imprint of Macmillan Publishers Limited, registered in England, company number 785998, of 4 Crinan Street, London, N1 9XW.

Palgrave Macmillan in the US is a division of St Martin's Press LLC, 175 Fifth Avenue, New York, NY 10010.

Palgrave is a global imprint of the above companies and is represented throughout the world.

Palgrave® and Macmillan® are registered trademarks in the United States, the United Kingdom, Europe and other countries.

ISBN 978-0-230-50642-8   ISBN 978-1-137-54792-7 (eBook)
DOI 10.1007/978-1-137-54792-7

This book is printed on paper suitable for recycling and made from fully managed and sustained forest sources. Logging, pulping and manufacturing processes are expected to conform to the environmental regulations of the country of origin.

A catalogue record for this book is available from the British Library.

A catalog record for this book is available from the Library of Congress.

Library of Congress Cataloging-in-Publication Data

Whitworth, Michael H.
  Virginia Woolf – Mrs Dalloway / Michael Whitworth.
    pages cm. –– (Readers' guides to essential criticism)
  Summary: "Virginia Woolf's Mrs Dalloway (1925) has long been recognised as one of her outstanding achievements and one of the canonical works of modernist fiction. Each generation of readers has found something new within its pages, which is reflected in its varying critical reception over the last ninety years. As the novel concerns itself with women's place in society, war and madness, it was naturally interpreted differently in the ages of second wave feminism, the Vietnam War and the anti-psychiatry movement. This has, of course, created a rather daunting number of different readings. Michael H. Whitworth contextualizes the most important critical work and draws attention to the distinctive discourses of critical schools, noting their endurance and interplay. Whitworth also examines how adaptations, such as Michael Cunningham's The Hours, can act as critical works in themselves, creating an invaluable guide to Mrs Dalloway"–– Provided by publisher.
  Includes bibliographical references and index.
  1. Woolf, Virginia, 1882–1941. Mrs. Dalloway. 2. Psychological fiction, English—History and criticism. 3. Married women in literature. 4. Modernism (Literature)—Great Britain. I. Title.
  PR6045.O72M739 2015
  823'.912—dc23   2015023933

For Roxanne and George

CONTENTS

ACKNOWLEDGEMENTS x

ABBREVIATIONS xi

INTRODUCTION 1

CHAPTER ONE 7
Early Responses

Examines the first reviews of *Mrs Dalloway* and the earliest works of scholarly criticism. It begins with reviews in British and American newspapers and magazines in 1925, before turning to treatments by major critics in the 1930s. It then considers the critical books by Bennett and Blackstone that appeared soon after Woolf's death, and three critical works that embody the close-reading methodology dominant in the 1950s and 1960s.

CHAPTER TWO 33
Recovering Woolf: Criticism in the Era of Second-Wave Feminism

Examines the recovery of Woolf's reputation in the late 1960s, occasioned by a revival of interest in the Bloomsbury Group and by the 'second wave' of feminism. It contrasts different approaches to the relation of *Mrs Dalloway* to James Joyce's *Ulysses*, and looks at the recovery of the political dimension to her work in criticism by Ralph Samuelson, Herbert Marder and Lee R. Edwards.

CHAPTER THREE 51
Woolf and Philosophy

Considers the various ways that Woolf's work has been related to systems of philosophy or has been understood as embodying a philosophy of her own. It looks at approaches to Woolf as a Bergsonian, an existentialist, a phenomenologist and an epistemologist.

vii

CHAPTER FOUR 74

Structuralism and Post-Structuralism

Looks at works from 1977 to 1991 that take structuralist linguistics and criticism and/or post-structuralist thought as their starting point. Beginning with David Lodge's use of the opposition of the metaphoric and metonymic, it turns then to Nancy Armstrong's article on Woolf's manipulation of literary convention, Teresa L. Ebert's article on metaphor and metonymy and Edward Bishop's article on writing, speech and silence. Finally it discusses pieces by Herbert Marder and Pamela Caughie that analyse the categories used in critical discourse.

CHAPTER FIVE 86

Woolf and Psychoanalysis

Considers various forms of psychoanalytic criticism as applied to *Mrs Dalloway*. Beginning with Mark Spilka on mourning, it turns to Suzette Henke's Freudian diagnosis of Septimus. It then considers several feminist critics who broke with Freudian assumptions: Elizabeth Abel's work on mothers and daughters, and the Kristevan work of Jean Wyatt and Makiko Minow-Pinkney. It looks at treatments of the problem of mourning in *Mrs Dalloway* by Susan Bennett Smith and Christine Froula, and work on trauma by Marlene Briggs and Karen DeMeester.

CHAPTER SIX 110

Sexuality and the Body

Considers questions of sexuality and the body. It begins with Emily Jensen on Clarissa Dalloway's lesbianism, and then turns to George Ella Lyon, Teresa Fulker and William Greenslade on the body. In the final section it turns to a historicized conception of lesbian culture in works by Patricia Cramer and Eileen Barrett.

CHAPTER SEVEN 124

Historicist Approaches

Surveys a range of historicist approaches, beginning with the historical recovery of the Bloomsbury Group, before turning to Alex Zwerdling's pioneering 1977 article on *Mrs Dalloway* and Jeremy Tambling's Foucauldian 1989 article. It then considers work on the themes of war, empire and global politics, and the city. In conclusion it examines more recent approaches to the Bloomsbury Group.

CHAPTER EIGHT 148

Mrs Dalloway and *The Hours*

Asks how creative adaptations – the principal example being Michael Cunningham's *The Hours* (1998) – can act as critical works, and looks at a range of recent criticism which has taken Cunningham's novel as its starting point.

CONCLUSION 157

Asks why perceptions of *Mrs Dalloway* have changed over the ninety years since its publication, and considers how and why critical agendas might change in the coming years.

NOTES 160

BIBLIOGRAPHY 169

INDEX 175

ACKNOWLEDGEMENTS

I'd like to thank the students who've studied Woolf with me, on the Woolf module at Bangor, for the Modern and Special Authors papers at Oxford, and on the M.St. and doctoral programmes at Oxford. I'd also like to thank the librarians at the Bodleian Library, Merton College Library and the English Faculty Library for their assistance. Thanks to all at Palgrave for their patience, and to the series editor Nicolas Tredell for his helpful feedback on the first draft. Thanks too to Kristin Ewins for encouraging words about an early draft of Chapter 7, and special thanks to Roxanne Selby for wisdom about the realities of publishing.

ABBREVIATIONS

In-text references to Woolf's works use the following abbreviations:

CSF *The Complete Shorter Fiction*, ed. S. Dick, revised edition. London: Hogarth, 1989.
D *The Diary of Virginia Woolf*, ed. A. O. Bell and A. McNeillie, 5 vols. London: Hogarth, 1977–84.
E *Essays of Virginia Woolf*, ed. A. McNeillie and Stuart N. Clarke, 6 vols. London: Hogarth, 1996–2011.
L *The Letters of Virginia Woolf*, ed. N. Nicolson and J. Trautmann Banks, 6 vols. London: Hogarth, 1975–80.
MD *Mrs Dalloway*, ed. D. Bradshaw. Oxford: Oxford University Press, 2000.
ROO *A Room of One's Own* in *A Room of One's Own and Three Guineas*, ed. M. Shiach. Oxford: Oxford University Press, 1992.
TL *To the Lighthouse*, ed. D. Bradshaw. Oxford: Oxford University Press, 2006.

In Chapter Eight, *Hours* denotes Michael Cunningham's *The Hours* (London: Fourth Estate, 1998); in other chapters, it denotes Helen Wussow's 1996 edition of the manuscript of Woolf's novel.

All quotations from *Mrs Dalloway* are referenced to David Bradshaw's Oxford World's Classics edition, regardless of the edition used by the critic. In a small number of cases, due either to critics misquoting, or to variations between editions, the quotations in the text are not identical to those in the Oxford World's Classics text. Similarly, references to Woolf's essays are keyed to the *Essays of Virginia Woolf*.

INTRODUCTION

■ The emphasis is laid upon such unexpected places that at first it seems as if there were no emphasis at all; and then, as the eyes accustom themselves to twilight and discern the shapes of things in a room, we see how complete the story is, how profound, [...]. (*E3* 35) □

Virginia Woolf's remarks in 'Modern Novels' (April 1919) about the story 'Gusev' by Anton Chekhov could equally well apply to the novel she would publish six years later, *Mrs Dalloway*. Without a plot in the conventional sense, and without chapter divisions, it lacks the conventional scaffolding of the novel as it was then understood; this, and the richness of its prose, allow readers great freedom about where to place the emphasis. Although the novel's focus on its titular central character makes *Mrs Dalloway* easier to discern than the crepuscular scene imagined by Woolf, readers have disagreed about the relative importance of Septimus Warren Smith and Peter Walsh; although readers have appreciated the clarity of temporal structure created by the chimes of Big Ben, they have recognized that clock time is an artificial structure.

When Woolf published the novel, the academic study of English literature was in its infancy, and the diverse approaches taken to *Mrs Dalloway* record the history of a discipline that has constantly innovated and that has been characterized by self-reflexive debate about its fundamental aims. The approaches taken also register, though not always directly, the changing social composition of the student body, and social movements and historical events from beyond the world of literature. It is unimaginable that a novel so concerned with women's place in society, with war, and with madness, could not have been interpreted differently in the ages of the second wave of feminism, the Vietnam War, and the anti-psychiatry movement.

When Virginia Woolf first conceived of *Mrs Dalloway* in August 1922, it was as a short story, 'Mrs Dalloway in Bond Street'; Clarissa Dalloway and her politician husband Richard had been minor characters in Woolf's first novel, *The Voyage Out* (1915). By October 1922, the narrative had developed into a book, though Woolf would still make use of the short story, publishing it in the American periodical *The Dial* in July 1923. By June 1923 she was referring to the book as

1

'The Hours', and it is under that title that her surviving manuscript draft has been edited by Helen Wussow. The discrepancies between the story, the manuscript and the published text have been valuable to scholars. Woolf finished her first draft in October 1924 (*D2* 316), and soon after began revisions; she had sent it off to the printers by the first week of 1925. Curiously, she could not leave the characters behind, and she wrote six more 'Mrs Dalloway' stories between March and May 1925, though they were not published in her lifetime; they were first gathered together as *Mrs Dalloway's Party*, in an edition by Stella McNichol, and are now reprinted in the *Complete Shorter Fiction*. *Mrs Dalloway* itself was published in Britain by Leonard and Virginia Woolf's own firm, The Hogarth Press, on 14 May 1925, and in America on the same day by Harcourt Brace.[1] In 1928 Harcourt Brace brought out the 'Modern Library' edition of the novel; in the introduction that she wrote specially for that edition, Woolf spoke of Septimus as Clarissa's 'double' (*E4* 549), a remark that has been particularly influential.

The remarks that Woolf made about *Mrs Dalloway* in her diaries have been important to critics. They first became widely available with Leonard Woolf's selection from the diaries, *A Writer's Diary* (1953), and available in full when the second volume of the five-volume edition appeared in 1978. Particular prominence has been given to her claim that 'I have almost too many ideas. I want to give life & death, sanity & insanity; I want to criticise the social system, & to show it at work, at its most intense' (*D2* 248). Such remarks have often been taken as insights into Woolf's true intentions, but it should be recognized that her diary was written with an audience in mind, at least indirectly. One such audience was an older Virginia, reading the diary as she wrote her memoirs; another was her husband Leonard. Moreover, her discussions of her works are often framed by references to other writers and to critical responses: the remark about having 'too many ideas' sprang from Woolf's seeing a posthumously published remark by her contemporary Katherine Mansfield; in the same entry, her remarks about creating memorable characters are in dialogue with the novelist and critic Arnold Bennett. The diaries are valuable sources, but need to be taken with a pinch of salt, understood not as direct revelations but as fragments of dialogues. And while Woolf's 1928 Introduction to the 'Modern Library' edition was intended as a public document, it does not necessarily embody the whole truth. Woolf's claim that Septimus was intended to be Clarissa's 'double' has generated as much disagreement as it has insight. It is worth remembering the remark about Woolf's friend T. S. Eliot: 'in the course of time a poet may become merely a reader in respect to his own works, forgetting his original meaning – or without forgetting, merely changing'.[2] On this basis, one might number Woolf's diary entries and her Introduction among the early responses.

Critical movements and practices do not appear and disappear instantaneously on the chime of midnight as one decade passes into another. Critics continue to work in an older mode, and to produce insightful work, even when critical trends have moved on; emergent critical practices sometimes articulate themselves in an inherited idiom; monographs rework critical articles published many years previously. For these reasons, the present guide divides Woolf criticism not into rigid chronological segments, but into eight phases.

Chapter One takes in a span of fifty years, from the first reviews of *Mrs Dalloway* to Avrom Fleishman's reading of it in *Virginia Woolf* (1975), and is itself chronologically subdivided. The first section examines the reviews that appeared on publication of the novel in 1925. The second considers comments that appeared during Woolf's lifetime in articles and in the first three critical books on her work, and sees the establishment of one line of opposition from the writers associated with the journal *Scrutiny*. The third section considers the sympathetic accounts by Bennett and Blackstone that appeared in the 1940s after Woolf's death. The final section of the chapter turns to three accounts of *Mrs Dalloway* that appeared when the close-reading mode of New Criticism was at its height.

It is widely accepted that Woolf's critical fortunes suffered in the twenty-five years after her death. Chapter Two examines the recovery of her reputation in the late 1960s, occasioned by a revival of interest in the Bloomsbury Group and by the 'second wave' of feminism. By this time, modernist literature had become part of the syllabus on most English literature degrees, but the canon was shaped around the poetry and criticism of T. S. Eliot and the fiction of James Joyce. One struggle for *Mrs Dalloway* was to be seen as something more or other than a copy of Joyce's *Ulysses*, and the chapter considers Patrick Parrinder and Hugh Kenner, of the hostile critics, and Carolyn Heilbrun and Harvena Richter of the sympathetic ones. The recovery of Woolf was a recovery of the political dimension of her work. While this recovery gathered pace in the late 1960s and through the 1970s, as far back as 1958 Ralph Samuelson had expressed frustration with the formalist mode of criticism, and his article is examined in some detail, followed by works by Herbert Marder (1968) and Lee R. Edwards (1977).

Another way of freeing Woolf from formalism, and of countering the *Scrutiny* charge that her work lacks a sense of values, was to relate it to a system of philosophy, and Chapter Three examines the various forms such work can take. It returns to the earliest reviews to establish the origins of this critical tendency, before making a survey of articles and books from 1946 to 2000; it takes in Woolf as a Bergsonian, an existentialist, a phenomenologist and an epistemologist.

Chapter Four turns to the influence of structuralist and post-structuralist literary theory in the period 1977 to 1991. Structuralism as a movement in linguistics began with the posthumously published lectures of Ferdinand de Saussure, and as a movement in anthropology it was established by the work of Claude Lévi-Strauss in the 1950s and 1960s; French literary critics, notably Roland Barthes, worked in a structuralist mode in the 1960s, but it became known as a movement in the English-speaking world only in the late 1960s and 1970s. It was soon overtaken by post-structuralist thought that was sceptical about the claims of structuralism to be a 'scientific' method and that questioned the stability of structure. The chapter considers works by David Lodge, Nancy Armstrong, Teresa L. Ebert, Edward Bishop, Herbert Marder and Pamela Caughie.

Chapter Five examines the history of psychoanalytic criticism of Woolf. While there was a brief flurry of interest in the 1950s centred on the journal *Literature and Psychology*, psychoanalytic work came into its own only when relevant autobiographical texts had been published in the 1970s. The chapter considers work by Mark Spilka and Suzette Henke in a Freudian tradition, before turning to critics who, under the influence of feminism and structuralism, broke with Freudian assumptions: Elizabeth Abel, Jean Wyatt and Makiko Minow-Pinkney. It then turns to the problem of mourning in *Mrs Dalloway*, as considered by Susan Bennett Smith and Christine Froula, and to work on trauma by Marlene Briggs and Karen DeMeester.

For many years Woolf's lesbian sexuality was ignored, or conflated with the ideal of androgyny that she advocated for writers in *A Room of One's Own* (1929). The turning point came with the publication of important theoretical works by Audre Lorde and Adrienne Rich in 1979 and 1980. Furthermore, under the influence of Michel Foucault, critics began to recognize the historical variability of conceptions both of sexuality and of the body, concepts previously understood as biological, natural and historically invariable. Chapter Six considers questions of sexuality and the body, beginning with Emily Jensen on Clarissa's lesbianism, turning to George Ella Lyon, Teresa Fulker and William Greenslade on the body, and then returning to a more historicized conception of lesbian culture in works by Patricia Cramer and Eileen Barrett.

Historicist approaches to *Mrs Dalloway* may be traced to Alex Zwerdling's pioneering essay 'Mrs Dalloway and the Social System' (1977), but the advance of historicist work was impeded by an association with stolidly traditional scholarship; however, in the course of the 1980s the New Historicism, beginning as a movement in early modern studies, won acceptance for historicisms old and new. Chapter Seven begins by tracing another origin of historicization in Woolf studies, the historical reconstruction of the Bloomsbury Group, before turning to Alex Zwerdling and the Foucauldian work of Jeremy Tambling. It then considers three themes that have been particularly important for historicist critics: war (in the work of Sue Thomas, Karen Levenback, David Bradshaw and Masami Usui); empire and global politics (in the work of Trudi Tate and Kathy Phillips); and the city (in the work of Susan Merrill Squier, Reginald Abbott, Leena Kore Schröder and Rachel Bowlby). Finally, it examines two historicist approaches to Bloomsbury in an essay by Brian Shaffer and a co-authored piece by Elyse Graham and Pericles Lewis. Creative works may constitute an oblique form of commentary on and criticism of earlier works, and in Chapter Eight I turn to criticism that takes as its starting point Michael Cunningham's *The Hours* (1998).

The conclusion asks why perceptions of *Mrs Dalloway* have changed over the ninety years since its publication, and considers how and why critical agendas might change in the coming years. It notes some recent trends in modernist studies, such as transnationalism, and recent growth areas in Woolf studies, such as ecocriticism and animal studies.

Mrs Dalloway has stimulated an extraordinary range of responses and interpretations. Nevertheless, certain scenes have been of recurrent interest: the scene in which Clarissa contemplates the 'something central which permeated', culminating in the image of 'a match burning in a crocus' (*MD* 27), which has been particularly important for considerations of sexuality; Clarissa's consideration of her dispersed identity, in her own thoughts (*MD* 8) and as recalled by Peter (*MD* 129–30); the scene in which Clarissa contemplates Septimus's suicide, the 'thing... that mattered' and the 'it' which he had flung away (MD 156); and the moment that follows in which she decides that she 'must go back' to her party (MD 158).

Moreover, certain questions about *Mrs Dalloway* have recurred through its history, sometimes tackled consciously by critics, sometimes answered implicitly. Critics have been unable to agree about whether the novel has one, two or three central characters. In 1945 Joan Bennett identified five, though she gave greater prominence to Clarissa and Peter than to the other three, Richard, Septimus and Rezia.[3] In 1960 Frank Bradbrook, a critic unsympathetic to Woolf, dismissed the Septimus scenes as a 'macabre ... episode'.[4] Others have seen the parallel between Clarissa and Septimus as essential. Critics have been uncertain whether the novel celebrates Clarissa as a heroine (see, for example, Lucio Ruotolo) or satirizes her (for example, Trudi Tate). They have been puzzled by the novel's unsympathetic presentation of Miss Kilman, given that it presents Clarissa's attraction to Sally Seton sympathetically. Readers of the present guide will discover other recurring points of interest.

CHAPTER ONE

Early Responses

Reviews (1925–1926)

Woolf's earliest reviewers were mostly writing for daily newspapers or for weekly reviews that combined political commentary with critical reviews of the arts. They were concerned to place *Mrs Dalloway* in relation to other works, to explain to their readers what kind of work it was, and to indicate where the centre of interest might lie. They were not, on the whole, concerned to make interpretative statements, though some reviews anticipate later critical concerns; nor were they particularly alert to the politics of the novel.

The title created the focus for many reviewers, with the result that most accounts fail to differentiate Septimus Warren Smith and Peter Walsh from the other more fleeting characters and observers, and so accord them little significance. The first review to appear, on 14 May 1925, in the English-language Welsh newspaper the *Western Mail*, registered some confusion: 'Mrs Dalloway doesn't interest us very much, nor do any of the characters drawn into this somewhat bewildering jumble. Something might have been made of Rezia Warren Smith, the Italian wife of a lunatic ex-soldier, if she had been allowed to evolve naturally. The remainder of the people, who skip into a page and out of it with no apparent purpose, are of no consequence.'[1] In a more perceptive review which appeared on the same day in the feminist political weekly *Time and Tide*, Sylvia Lynd (c.1888–1952) took Woolf to task for imposing Septimus on the narrative. Whenever Clarissa appears, she said, 'we, like her friends and lovers, rejoice and admire her'.[2] Lynd believed that Clarissa should have dominated the narrative.

■ As it is, some of the minor characters take far too much room. Septimus Warren Smith, the wretched neurotic, is a huge piece of irrelevance. I don't believe in the coincidences of Peter Walsh's seeing him on his way to visit the mental specialist in the morning and on the way to the mortuary after committing suicide in the afternoon. I refuse to accept him from Mrs Woolf as a character at all. □

7

She felt that Septimus was an unconvincing copy of Leonard Bast in E. M. Forster's *Howards End* (1910), and implied he better belonged in one of John Galsworthy's realist and socially committed novels: 'He lives in "Howards End" talking about "dear R. L. S." [i.e. Robert Louis Stevenson] and for the last dozen years he has been visiting Mr Galsworthy.' In a remark that anticipates the concerns of later critics, she recognized that he brought 'a touch of the dark tragic side of things'; but she felt that 'his appearance as the thought of a doctor and the "news-item" of a bore would have been enough'.[3]

Another perceptive and reflective review, by the novelist and critic Richard Hughes (1900–76), appeared on 16 May. However, for all his perceptiveness, when Hughes turned to summarizing the story, he identified the 'sole principal event' as the return of Peter Walsh. He went on to explain that other characters 'are in many cases not even acquainted with the principals – sometimes simply people they pass in the street, or even people who merely see the same aeroplane in the sky. Towards the end, one of these strangers flings himself from a window.'[4] The dismissive description partly serves to demonstrate the inadequacy of a plot summary to this novel – 'Chronicle is an ass', says Hughes – but Hughes's near-omission of Septimus suggests that he failed to perceive the character's place in the pattern. On 21 May, the *Times Literary Supplement*'s reviewer, Arthur Sydney McDowall (1877–1933), while recognizing that Septimus has his own distinct story, and that it made a 'poignant' contrast to that of Clarissa, nevertheless expressed the view that it compromised the design of the novel; McDowall had emphasized the importance of fluidity in the novels; Septimus's tragedy made 'a block in the tideway now and then'.[5] The *New Statesman*'s reviewer gave a fuller account of Septimus's story than many, but, like Sylvia Lynd, was not altogether convinced of its place in the novel. Quoting the passage in which Clarissa reflects that Septimus's death was 'somehow her disaster—her disgrace' (*MD* 157), the reviewer remarks that 'any tragedy would have served for that contrast; the artificial link is purely redundant, purely improbable, purely pointless. It is the sort of coincidence which mars the conventional novel; but it is less distracting there, because there it at any rate serves a purpose.'[6]

In defining what kind of work *Mrs Dalloway* was, many reviewers identified it with Woolf's technical experiments. However, many recognized that Woolf's experiments were not entirely unprecedented. Arthur McDowall noted that the idea of compressing the action into one day, 'though new enough to be called an experiment', was 'not […] unique in modern fiction', and pointed to the precedent of James Joyce's *Ulysses* (1922). An American reviewer of *Mrs Dalloway*, Joseph Wood Krutch, later described Woolf as 'a sort of decorous James Joyce', and in doing so anticipated a line of criticism that saw the novel as an imitation of Joyce's work.[7] In the *Daily News* on 28 May, Naomi Royde-Smith (1875–1964) highlighted what we would now call interior monologue or free indirect discourse, the 'method of telling a story in the medium of the unspoken thought which runs along just below the surface of our apprehension of events'.[8] The method was no longer new, any more than the method of 'filling a full-length novel with the contents of one single day'; Royde-Smith pointed not only to the precedent of *Ulysses*, but also to *Pilgrimage* (the first volume of which had appeared in 1915) by Dorothy Richardson (1873–1957), and to *Mary Olivier* (1919) by May Sinclair (1863–1946). Nevertheless, Royde-Smith felt that Woolf had used these devices 'with a difference'. She remarked upon the complex combination of tones and modes that the novel embodied:

■ The book is a satire, it encloses a raw and jagged tragedy, it flays a sentimentalist and exposes a professional incapacity as it gathers momentum for the evanescent thrill of the party which is its climax. But all these things are accomplished in an atmosphere of sunlit retrospect, prosperous and intelligent enjoyment of the moment, laughter, and the clear beauty of an ordered household, an inherited culture, a gay considerate civilisation; and they combine and coalesce in a whole the completed effect of which is the most finished Mrs Woolf's individual and careful art has yet so far achieved.[9] □

In seeking to place the quality of Woolf's experimentation, several reviewers reached for other arts. Richard Hughes noted that Woolf not only portrayed London vividly, but she did so with a sense of form: 'As well as the power of brilliant evocation she has that creative faculty of form which differs from mechanism: the same quality as Cézanne.' Hughes would probably have known of the importance of Paul Cézanne (1839–1906) to Woolf's circle, and of his prominence in the Post-Impressionist exhibitions in 1910 and 1912 organized by Woolf's friend, the art theorist and painter Roger Fry (1866–1934). Though form in a novel was different from form in a painting, Hughes argued that 'it is not by its vividness that [Woolf's] writing ultimately stays in the mind, but by the coherent and processional form which is composed of, and transcends, that vividness'. The complexity of structure and of movement in the novel led Woolf's friend Gwen Raverat to remark that 'it's like a ballet [...] All the movements in different directions both in time and in space.'[10] For Helen McAfee writing in *the Yale Review* in January 1926, 'In the structural perfection with which the themes are developed and held together, it is akin to an orchestral composition.'[11]

Comparisons to other arts were not always flattering. The *New Statesman*'s reviewer suggested that Woolf's method was not as original as many had claimed, and that the precedents were to be found not only in *Ulysses*:

> ■ People will tell you, with a face of praise, that the whole action of *Mrs Dalloway* passes in one day. But it doesn't pass in one day. In order to create that impression, Mrs Woolf makes her characters move about London, and, when two of them come into purely fortuitous and external contact, she gives you the history of each backwards. She might just as well – better – have given it forwards. The novelty [is] not a novelty. It is a device that is used constantly, especially on the 'pictures', where the hero closes his eyes, a blur crawls across the screen, and the heroine is seen in short skirts and ringlets, as he knew her in the old home-village before she was betrayed.[12] □

Woolf had imposed 'a purely artificial unity' onto several different stories, the reviewer claimed.

Many reviewers recognized that there was a philosophical dimension to Woolf's representation of reality, and in trying to explain her experimentalism, many tentatively contextualized her work. Richard Hughes claimed that Woolf implicitly touched on 'the problem of reality':

> ■ In contrast to the solidity of her visible world there rises throughout the book in a delicate crescendo *fear*. The most notable feature of contemporary thought is the wide recognition by the human mind of its own limitation; i.e., that it is itself not a microcosm (as men used to think) but the macrocosm: that it cannot 'find out' anything about the universe because the terms both of question and answer are terms purely relative to itself: that even the key-words, *being* and *not-being*, bear no relation to anything except the mind which formulates them. [...] In short, that logical and associative thinking do not differ in ultimate value – or even perhaps in kind. So, in this book each of the very different characters – Clarissa Dalloway herself, the slightly more speculative Peter, the Blakeian 'lunatic' Septimus Warren Smith, each with their own more or less formulated hypothesis of the meaning of life – together are an unanswerable illustration of that bottomlessness on which all spiritual values are based. This is what I mean by fear.[13] □

While Hughes's starting point is no doubt the refrain of 'Fear no more the heat of the sun', in his account the theme of fear takes on philosophical dimensions. That human thought was essentially anthropomorphic was an idea that had been advanced by many philosophers in the late nineteenth century, notably Friedrich Nietzsche (1844–1900).

McDowall also noted the peculiar quality of reality in *Mrs Dalloway*, and did so in a vocabulary that recalled contemporary philosophy. 'People and events here have a peculiar, almost ethereal transparency, as though bathed in a medium where one thing permeates another. Undoubtedly our world is less solid than it was, and our novels may have to shake themselves a little free of matter. Here, Mrs Woolf seems to say, is the stream of life, but reflected always in a mental vision.'[14] The 'stream of life' was a phrase found in *Creative Evolution* (1911), the English translation of *L'Évolution créatrice* by the French philosopher Henri Bergson (1859–1941).[15] McDowall had reviewed works by and about Bergson, and was certainly familiar with such phrases.

In the *Nation* (New York), Krutch traced a different lineage, though one closely related philosophically to Bergsonian thought. He contrasted an 'older method of writing novels', one which imagined the human ego as a 'unified, self-consistent thing', with the 'modern method', which resembled the psychology of the American philosopher and psychologist William James (1842–1910). James saw the ego as 'a figment of the imagination', and believed the fundamental truth about the human mind to be the 'stream of consciousness'. The stream of consciousness is never stable. Krutch noted the larger implications of this view of the mind. It meant that in considering a sequence of events we could 'dispense with' the need to find a 'logic' which would represent 'the working out of a plan or a meaning in existence'. Life was not the working out of a divine purpose in which the artist must aim to discover a 'hidden significance and harmony'; rather it was 'an unending sequence of events', the only significance of which 'lies in its fertility and its contrasts'. There was no need to think of there being a 'soul' within human beings or within the universe.[16]

Although Krutch invokes William James, the underlying notion that life is a continual process is similar to the Bergsonian philosophy, as is the vocabulary of life being a 'stream'. The phrase 'stream of consciousness' had originated with James as a psychological hypothesis; and although it had been applied to a literary technique of narration by May Sinclair in 1918, Krutch appears to be using the phrase in its psychological sense.[17] Krutch also implicitly makes a case for Woolf as an atheist and existentialist novelist, which anticipates studies which are covered in Chapter Three.

The earliest reviews, where they praised Woolf, praised her for the vividness of her writing and its truth to the processes of the mind. Their tacit assumptions about the purpose of literature did not include politics, and they make no explicit remarks about the feminist or other politics that have informed later critical work. In any case, because the reviews appeared in ephemeral publications, most were not readily available for consultation, so their influence on later criticism was indirect. Nevertheless, they give some indications of the readership that Woolf was writing for, and the expectations they had about novels.

Literary Criticism (1928–1937)

During Woolf's lifetime there appeared a small number of articles and books on her work. The character of such works and their intended readerships were different from contemporary literary criticism. Although there were university degrees in English literature, their syllabuses generally avoided living writers; similar restrictions tended to apply to scholarly journals and academic book publications. Literary criticism of living authors tended to be directed towards a non-specialist educated readership. Critical articles on Woolf appeared in forums such as T. S. Eliot's journal *The Criterion* (1922–39), F. R. Leavis's *Scrutiny* (1932–53), and *The Yale Review* (1892–).

Although early reviews of *Mrs Dalloway* had been largely appreciative of Woolf's experimentalism, later in her career a critical note was sounded more often. An early hint of such criticisms comes in an undergraduate overview from 1928 by G. M. Turnell. Under the name Martin Turnell, the author was to become a frequent contributor to Leavis's *Scrutiny*, the journal which did most to mount a critique of Woolf's works and values. Turnell's undergraduate piece goes some way to defending Woolf from criticisms of 'unreality'. Woolf's, he explains, 'is a new kind of realism; it does not give us an accurate picture of things that we have all seen [...]; it tells us things about other people's existence that we cannot discover for ourselves [...]'.[18] However, Woolf's attention to consciousness had concomitant faults: 'the writers who study the mind so carefully cannot give us creatures of flesh and blood'. The same quality that McDowall had praised as 'transparency' was less satisfactory to Turnell: 'After all, Mrs Woolf's characters remain ghostly emotions that flit through the pages. This, it is true, does not make our experience of reading the book less vivid, but it does give a sense of impermanency to all that she writes. Her characters do not stay in the mind like those of Mr Hardy or any other great English novelist. They fade away like a photograph that has not been fixed.'[19] (The remark about character echoes the novelist and critic Arnold Bennett [1867–1931], who had written in 1923, with reference to *Jacob's Room*, that 'the characters do not vitally survive in the mind'.)[20] Later in his career, in 1950, Turnell apparently thought better of the appreciative remarks he had made, describing Woolf as having been 'overrated' during her lifetime.[21]

Though for Turnell, James Joyce had also failed to create 'creatures of flesh and blood', such criticisms were often directed at Woolf by way of a contrast with Joyce. Joyce's fearless representations of the body in *Ulysses* were used to make Woolf's novels appear bloodless, shy of confrontation with the modern world. This was the line taken by the artist, novelist and cultural critic Wyndham Lewis (1882–1957) in *Men Without Art* (1934).

Lewis takes his cue from Woolf's essay 'Character in Fiction' (1924); in his case, he objects particularly to Woolf's prediction that her contemporary period, as it struggles to escape from Edwardian realism, will be 'a season of failures and fragments', and that the truth will reach us 'in rather an exhausted and chaotic condition', 'a little pale and dishevelled'.[22] *Ulysses*, Lewis asserts, may be a failure, but it is certainly not a fragment, and it cannot be called pale. Nor can D. H. Lawrence's novels: 'Far from being "pale", they are much too much the reverse.'[23] Such a view of the contemporary scene, Lewis declares, could only be advanced by those wishing to excuse their own 'mediocrity'.[24] A similar dismissive and robustly assertive tone characterizes Lewis's criticism of Woolf's novels. They lack the 'realistic vigour' of Joyce; the scene of the car in Bond Street (*MD* 12–15) is merely 'a sort of undergraduate imitation' of Joyce's depiction of the Viceroy's progress through Dublin. Lewis uses the scene of Clarissa at the gates of St James's Park (*MD* 7) as the basis for his satirical account of Woolf. Clarissa 'looking at the omnibuses' should really have been 'peeping', he suggests. Of Clarissa's sense that 'it was very, very dangerous to live even one day' (*MD* 7), he jeers:

■ To live *outside*, of course that means. Outside it is terribly *dangerous* – in that great and coarse Without, where all the he-men and he-girls 'live dangerously' with a brutal insensibility to all the *risks* that they run, forever in the public places. But this *dangerousness* does, after all, make it all very *thrilling*, when peeped-out at, from the security of the private mind.[25] □

Lewis mistakes the character for the author, identifying Clarissa Dalloway's nervousness with Woolf's worldview. Such a critique might have some validity if one could demonstrate that Clarissa's existential anxiety is omnipresent in Woolf's works. Lewis, however, is not engaged in an analytical criticism, and his insights are difficult to separate from a misogynistic attitude and hectoring tone, as becomes clear in the next paragraph:

■ Those are the half-lighted places of the mind – in which, quivering with a timid excitement, this sort of intelligence shrinks, thrilled to the marrow, at all the wild goings-on! A little old-maidish, are the Prousts and sub-Prousts I think. And when two old maids – or a company of old maids – shrink and cluster together, they titter in each other's ears and delicately tee-hee, pointing out to each other the red-blood antics of this or that upstanding figure, treading the perilous Without.[26] □

Although the tone has largely disappeared from criticism, critics hostile to Woolf still occasionally characterize her fiction in terms of a timid femininity.

A longer-lasting and more prominent line of criticism found its home in the literary critical journal *Scrutiny*, founded by F. R. Leavis (1895–1978).[27] In 1932, the first issue identified *Scrutiny*'s opposition to Woolf in Muriel Bradbrook's 'Notes on the Style of Mrs Woolf'. Bradbrook begins from a stylistic observation: the tendency of Woolf's 'little asides' to 'deflate' the authority of a statement.[28] Her examples, from *To the Lighthouse*, are of characters making general, almost philosophical statements, for example about the 'stability' of the world, while engaged in ordinary activities such as serving dinner. The 'affirmation', Bradbrook complains, 'is given a relative value only'. 'Affirmation' was an important term in *Scrutiny*'s critical vocabulary. D. H. Lawrence (1885–1930), whose work F. R. Leavis championed, was seen as an affirmative novelist, though more recent criticism has emphasized his relativistic and dialogic qualities.[29] In Bradbrook's view, Woolf's evasiveness prevented her from achieving all that a novelist should achieve.

> ■ Mrs Woolf refuses to be pinned down [...] and consequently she is debarred from a narrative technique, since this implies a schema of values, or even from the direct presentation of powerful feelings or major situations. In *Mrs Dalloway* the most powerful feelings depend on more powerful feelings long past: the old relationships between Clarissa, Peter, and Sally Seaton [sic], the war experiences of Septimus Warren Smith.[30] □

Bradbrook extends the second sentence to a more general statement: 'Whenever the direct presentation of powerful feelings or major situations is inescapable, Mrs Woolf takes refuge in an embarrassing kind of nervous irony.'[31] Though Bradbrook's approach to Woolf reaches a foregone conclusion, her remark about the relation of narrative to 'a schema of values' raises large questions about the nature of narrative. Similar considerations informed the 1937 overview of Woolf's work by another *Scrutiny* critic, W. H. Mellers. Acknowledging that Woolf was often praised as a 'poet' on account of her ability to record 'sensuous impressions', Mellers argued that though impressions were 'the only means whereby a poet can make his apprehensions and his attitudes concrete and comprehensible', they were not enough in themselves: 'if they were, most normally sensitive children would be great poets'.[32] Mellers diagnosed a kind of immaturity in what he felt was the formlessness of Woolf's writing. The only exception he would allow was *To the Lighthouse*, the one novel in which Woolf had been able to use her impressions 'to form an organization'.[33] Though Mellers is not explicit about what might have brought form to Woolf's novels, by implication he follows Bradbrook's diagnosis, that she lacks a mature sense of values.

Following Woolf's death, F. R. Leavis was to endorse Mellers's identification of *To the Lighthouse* as the one acceptable novel in Woolf's oeuvre, and to present his own version of the critique. Leavis took as his text Woolf's injunction, in 'Modern Fiction', to the novelist who wished to escape the predetermined forms of Edwardian fiction:

> ■ Look within and life, it seems, is very far from being 'like this'. Examine for a moment an ordinary mind on an ordinary day. The mind receives a myriad impressions – trivial, fantastic, evanescent, or engraved with the sharpness of steel. (*E4* 160) □

Leavis observed that it was not enough for the writer's mind to 'receive' impressions: it must 'form' them as well.[34] To arrange the impressions into a pattern, the mind must have 'a very positive and active bent of interest'. Leavis continued: 'And to achieve the kind of order necessary to a good novel, the mind would have to have not only a strong positive bent of interest, but a kind of interest in the world "out there" that Mrs Woolf's injunction to "look within" for "life" among the "innumerable atoms" of "impressions" hardly suggests.'[35] For Leavis, Woolf's mode of narration paid too much attention to the perceiving consciousness, too little to the perceived world. Woolf tended 'to shut out all the ranges of experience accompanying those kinds of preoccupation, volitional and moral, with an external world which are not felt primarily as preoccupation with one's consciousness of it. The preoccupation with intimating "significance" in fine shades of consciousness, together with the unremitting play of visual imagery, the "beautiful" writing and the lack of moral interest and interest in action, give the effect of something closely akin to a sophisticated aestheticism.'[36]

Leavis's explicit diagnosis of the cause of the problem was the place of the artist in modern society: because the artist appeared irrelevant, he or she was more likely 'to cultivate [...] the "bubble of the private consciousness"'.[37] But implicit was class-based antagonism: Leavis implies that Woolf's impressionist subject position is that of someone protected by economic privilege from the external world; the position of someone who can afford to pay attention to their own private consciousness. Such class antagonisms were plain to see in Q. D. Leavis's influential review of Woolf's *Three Guineas* (1938), of which Woolf remarked: 'I read eno[ugh] to see that it was all personal' (*D5* 165).[38] One of the key tasks for the next generation of Woolf critics was to establish that she possessed a mind as well as a sensibility. Harder to dislodge were the ideas of Woolf as the invalid of Bloomsbury, and of Bloomsbury writers as having avoided real engagement with the world.

Woolf's lifetime also saw some more positive critical accounts of her work, both in Britain and in continental Europe. The 1932 study by the novelist Winifred Holtby (1898–1935) saw *Mrs Dalloway* and *To the Lighthouse* as the justification of the experimental phase that had begin with the short fiction *Kew Gardens* (1919) and *Jacob's Room*. Holtby acknowledged the complex multifariousness of *Mrs Dalloway*:

> ■ Into those hours of one London day are enclosed beauty and horror, gaiety and madness, jealousy stirring like a snake under the flowers, all time past remembered by each of the characters, so that no page can be opened without finding the full orchestra in full swing—mind, senses, the memory, external action, reference, like so many instruments, flutes, violins, drums, trumpets, playing together.[39] □

But she was also concerned to identify what unified the novel. There was, Holtby suggested, a unity to the novel which might be termed 'metaphysical' or 'philosophical', for example, the unity which makes Clarissa feel that Septimus's death was somehow her death.[40] Holtby was also interested in the paradox that novels that had so little by way of conventional narrative could yet be so rich. Like Richard Hughes before her, she provided a plot summary of *Mrs Dalloway* and *To the Lighthouse* as a means of indicating the inadequacy of such an account. Yet, she continued, the two novels 'contain as much of character-drawing, of moment-creating, of tension and of revelation, as any written in their time'.[41]

Outside Britain, Woolf's novels had become the object of academic attention. *Le Roman psychologique de Virginia Woolf* (1932), by Floris Delattre, a professor of literature at the University of Lille in France, pursued Woolf's connection to the intellectual context of her time, and argued that Woolf had applied the theories of Bergson and William James to the novel.[42] Delattre distinguishes *Mrs Dalloway* (along with *Jacob's Room* and *To the Lighthouse*) as a mature novel, by contrast with *The Voyage Out* and *Night and Day*; it is a novel in which Woolf is in full command of her medium and in which the experiments of her shorter fiction bear their fruits. The main argument that Delattre makes for the novel concerns Woolf's grasp of psychological realism and complexity: unlike *Jacob's Room*, in which we hardly know the titular protagonist, *Mrs Dalloway* presents a persuasive and complex portrait. He particularly focuses on Clarissa; his accounts of Septimus and Peter are brief. Woolf, he argues, presents two aspects of Clarissa: one, the superficial aspect of the society hostess with a settled position in the governing classes, the other, the unique personality with her love of life, her vitality and her sensitivity. This dualism is consistent with Delattre's regard for Bergson, though he does not explicitly theorize it as Bergsonian in the paragraphs on *Mrs Dalloway*. It also allows him to avoid having to choose between a conception of the novel as satirical of Clarissa and the opposing conception of it being a sympathetic presentation. What such a character-based account leaves out is any recognition of the internal patterning of the novel, quite apart from matters that were not widely discussed in criticism at the time, such as its politics.

In the year that Holtby's and Delattre's books appeared, a young American graduate student, Ruth Gruber, submitted a Ph.D. thesis at the University of Cologne (Köln) in Germany, at the unprecedentedly young age of 20. The thesis, *Virginia Woolf: A Study*, was published in 1935. Its main argument presents Woolf as a writer struggling heroically to forge a style which will enable her to 'write as a woman'.[43] In the absence of any published criticism, Gruber takes her critical cues from *A Room of One's Own*, and particularly Woolf's insistence that female writers must think back through their mothers (*ROO* 99). Gruber begins with a crudely reductive notion of a 'feminine style': it is 'lyrical' (7), 'rhythmic' (8), and is an 'emotional romantic style' (8); the masculine style is 'abstract, structural and urgently clear' (8). These categories take a conventional patriarchal binary of woman as irrational, man as rational, and invert the values attached to each side; they do not fundamentally deconstruct or complicate the binary. Within her broad narrative of development, *Mrs Dalloway* features as the novel in which Woolf successfully formed a style.

In the ten pages devoted to *Mrs Dalloway* Gruber's essentialist ideas about gender and style are still clearly visible. Commenting on the novel's sixth paragraph ('For it was the middle of June... the admirable Hugh!', *MD* 4–5), Gruber comments that 'The thoughts run on like a gossipy woman; the long full sentence is less a structural feat than a psychologic one, giving the hurrying, bustling tokens of the hurrying, bustling observations and ideas' (47). Labelled as 'gossip', the idea of an essentially feminine volubility does not escape its misogynist origins. However, elsewhere Gruber is subtler. She argues that in *Mrs Dalloway* Woolf becomes less concerned with individual details of vocabulary, the Flaubertian *mot juste*, and more concerned with shaping sentence rhythms 'which convey the rise and fall of thoughts themselves' (50). In this, like Delattre, she discerns the influence of Bergson, or at least a parallel to his thought; she is primarily interested in Bergson as a thinker who believed in the value of 'poetic intuition' (49), although she also considers Woolf's treatment of clock time from a Bergsonian point of view.

The critics of the 1930s were engaging with Woolf on several different levels: they engaged with Woolf as one who experimented in the art of fiction, particularly with regard to psychological truth, but they also engaged with what they believed were the values and theories underlying her work.

Posthumous Accounts (1945–49)

Within a few years of Woolf's death in 1941, there appeared several introductory books on her fiction. The first of them, Joan Bennett's *Virginia Woolf: Her Art as a Novelist* (1945), subtly refutes the criticisms of the *Scrutiny* critics. By dedicating the study to George Rylands, Bennett hints at an affiliation with Bloomsbury: Rylands (1902–99) had been introduced to Leonard and Virginia Woolf by Lytton Strachey, and had worked at the Hogarth Press for six months in 1924; by 1945 he was a Fellow of King's College Cambridge, a college closely associated with Woolf's circle. In her prefatory note Bennett apologises for not having included a chapter on Woolf's style, and defines the book as being about Woolf's 'vision of human life', and 'her sense of values'.[44] The latter remark clearly responded to *Scrutiny*'s objection that Woolf lacked a 'schema of values'. Bennett also declared her intention to analyse the form of Woolf's novels, and this too responded to the Leavisite belief that her novels were formless and impressionistic. 'All art', Bennett asserts, 'implies selection, arrangement, order, and therefore conventions' (13). While Leavis and his followers would have argued that Woolf did not select, and was therefore not an artist, Bennett argued that even though Woolf had destroyed the existing conventions of the novel, she had invented her own new conventions. She identifies these conventions by differentiating Woolf's method from Joyce's. Like many critics, Bennett takes 'Modern Novels' as a starting point, and quotes Woolf's praise of *Ulysses*. But she also draws attention to Woolf's misgivings about Joyce's method: 'Is it the method that inhibits the creative power?' Woolf had asked. 'Is it due to the method that we feel neither jovial nor magnanimous, but centred in a self which, in spite of its tremor of susceptibility, never embraces or creates what is outside itself and beyond?' (*E*4 162). Bennett comments that the 'intricate and disciplined form' of Woolf's own novels 'is a means of escaping from a single point of view and creating "what is outside and beyond". Form enables her [...] to move from mind to mind without confusion, to present diversity of experience within a single design' (17). The remark about the 'outside' world clearly opposes the Leavisite assertion that Woolf's works were inward looking.

Bennett expounds Woolf's values in the course of interpreting her novels. Bennett's Woolf is concerned with the inner essence of life: 'it is not the width and variety of the human comedy, nor the idiosyncrasies of human character, that most interest her. Rather it is the deep and simple human experiences, love, happiness, beauty, loneliness, death' (3). She is relatively uninterested in the social and economic circumstances that surround her characters, except as they impinge on their lives. Bennett's Woolf is also implicitly a follower of the Cambridge ethical philosopher G. E. Moore, who had attempted to define the essence of 'the good', and had concluded that the most valuable things were 'certain states of consciousness, which may be roughly described as the pleasures of human intercourse and the enjoyment of beautiful objects'.[45] When Bennett writes that in Woolf's first novel, 'what we actually see [the characters] doing is living a life bounded by personal relations', she is implying that Woolf's values are those of Moore. Woolf's desire to reach the essentials is also seen in her awareness of 'the strangeness of human life, as though there were some other life guessed at, more ordered and significant, of which men catch an occasional glimpse' (18).

Bennett's chapter on Woolf's 'Morals and Values' continues the critical engagement with the *Scrutiny* critics. Bennett observes that Woolf believed that 'philosophy' must be 'consumed' in a novel, so that statements of doctrine do not obtrude (64).[46] Woolf's values are not always immediately apparent in her novels, because her 'whole endeavour' is directed towards 'understanding rather than judgment, and it is from the judgments, pronounced or implied by authors, that we usually extract their own views upon ethical or philosophical questions' (64). Nevertheless, Woolf's characters often recognize the duality of life: on the one hand, its ugliness and chaos, and on the other, its joyfulness and 'magnificence' (65, 67). In *Mrs Dalloway*, not only is 'the exquisite joy of life' presented to us, but 'side by side with it stalks the horror and the chaos; Septimus is over-whelmed by it and courts death' (69). Given that many of her contemporaries separated art and politics (equating the latter with propaganda), it is noteworthy that Bennett also recognizes the political dimension to Woolf's values: the 'two forms of human misery' most often found in her books are, Bennett remarks 'poverty and war'. Moreover, Bennett acknowledges the depth of Woolf's commitment to the feminist cause, and the presence of ambivalence.

Bennett also wished to demonstrate that Woolf's best novels had a coherent aesthetic form. Though she felt that *Jacob's Room* 'falls apart', consisting of vivid episodes that did not form a memorable whole, *Mrs Dalloway* was among those that cohered. In Woolf's successful novels, which Bennett took to be *Mrs Dalloway*, *To the Lighthouse*, *The Waves* and *Between the Acts*, 'a small group of people is selected, and through their closely interrelated experience the reader receives his total impression. In each case also certain images, phrases and symbols bind the whole together' (98). In the idea that imagery brings unity to the work, Bennett has something in common with the New Criticism, a primarily American school of criticism which was to dominate the 1940s and 1950s.

In considering the unity of *Mrs Dalloway*, Bennett finds a significant place for Septimus. His story introduces 'a darker side of life, and a more profound sense of the historic background against which the whole is set' (99). In any case, Bennett argues that the real 'subject' of the book is not one character or the other, but a timeless abstraction, 'human life itself, its tension between misery and happiness and its inevitable consummation in death' (100). Bennett's discovery of unity in a timeless theme is consistent with her belief that Woolf persistently searches for the essences beyond historical contingencies, as well as being consistent with the then widely prevalent idea that what is most interesting in literature are its timeless and universal aspects, not its historical specificities. The novel's quotations from *Cymbeline* and *Othello* both belong to the characters who think them, but also evoke their own associations. 'For within the book there is a poetic pattern, probing to that deeper level at which the mind apprehends timeless values, as well as the prose pattern wherein the reader is given a picture of the modern world with its destructive forces of class-struggle, economic insecurity and war' (100). In effect, Bennett distinguishes between two levels of *Mrs Dalloway*: one is the 'prose plane', a novel that makes satirical reference to the modern world, 'with its destructive forces'; the other is the 'poetic plane', on which we find the tragic aspect of Septimus, and where there is 'love and death and the evanescent beauty of the world' (100). While Bennett in no way belittles Woolf's achievement in the first plane, there is little doubt that, in 1945, any claim for the significance of a writer required her to achieve something more timeless.

Bernard Blackstone's *Virginia Woolf: A Commentary* (1949) is a less sophisticated work than Bennett's, but is worthy of attention because it illuminates one of the difficulties of writing about *Mrs Dalloway*.[47] In his introduction Blackstone presents Woolf as a writer focused on the inner life, 'an explorer of different worlds of experience' (9). He invokes the myth of the invalid of Bloomsbury, saying that she was 'forced back by ill-health on the inner world' and so became interested in 'the subtle world where the springs of action lie' (10). 'Her novels are not novels of action, or even of character in the ordinary sense. They are evocations of moods: of experiences which, though fleeting, have about them an eternal quality and seem to point to a meaning underlying them all' (10). He sees her as finding 'patterns in human experience'. In her middle period (beginning with *Jacob's Room*), she 'presents us with situations in which various kind of truth are examined in their relation to the compromises of married life' (11). In *Mrs Dalloway* and *To the Lighthouse*, characters experience 'the tension between family life and clear-sightedness' (12).

Throughout the book, Blackstone's discussion is directed much more towards character and theme than Bennett's, and much less towards an analysis of fictional experiments. His chapter on *Mrs Dalloway* begins by leading us through the main scenes of the novel and the characters they introduce. He tends to summarize characters: for example, having quoted Peter Walsh's reflections on Clarissa, he comments, 'An admirable person this Peter Walsh, we perceive! He is critical, aware, detached, and holds to the supreme virtues of truth and reality' (81). At certain points, Blackstone attempts to relate Woolf's characters to a 'type' that the reader is believed to recognize: 'Sir William Bradshaw is Virginia Woolf's portrait, complete and of a certain magnitude, of the professional type' (83). Bradshaw, for Blackstone, is an index of modernity: 'He is the product, that is, of spiritual apathy, of ignorance, of the brute weight of non-awareness that afflicts our twentieth-century world' (84). Turning to Miss Kilman, Blackstone remarks that Woolf 'is making her criticism of an all-too-common religious type; to which, she believes, not only frustrated women like Doris Kilman belong but also a good number of clergymen. It is a type in which the love of power is hidden under a religious cloak: a love of power mingled with invincible stupidity' (89). As Jean Guiguet noted in his penetrating critical survey, Blackstone's starting point is one of 'traditional realism'.[48] By relating characters to recognizable types, and by speaking confidently in the first-person plural (e.g. '*our* twentieth-century world'), he supplements Woolf's novel with the kind of omniscient narrator to be found in the realist fiction of George Eliot.

One of Blackstone's starting points concerning Woolf is that she is – in the philosophical sense – a 'sensationalist': she believes 'that through a direct, immediate apprehension of the thing-in-itself we get our closest glimpses of reality. This sensationalism, this entranced attention to the forms, shapes, colours, feel, and scents of *things*, is for Virginia Woolf the one certain good in life' (12). One of his conclusions concerning *Mrs Dalloway* is that love is 'as detestable as religion' (95) because it limits our access to reality. Considering Clarissa's love for Sally, for Peter and for Richard, and Peter's love for Clarissa and other women, and Miss Kilman's love for Elizabeth, Blackstone asks, 'Is is possible to have the clear vision of reality when such disturbing colours flash in front of the eyes?' (94). This negativity about love emerges in his commentary on the passage in which Clarissa considers her sexual feeling for other women. He recognizes that the passage embodies a large concern for Woolf, 'that the novel as constructed by male writers is not a wholly satisfactory medium for the woman novelist'; but rather than recognize the passage as being about lesbianism, he can go no further than concede (with implicit allusion to *A Room of One's Own*) 'that there is something androgynous in the nature of the artist' (74). It is impossible to be sure whether Blackstone's 'androgyny' is a euphemism for bisexuality, or for lesbianism, or whether he simply does not acknowledge same-sex relationships. When considering Clarissa's feeling for Sally more specifically, he sees it not as something that might be celebrated, but as part of a larger problem of the conflict between emotion and truth in Woolf's work. 'How reach an adequate solution, she now asks, when there is this further complication of a love between women and an understanding of what men feel for women – which one certainly cannot share with one's husband? For too intense an understanding is disruptive of spontaneity, utterly destructive' (75). While Blackstone's enthusiasm for Woolf's writing is palpable, his critical voice is often moralizing, in a tone at odds with Woolf's own.

Close Reading (1951–75)

Criticism in the 1950s and 1960s was dominated by the assumption that the proper focus of literary criticism was the text in itself. The best-known embodiment of this assumption was the primarily American school of criticism known as the New Criticism, but the assumption and its corollaries were shared by many critics who would not have identified themselves as 'New Critics'. Because several generations of critics were educated on this basis, its characteristic methods survived well into the 1970s and may even be detected in some 1980s work. Studying the text 'in itself' primarily meant studying it in isolation from authorial intentions and authorial biography, and from social context. The exclusion of authorial intention was codified by Wimsatt and Beardsley in their article 'The Intentional Fallacy' (1946).[49] The *form* of the text was important above all: 'pattern' and 'structure' were other key words. While the emphasis on form meant that lyric poetry was the primary focus of New Critical attention (as in Cleanth Brooks and Robert Penn Warren's classroom text *Understanding Poetry* (1938) and Brooks's collection of critical essays *The Well Wrought Urn: Studies in the Structure of Poetry* (1947)), the novel was a legitimate object of study, and the modernist novelists' self-conscious attention to form meant that they were particularly prized. Although intention and biography were excluded, there was a place for the author as a detached shaper of aesthetic form. The New Criticism also drew a sharp division between art and propaganda, and therefore between art and politics. The political content of works was either ignored, or treated as a blot on their artistic integrity.

Reuben Brower's 'Something Central Which Permeated: Virginia Woolf and *Mrs Dalloway*' (1951) exemplifies many of these tendencies.[50] In his introductory note to the book in which it first appeared, Brower presents his essays as 'an experiment' because he sees literature as 'an active engagement between the reader and the printed page' (p. xi), and in saying this he implicitly acknowledges a break with the New Critical exclusion of the reader's response, which had been codified in Wimsatt and Beardsley's 'The Affective Fallacy' (1949).[51] But in practice in the Woolf essay, Brower's recognition of the reader's active role in making connections between parts of the text does not amount to a legitimization of the reader's personal emotional response as a basis for criticism. Elsewhere in the note, Brower declares his aim as being to discover 'designs of imaginative organization' (p. xi) (in other words, form or pattern), and he understands literary criticism as a matter of 'finding order in experience': it is another key tenet of New Criticism that experience (the real world, and especially the modern real world) is chaotic, while art is orderly. Finding order is 'among the primary activities of civilized men' (p. xii).

Brower's chapter on *Mrs Dalloway* follows one on *The Tempest*, and he claims that the best approach to reading Woolf's novel is to read it like a Shakespeare play – by which he means, to read it as critics in the mid-twentieth century read a Shakespeare play. At this point in Shakespeare's critical history, he was far more a poet than a writer for the stage. Works such as Caroline Spurgeon's *Shakespeare's Imagery* (1935) had brought imagery, metaphor and symbol to the centre of Shakespearean studies. The neoclassical criticism of Shakespeare, that his plays lacked 'unity of action' (they did not subscribe to the Aristotelian unities of action, place and time), was dismissed by appeal to their 'unity of design'; the phrase is echoed in Brower's essay. Brower introduces Woolf's novel by saying that it has 'a story and some characters', but only a 'fragmentary dramatic design'. What it has instead is imagery:

■ The dramatic sequences are connected through a single metaphorical nucleus, and the key metaphors are projected and sustained by a continuous web of subtly related minor metaphors and harmonizing imagery. (123) □

Brower begins from the assumption that a bare 'outline' of the events of the novel is very remote from the 'remembered experience' of reading *Mrs Dalloway*. (Notably at this point, Brower fleetingly allows reader response a place in his argument.) The 'outline' and the 'peculiar texture' of the novel are at odds, and the latter is the more important. It includes 'The ebb and flow of her phrasing' – though this plays little part in his analysis – 'and the frequent repetition of the same or similar expressions'. The repetitions that interest Brower are 'Fear no more' from *Cymbeline*, and less conspicuous words such as '"life," "feel," "suffer," "solemn," "moment," and "enjoy"' (124).

Brower begins his detailed analysis with 'solemn' and 'solemnity', looking at its appearance in the third paragraph (*MD* 3), in the description of Westminster before Big Ben strikes (*MD* 4); its three appearances in the scene of Clarissa looking at the old lady across the road (*MD* 107–8); and its appearance again as Clarissa looks across the road (*MD* 158). Brower comments that in all but the last, 'there is some suggestion in the imagery of Big Ben's stroke coming down and marking an interruption in the process of life' (126). The suggestion emerges from a set of associations: 'association' and 'connection', for all their vagueness, are important concepts for this kind of criticism. Brower connects the terror symbolized by Big Ben's pause with childhood, 'one's parents giving it into one's hands' (*MD* 157), and he also notes the recurrence of wave and water imagery in other 'solemn' passages. He concludes that '"solemn" acquires symbolic values for the reader: some terror of entering the sea of experience and of living life and an inexplicable fear of a "suspense" or interruption' (126).

In the next phase of Brower's essay, he argues that various expressions such as 'solemn' all lead towards 'the key metaphor of the book' (126). It is not 'a single, easily describable analogy', but two complementary analogies or 'metaphorical poles' (126–7). (Brower's essay often pushes 'analogy' and 'metaphor' beyond their conventional meanings.) The first pole clusters around 'life' and the phrase 'they love life' (*MD* 4): life in *Mrs Dalloway* is associated with 'the doings of people and things' (127). Brower suggests that the deictics in *Mrs Dalloway* are frequently associated with 'life' ('this' and 'all this'), though he stretches the term 'metaphor' when he calls deictics 'metaphors for life' (127). The other metaphorical pole is the fear of being excluded or interrupted. In summary, the central metaphor of the novel is 'twofold': 'the exhilarated sense of being a part of the forward moving process and the recurrent fear of some break in this absorbing activity, which was symbolized by the "suspense" before Big Ben strikes'. The central metaphor is expressed 'through countless variant minor metaphors and images' (128).

In the light of this definition, Brower goes on to examine the scene of Clarissa sewing ('Quiet descended on her... barking', *MD* 33–4). In relation to the calm of this scene, Peter Walsh's arrival marks him as an interrupter, and an instance of what Brower terms the 'destroyer' theme in *Mrs Dalloway*. The 'destroyer' is seen in its most prominent form – 'an almost allegorical representation' (132) – in Sir William Bradshaw. However, Brower notes that Peter also participates in the 'key figure' of 'life', as do others like Septimus and Miss Kilman, even though they are 'unable to "live" as Clarissa does' (130).

Like many critics, Brower attempts to find a place for Septimus's death in his interpretative scheme. He focuses not on the suicide itself, but on Clarissa's learning of it. All of the analogies that comprise the 'key metaphor' come together in the final scene of the novel. By killing himself, Septimus has avoided the loss of his 'independence of soul': 'This (in so far as we can define it) is "the thing" he had preserved.' Clarissa, by contrast, has 'made compromises for the sake of social success'. The old lady opposite, in her second appearance, 'symbolizes the quiet maintenance of one's own life, which is the only counterbalance to the fear of "interruption" whether by death or compulsion' (133).

In his closing paragraphs, Brower supplements his essentially sympathetic account of the novel with a few critical remarks, primarily aesthetic in nature. The first concerns Peter Walsh's pursuit of young woman from Trafalgar Square to Oxford Street (*MD* 45–6). Brower's criticism of this 'embarrassing' episode is not an ethical one about Peter's behaviour, but an artistic one. Brower believes that Woolf is apparently attempting to portray Peter's passionate side, but the lack of 'lively sensuous detail' in the narrative contrasts badly with the 'glowing particularity' (134) of Clarissa in Bond Street or Peter's later impressions of a London evening (*MD* 137–40). A further criticism, and one more specifically connected to Brower's main idea, is that Woolf occasionally 'elaborates [a] metaphor out of all proportion to its expressive value' (135), most notably in Peter's 'solitary traveller' passage (*MD* 48–50). Brower sees it as an 'enlarged symbolic version of Peter's experience with the girl'; while it is 'in a picturesque sense a beautiful passage', it is merely decorative, and 'does not increase or enrich our knowledge of Peter or of anyone else in the book' (135). Brower's final objects of criticism are the novel's 'super-literary, pseudo-Homeric' similes, such as the one describing Clarissa and Peter sitting side by side on a sofa: 'So before a battle begins, the horses paw the ground; [...]' (*MD* 37–7). He contrasts it with the earlier, successful scene of Clarissa sewing. The problem with this epic simile is that the images 'are not grounded on the dramatic and narrative level' (135–6); there has been no preparation for it in the description of Clarissa and Peter, and so the reader cannot 'take the further jump to the psychological levels of the metaphor' (136).

These criticisms ultimately serve to reinforce Brower's point that, for most of the novel, that which is 'vital' in the writing of *Mrs Dalloway* is both 'omnipresent' and 'unobtrusive' (136). His final illustration of the success takes an example more prominent and obvious than 'solemn', which is the recurrence of the word 'plunge' and its cognates, from Clarissa's opening 'plunge' (*MD* 3), to her hesitating before 'plunging' into a room (*MD* 26), through to Clarissa's use of 'plunged' (*MD* 156) in her reimagining of Septimus's death.

Brower's essay is outstanding in its attention to verbal detail, and its patient tracing of interconnections; and while its account of the 'central metaphor' risks reducing the novel to a simple binary contrast between 'life' and 'interruption', it has the merit of providing a clear map with which to negotiate the fine detail. Brower's approach allows him to make an implicit claim for the value of Woolf's work: her metaphorical intricacy and her unity of design are Shakespearean in their qualities. The limitations of his account are, for the most part, typical of his era: he is concerned only to trace connections within the text, and never to consider anything outside it, even within the limited sphere of the literary canon. Moreover, he is interested only in what is present in the text: the idea that a text might have – on a psychoanalytical model – repressed or displaced elements is not part of his interpretive programme. Finally, Brower's commitment to arguing for unity of design means that he essentially sees the text as a unity. He recognises some blemishes, but they do not lead to any larger questions about Woolf's understanding of her subject matter or of her audience.

While Brower's study adheres relatively closely to a single method, Jean Guiguet's study of Woolf is far more eclectic. First published in French as *Virginia Woolf et son oeuvre* (1962), and published in an English translation, *Virginia Woolf and her works*, by the Hogarth Press in 1965, at 464 pages Guiguet's study was by a significant margin longer than any previous critical work on Woolf. It was also the first study to make substantial reference to Leonard Woolf's selection from Virginia's diaries, *A Writer's Diary* (1953). The availability of the diaries means that Guiguet could be more accurate than previous critics about the genesis of *Mrs Dalloway*. However, he does not make reference to the manuscript versions, and although he was aware of the existence of 'Mrs Dalloway in Bond Street' and 'The Prime Minister' from the diaries, he does not discuss the texts themselves, which were at that time unpublished. Guiguet also discusses Woolf's formal innovations, their relation to her underlying theme, and the relation of *Mrs Dalloway* to the works of James Joyce and Marcel Proust. French literary criticism was relatively untouched by the Anglo-American New Criticism, and while Guiguet's interest in formal innovation has some similarities with contemporaneous Anglophone work, he is less concerned to root his account of form in close reading. The present summary focuses on his discussion of form.

Guiguet gives prominence to a passage from Woolf's diary in January 1920, written at a time when she had recently completed her relatively traditional novel *Night and Day* (1919), and had also written the more experimental short fictions 'The Mark on the Wall', 'Kew Gardens' and 'An Unwritten Novel.' In it she anticipates the form of *Jacob's Room*, but also that of *Mrs Dalloway*:

■ Suppose one thing should open out of another – as in An Unwritten Novel – only not for 10 pages but 200 or so – doesn't that give the looseness & lightness I want; doesnt that get closer & yet keep form & speed, & enclose everything, everything? (*D2* 13) □

These reflections led immediately to *Jacob's Room*, but less directly to *Mrs Dalloway*. In his discussion of *Mrs Dalloway*, Guiguet understands Woolf as attempting to build on the successes of *Jacob's Room* while avoiding the weakness of her previous compositional process. In particular, he emphasizes her having conceived the book as a whole, whereas *Jacob's Room* had been written 'somewhat at random', with Woolf 'solving problems as she met them' (228). He particularly emphasizes the breadth of her project, noting two diary entries in which she speaks of wanting to devise a structure that will accommodate 'everything' (229, with ref. to *D2* 272 and *D2* 302).

The form itself allows Woolf to tell, as a framework, the story of what happens on one day in the middle of June, while also telling the past stories of Clarissa and Septimus: Woolf's important discovery is the 'integration of past with present'. Guiguet is particularly interested in what Woolf called her 'tunnelling process', 'by which I tell the past by instalments, as I have need of it' (*D2* 272), and in another passage where she speaks of digging out 'beautiful caves' behind her characters which come 'to daylight at the present moment' (*D2* 263). In Guiguet's account Woolf reveals the interiors of characters 'by a succession of interior monologues, set off by some sensation which brings back its homologue from the past and, with it, an associated train of places and people, feelings and thoughts' (233).

■ It is in the most intimate depths that the 'caves connect'. The casual and meaningless way in which the heroes' lives are reconstructed – when the caves 'come to daylight at the present moment' – reveals the shallowness of apparent contacts, and on the other hand emphasizes the profound unity that comes from participation in the inward experience of life. In fact these beings, Clarissa and Septimus, not only communicate with one another through identical emotions but are superimposed on one another to the point of identity. (234) □

As is clear from this last remark, Guiguet draws to some extent on Woolf's 1928 Introduction to the American edition. Septimus, 'through his neurosis',

■ amplifies all Clarissa's reactions, and plays in the novel the role of an echo chamber. The explosion from the Prime Minister's car startles Clarissa, who thinks of a pistol shot; for Septimus, 'The world has raised its whip; where will it descend?' (*MD* 12). (234) □

Guiguet goes on to note other respects in which Septimus does not simply parallel Clarissa (a common enough observation), but amplifies her. They contrast, however, in that Clarissa has condemned herself to a compromise by marrying Richard, while Septimus remains an outcast. Commenting, Guiguet remarks that Woolf's 'social criticism' is 'grafted on to the psycho-metaphysical theme of the novel':

> ■ Politics, money, religious intolerance, everything in our civilization which is built on ready-made ideas into which feeling does not constantly infuse fresh life and significance, creates around human beings a prison parallel to that in which our own nature confines us – so closely parallel indeed that, to Septimus's visionary mind, it becomes its concrete embodiment. (235) □

Although 'psycho-metaphysical' is an ungainly phrase, what Guiguet gestures towards with it is the intersection of the personal and the political that characterized late 1960s and early 1970s second-wave feminism and which has sustained politically oriented Woolf criticism ever since. Although the political aspects of Woolf's writing are not foregrounded by Guiguet, his account recognizes that she had aims beyond devising new structures for fiction.

Avrom Fleishman's *Virginia Woolf: A Critical Reading* (1975) represents the final phase of approaches that were concerned primarily with the structure of the text itself.[52] By the date of its publication, biographical materials had begun to appear that changed the nature of Woolf criticism, and the political upheavals of the 1960s had begun to change the scope of literary criticism; those developments will be examined in later chapters. In his Foreword to the book, Fleishman describes his approach as eclectic: he recognizes that New Critics might reject his use of biographical materials, and that historicists might be unsympathetic to his use of myth (p. xii). However, in other statements his sympathies become clear. He sees Woolf as similar to other high modernist writers (Eliot, Joyce, Pound and Yeats), and by that he means that she had 'a fundamentally literary sensibility'; her informal but wide-ranging literary education means that she forms her works 'around metaphors, allusions, and quotations drawn from the classics – ancient and modern' (p. x). In a critical context that differentiated sharply between scholars and critics, the importance attached to Woolf's literary knowledge might seem to place Fleishman on the side of the scholars, but he sees knowledge of 'intellectual context' as only a preliminary to the real work, 'the criticism of individual works of art' (p. xi). In the context of the time, Fleishman's references to 'works of art' and to 'literary sensibility' imply that Woolf was not producing works with political intentions. Elsewhere Fleishman explicitly rejects approaches that try to make 'a philosophical analysis' about Woolf's writings as a whole: such approaches fail to account 'for the multifarious verbal events in a work of fiction' (p. xii). Fleishman's primary focus is on entire novels (each of his nine chapters deals with a separate novel) understood as unified wholes. He is not interested in themes that run from one novel to another, or in the ways that the novels illuminate each other. In his discussion of *Mrs Dalloway* he speaks of its 'compelling unity' rooted in its being 'the fictional biography of a single character'. Its form is that of 'a center' (Clarissa) with 'radial links to a number of points on the circumference' (80). He shares with the New Criticism an interest in the verbal surface or texture of the work, with 'verbal events', and an interest in unified form; however, his interest in symbols, archetypes and mythologies leads those events to different places.

The beginning of Fleishman's chapter on *Mrs Dalloway* downplays the significance of technical innovation, asserting that the work is above all a novel, rooted in 'social life' and 'close character study' (69). Fleishman begins his reading with a systematic account of the novel's treatment of time and space, including a tabulation of its 21 unmarked sections. He pays close attention to verbal detail, and particularly the repetition of details that he tends to speak of as symbols: thus illness, for example, through frequent repetition, becomes a symbol 'of the state of society' (75). The 'cumulative effect' of such repetitions

> ■ is to establish a systematic network of social elements – human time, city space, personal relationships, professional and institutional activities, publicly shared symbols, political issues – so as to arrive at a vision of modern life on a national scale. (76) □

Such a verdict might suggest that Woolf was writing a condition-of-England novel for the 1920s, developing a form exemplified in the mid-nineteenth century by Elizabeth Gaskell's *North and South* (1854) and revived by E. M. Forster's *Howards End* (1910), but Fleishman remarks that Woolf does not apprehend the nation's collective existence 'externally', as would a social scientist or naturalist novelist, but internally, through internal monologues. He acknowledges that Woolf had 'highly developed' conceptions of collective existence, but states that what is 'of interest' in *Mrs Dalloway* is 'the form that such beliefs take in characters of different kinds' (76).

The designation of Septimus (in his own mind) as 'the greatest of mankind', 'the Lord who had come to renew society' and 'the scapegoat' (*MD* 22) is important for Fleishman's argument, as it justifies the discussion of the text in terms of archetypal symbolism. Of the 'scapegoat' passage, Fleishman comments that

> ■ Woolf deepens her portrait of the outsider by relating him to the archetype of the scapegoat, which has traditionally accompanied the communal ideal. By the exclusion, sacrifice, or crucifixion of one of its members the group establishes or reaffirms its own organic ties. (77) □

Septimus's last words ('I'll give it you', *MD* 127) signify his 'yielding his own life for mankind' (77).

While Fleishman does not use the word archetype in the discussion of Clarissa at this point, his focus on her 'strong instinct of withdrawal from others' (78) and the images of 'cloistral isolation and virginal inviolability' associated with her (79) suggest that she is halfway to being a symbol. On the basis that the novel is a biography of Clarissa and Clarissa alone, Fleishman describes the narrative as moving towards her 'enlightenment and imaginative expansion' in its closing scenes. *Mrs Dalloway* uses 'the conventions of the English social novel' for a 'metaphysical aim': 'the dawn of an individual's conviction of her own reality and the simultaneous evocation of that sense in the reader'. By 'reaching toward the epiphany of a human subject rather than of a god', Woolf is engaged in the 'secularization of traditional religious concerns' (80).

Fleishman's interest in archetype also finds the 'solitary traveller' passage (*MD* 48–50) particularly fertile ground. He focuses on a passage in the manuscript drafts of the novel which says that the benign divine power 'is my embodiment of an instinct' and 'the complement of his own person' (quoted 82–3), which he interprets in terms of a 'universal impulse' towards 'completion and security with the feminine aspect of oneself' (83). For Fleishman, the 'apparition' in the passage 'combines elements of Peter's imagination [...] with elements of Clarissa's' (83), and could be related to 'archetypes of the eternal feminine or *magna mater*' (84). It seems that this recognition occasions a small crisis of principle in Fleishman's method, as he asserts that the 'configuration of images' 'need not be pursued outside the text to reveal its powerful local significance' (84): Fleishman's method is essentially to treat the text as self-sufficient, but the invocation of archetypes requires one to consider what the archetype means or has meant in wider culture.

Fleishman suggests that repetition of images from one character to another, which many critics up to that date had seen as serving to give the novel a formal pattern, indicates that they are 'collective images, drawn from a larger community of mind' (84), although their immediate function in the text is to characterize the main figures. Fleishman looks in detail at the most prominent instance, the bird imagery that connects Clarissa and Septimus. 'This image of the characters assumes more than metaphorical significance, however, as the bird becomes a complex symbol through repeated and diverse uses.' It is in particular 'a means of communication with the universe' (85). The bird is identified with the street singer (who has a 'bird-like freshness', *MD* 70), 'adding to her connections with an ancient spring and with the great mother archetype' (85).

Fleishman also finds mythic significance in the narrative patterns of the novel. The sacrifice theme that is explicit in Septimus's status as scapegoat is also hinted at in Clarissa's consideration of her parties as 'an offering' (*MD* 103). Clarissa's contemplation of Septimus's suicide is also open to mythic interpretation. Fleishman quotes Northrop Frye's insight that many comic narratives 'approach a potentially tragic crisis' near the end (quoted 88), and that Clarissa's hearing of Septimus's death is 'a meeting with and release from the threat of death' (quoted 88). Fleishman says that

■ In recent studies of myth and archetype, such movements of the hero are called patterns of 'withdrawal and return'—a temporary removal from the active role, a pause for meditation and inspiration, and a rededication to the social group and its destiny. (88) □

He does not specify which studies are intended, but he may have had in mind works by Mircea Eliade and Mary Louise Lord.[53] Fleishman sees Clarissa and Septimus as a single 'conjoint protagonist' (88), with functions divided between them: 'while Septimus plays the role of sacrificial object [...] Clarissa plays the role of the social leader who temporarily withdraws for insight into the true significance of a leader's role and for rededication to it' (88–9).

While Septimus and Clarissa may contrast as drawn to death and life, respectively, they are not at odds with each other: both are 'healers', and are set against the 'forcers', Miss Kilman and Sir William Bradshaw. Fleishman acknowledges that the portrait of Bradshaw is 'wittily satirical', but argues that Woolf has connected it to the 'deepest themes of the work' by posing it in 'mythic terms'. Bradshaw is 'a figure of some permanence in the human imagination', a figure with a 'symbolic connection' with 'bewitchment, hypnotism, and other ritual practices' (89); he is not merely 'an authoritarian bully', but 'a shaman' (90). Set against him are Septimus, whose name suggests the seventh son of folklore, often gifted with 'restorative powers', and Clarissa, who Fleishman associates with the figure of Flora: she begins the story with a promise to bring flowers, and she stages her social triumph dressed in green (91).

For Fleishman, there are two stylistic modes in the novel: its 'tendency' is 'to assimilate its protagonists from their initially realistic mode to archetypal stature' (92). What this account omits is the question, first, of how far the archetypal status of the characters is simply a product of Fleishman's willingness to read them that way, and secondly, what to do with another mode of writing in *Mrs Dalloway*: the satirical. What if the exaggerated or unrealistic qualities that Fleishman reads as signalling archetypal status might be signalling satire? Fleishman's discomfort with the satirical aspect to the portrait of Bradshaw typifies a larger blind spot in his reading: any reading of Clarissa or Septimus as archetypes is undermined by their incomplete self-knowledge, and by the possibility that we should not take them at their own estimation.

There are continuities between the critical concerns of the earliest academic critics, like Bennett, and work as late as Fleishman's, in their largely unstated beliefs about the aims and limits of literary criticism, and their concern for finding pattern in the work itself. There are, indeed, continuities between such approaches and Woolf's own informal critical vocabulary of rhythm and pattern. But Woolf had other concerns, which a critical focus on form cannot do justice to, and which needed a new critical vocabulary. As we shall see in the next chapter, discussion of 'form', 'technique' and 'pattern' gave way to, or coexisted with, discussions of society, social roles, power and inequality. And to make such discussions possible, it was necessary to rescue Woolf from biographical accounts of her as an apolitical being, and to distinguish her modernism from that of her male contemporaries, particularly James Joyce.

CHAPTER TWO

Recovering Woolf: Criticism in the Era of Second-Wave Feminism

Biographical Accounts

Crucial to the revival of interest in Bloomsbury, and therefore Woolf, was Michael Holroyd's 1967 biography of Lytton Strachey. However, Holroyd presented Woolf in terms that were severely limiting to anyone who wished to take her seriously as a politically engaged writer.

> ■ Early photographs of Virginia Stephen show her as less robust and comely than Vanessa, rather anaemic and ethereal. From out of a thin anxious face, her enormous green eyes gaze out fearfully at the cold, slow terrors of the universe. There was always something unsubstantial and impalpable about her. She appeared to glide below the turbulent seas of life as in a dream that would pitch without warning into the terrifying troughs of nightmare. The mystic aura that during her life enveloped her fragile being like a cocoon has caused many of her friends' retrospective memories to take on the illusion of reverie. For though she could be as animated as her sister, when her haunted, melancholy expression would suddenly light up with a smile, making her face look oddly different, yet her nature was perpetually clogged with morbid self-obsession, the intensity of which would recurrently build up and explode, leaving her in a shattered state of sick, mental collapse. Even in lighter moments, her compulsive fits of vitality seemed to come not from her physical resources, but through a painful, electric system of nerves.[1] □

The idea of Virginia Woolf as the 'invalid Lady of Bloomsbury' had been in circulation even in her lifetime – E. M. Forster had attempted to rebut it shortly after her death – but Holroyd's account only reinforces it.[2] While Holroyd's remarks do not ostensibly concern Woolf's fiction, by emphasizing her delicacy, they reinforce the expectation that her fiction could not have engaged with the world, that, as Wyndham Lewis had claimed in 1934, she merely 'peeped' out at the world. The idea that her nerves were hypersensitive allows her to be a novelist of sensibility, but not a novelist of ideas. Holroyd's few remarks on Woolf's fiction build upon this idea of her: 'Virginia's strong masculine intelligence and heightened female sensibility seemed almost to cancel each other out, producing a sort of eddying, cross-current of nihility, a bleak no-man's-island that is reproduced in the aseptic, vestal texture of her fiction [...].' Hers are novels of 'anguished self-observation'; they are 'delvings into the sick, neuraesthenic depths of her nature'.[3] A reader of *Mrs Dalloway* starting from this biographical sketch would be unsurprised by Septimus's mental illness, and would be likely to read it biographically, but would not expect it to be a novel engaged with the texture of London life in the 1920s, still less with contemporary political realities.

In the same year as Holroyd's biography, Leonard Woolf published the volume of his memoirs covering the years 1919 to 1939. In it, he wrote that Virginia Woolf was 'the least political animal that has lived'. The phrase has frequently been employed by those who wish to minimize the political aspect of Woolf's art, and also by those who believe that Leonard Woolf failed to recognize Virginia's political understanding. But Leonard Woolf has been quoted selectively: he went on to refute the representation of her as 'a frail invalidish lady living in an ivory tower in Bloomsbury'. Rather, she was 'intensely interested in things, people, and events', and 'highly sensitive to the atmosphere which surrounded her, whether it was personal, social, or historical. She was therefore the last person who could ignore the political menaces under which we all lived.'[4] Leonard Woolf's account, and the different ways it has been taken, neatly encapsulates divergent versions of Virginia Woolf.

Quentin Bell's 1972 biography of Woolf presented a more complex and multi-faceted picture than Holroyd's vignette. However, although Bell acknowledged Woolf's political interests, he tended to diminish them or to patronize her. He records her menial work stuffing envelopes for a suffrage organization in 1910, but also brings to attention her severe reservations about political activists.[5] He notes her work as Secretary of the Rodmell branch of the Labour Party, but in doing so recalls an incident when she diverted discussion of a pressing political issue into 'an exchange of Rodmell gossip'. He also suggests that her world-view was closed to conventional political thinking. As a young man, Bell had tried to explain the 1930s political crisis to her as something deriving from an economic cause:

■ She was frankly amazed, neither agreed nor disagreed, but thought it a very strange explanation. To her, I think, it appeared that the horrible side of the universe, the forces of madness, which were never far from her consciousness, had got the upper hand again. This to her was something largely independent of the political mechanics of the world. The true answer to all this horror and violence lay in an improvement of one's own moral state; somehow one had to banish anger and the unreason that is bred of anger.[6] □

Echoing Holroyd's view of Woolf as someone who engaged with a metaphysical 'universe' and with private consciousness, but not with the political world, Bell personalizes the limitations of Woolf's political outlook. Bell also echoes Holroyd's view of Woolf as a writer when he argues that her characteristic prose style was unsuited to the urgent crises of the 1930s: 'Her gift was for the pursuit of shadows, for the ghostly whispers of the mind and for Pythian incomprehensibility, when what was needed was the swift and lucid phrase that could reach the ears of unemployed working men or Trades Union officials.'[7] Even if we concede that Woolf's gift was not for propaganda, it does not follow, as Bell would have it, that her prose 'could never be an effective vehicle for conveying political ideas'.[8] Conceding something to Bell, one might better say that her prose was an effective vehicle for prompting political reflection; that Woolf's political project presupposes a longer time scale than the political activists of the 1930s allowed themselves.

In the Shadow of *Ulysses*

In the 1950s and 1960s, a consensus emerged as to the nature of literary modernism and the works that defined it. The modernist canon that emerged was dominated by poetry, with T. S. Eliot's *The Waste Land* the central text, and with Ezra Pound and the later W. B. Yeats granted great importance. The emphasis on poetry was due to the characteristic focus of scholarly writing at the time: the novel was only slowly winning credibility as a focus for academic study; the New Critical emphasis on close reading tended to favour lyric poetry. The exception, the one work of fiction which was allowed to define the nature of modernism, was James Joyce's *Ulysses*. The importance accorded to *Ulysses* had significant effects on the critical acceptance of Woolf's novels, and particularly of *Mrs Dalloway*. Though the received assumptions about the modernist canon hindered the acceptance of Woolf as a modernist, champions of Pound and Joyce maintained that, conversely, Virginia Woolf and Bloomsbury had shaped mainstream English literary tastes to such an extent that the modernist experiment had never been properly accepted.

In 'The Strange Necessity' (1982), an article taking its name from Rebecca West's 1928 critical appraisal of Joyce, Patrick Parrinder traces the history of Joyce's rejection in England. In Parrinder's view, the English literary tradition assimilated only 'those elements of the modernist movement which could be reconciled with the dominant image of English cultural identity'.[9] Parrinder is interested less in those critics who rejected modernism outright, and more in those who were ostensibly aesthetically progressive, but who expressed criticisms of, or at least reservations about, Joyce's experiments.

> ■ We should look [...] at figures like Clive Bell, a leading member of the Bloomsbury circle and propagandist for post-Impressionist art, who in 1921 dismissed Joyce as an untalented mediocrity; at Desmond MacCarthy, who found Work in Progress [the drafts of *Finnegans Wake*] a 'physical impossibility to read'; at Richard Aldington, co-author of Pound's Imagist manifesto in 1913, who described *Ulysses* as 'a tremendous libel on humanity'; at E. M. Forster, who misread *Ulysses* in *Aspects of the Novel* (1924) as a 'dogged attempt to cover the universe with mud'; at John Middleton Murry, who spoke of Joyce's 'inspissated obscurities'; and, above all, we should look at Virginia Woolf. (161) □

Parrinder's examination of Woolf begins with her account of *Ulysses* in 'Modern Fiction' (1925). The Edwardian novelists (Bennett, Galsworthy, and Wells) are 'materialists', while the moderns are more spiritual. According to Parrinder, as soon as Woolf asks whether Joyce is really as spiritual as a novelist ought to be, her reservations begin to appear.

> ■ He may be the best of the moderns, but he is not in her view as great as Hardy or Conrad. The episode of Paddy Dignam's funeral fails, she says, 'because of the comparative poverty of the writer's mind – we might say simply and have done' [E4 161–2]. Joyce's supposed mental poverty is connected with another matter – a failure in taste. This is something that Woolf alludes to with more delicacy than Wells [who had once described Joyce as having a 'cloacal obsession'], with far more delicacy than vulgar, unbuttoned Ezra Pound, but the reference to an insalubrious 'obsession' is nevertheless unmistakeable. 'Does the emphasis', she writes, 'laid, perhaps didactically, upon indecency, contribute to the effect of something angular and isolated?' [E4 162]. In the privacy of her diary she was a good deal less circumspect than this. *Ulysses*, she noted, was the 'underbred' book [D2 199] of a 'self-taught working man', or perhaps of a 'queasy undergraduate scratching his pimples' [D2 188–9]. □

The references to Woolf's 'delicacy' are worth noting: while the word explicitly refers to her reluctance to name the problem directly, it also insinuates that she felt a physical aversion to the bodily functions described. With her aversion to the 'vulgar', Parrinder's Woolf is another version of Holroyd's anaemic and invalid lady of Bloomsbury. Parrinder's account of *Mrs Dalloway* echoes Wyndham Lewis's idea that Woolf's novel is merely an imitation of Joyce's:

> ■ Poor Joyce: once again his obscenity has been found reprehensible, not by a spokesman for conventional morality, but by a leading avant-garde artist – though admittedly this epithet seems a bit strong when Woolf is put beside Pound or Lewis. Woolf was unwilling for the Hogarth Press to try the experiment of publishing *Ulysses*, but she did borrow many of Joyce's procedures, such as the stream-of-consciousness monologue, the use of city streets as a setting, and the 'day in the life' of a number of characters, when writing *Mrs Dalloway* [...]. (162–3) □

The modernism of *Mrs Dalloway*, Parrinder concludes, is 'diluted' and 'anglicised'. Parrinder's assumption that the 'English' version is weaker, in contrast to its Irish other, is an interesting one, and possibly little more than an inversion of an English colonial belief about the passionate and unbalanced nature of the Celt.

Dismissive references to *Mrs Dalloway* may be found elsewhere in critical works by those committed to the Eliot–Pound–Joyce version of modernist literature. Hugh Kenner was a particularly prominent champion of this construction of modernism: his *The Pound Era* (1975) asserts Pound's centrality; in *Joyce's Voices* (1978), he claims that Ulysses was 'the decisive English Language book of the century', 'the first pivotal book in English since *Paradise Lost*' (p. xii). In *A Sinking Island* (1988), a critical study that aims to belittle English modernist writing, Kenner treats *Mrs Dalloway* dismissively. Like Parrinder, Kenner quotes Woolf's 16 August 1922 account of Joyce as a 'queasy undergraduate', and remarks:

> ■ She adds that she is even then 'laboriously dredging [her] mind for Mrs Dalloway' [D2 189], and there'd not have been a *Mrs Dalloway* but for *Ulysses*. The mid-August diary entry, the one that dismisses Joyce's monster, contains her first mention of her new undertaking. She meant to call it *The Hours*, and through its early pages clocks chime as they do in Joyce's.[10] □

It is difficult to determine whether the worst effect of such criticisms was that *Mrs Dalloway* was deemed not worthy of study, or that it was deemed worthy, but only as an adjunct to Joyce's masterpiece. In the American university system, there were reports from as late as 1989 of Woolf not being counted as a 'major' author for doctoral study: such institutionalized value judgements shape what is written about and what is published, and can shape a scholar's entire career.[11]

In parallel with the critical tradition of measuring *Mrs Dalloway* against *Ulysses* and finding it wanting was a tradition of trying to understand Woolf's novel on its own terms, while recognizing the presence of Joyce's. Carolyn Heilbrun's 'Virginia Woolf and James Joyce: Ariadne and the Labyrinth' was written around 1982, and circulated in manuscript form before being published in 1990.[12] Heilbrun is generous in her acknowledgement of earlier critics who had defended Woolf from the charge of copying: James Hafley, Jean Guiguet, James Naremore and Maria DiBattista. She notes that Woolf's critics often confine themselves to Woolf's 'snobbish' response in her diary. Heilbrun is a subtler reader of Woolf's diary than most, and argues that T. S. Eliot, as an early champion of *Ulysses*, is an unspoken presence in Woolf's responses: 'almost every time Woolf mentions *Ulysses* in her diary, she does so in the presence, so to speak, of T. S. Eliot, of his admiration and her distrust of Joyce, a distrust not only of what she called "underbred," but also of what she found egotistical, narrow, restricting' (60). Woolf's 'oft-quoted tirade against *Ulysses* as the book of a self-taught working man' is, Heilbrun notes, written in the same diary entry as a judgement about Eliot as one who is 'anaemic' and who therefore finds 'glory in blood' (*D2* 189). Heilbrun also notices that Woolf was interested in *Ulysses* up to the end of 'the cemetery scene' (also known as 'Hades'), and that only thereafter did she become 'bored, irritated, & disillusioned' (*D2* 188). The fear she feels is not snobbery, but 'terror before the raw masculinity, the male sexual fantasies that confront her – and all that such male fantasies imply for women' (62). After 'Hades' we find ourselves in the 'wholly masculine' worlds of the newspaper offices ('Aeolus') and the eating-houses ('Lestrygonians'). At the time of these remarks, Woolf had already begun writing *Mrs Dalloway*. While this fact does not entirely dismiss the charges of copying, as Woolf had been aware of the chapters of *Ulysses* serialized in the *Little Review*, it does put Woolf's remarks into perspective:

> ■ How could she have failed to perceive *Ulysses*, with its arrant masculinity and steaminess, with its drinking and swearing and eating and fornicating, but as a direct attack on her own aims for *Mrs Dalloway*, whose central character, a society lady, Woolf already feared would be too 'tinselly,' too 'feminine?' (62) □

(In fact Woolf recorded her specific doubts about the tinselliness of Clarissa over a year later [*D2* 272], but Heilbrun's larger point about self-doubt remains valid.)

> ■ Was Mrs Dalloway, her world far removed from the world of Blazes Boylan and his confreres, to seem unreal? Was it a failure? Feeling thus assaulted by *Ulysses*, she spoke of it thoughtlessly and brutally in her diary, using the

sort of epithets – racial, sexual, physically descriptive – that come to us when we are afraid, and angry, and not engaged in public discourse. (62)

Heilbrun argues that Joyce is not as innovative as Eliot believed, and that, in a resemblance to *Paradise Lost* that Kenner did not intend, *Ulysses* 'looks back to an old cosmology and an old faith' (60), while Woolf attempted to invent a new one (65):

> ■ *Ulysses* recreated, reworked one of the great epics: it reflected, in the mirror of a new technique, an old and long-known text. But however modern Joyce's technique, his art was profoundly conservative. Moreover, his characters were unaware of the ancient text against which they spoke: Bloom is not conscious of the classical forebears in whose steps he treads. [...] □
>
> ■ Woolf's characters, on the contrary, are aware of all the texts which preceded them – including those which were, like the female authors who probably wrote them, anonymous and little known. Aware of the entire western culture behind them, Woolf's characters are also aware it is not for them: it does not serve their lives. [...] It was, of course, inevitable that while Eliot praised the scaffolding that Joyce had employed for the writing of *Ulysses*, the use of an ancient text which alone made the novel possible in modern times, he scarcely noticed the equally arduous labors of the woman who was his friend: to write without scaffolding, knowing that none of the ancient texts would serve as one tried to net 'that fin in the waste of water'. (65–6) □

Heilbrun's final image is one that Woolf associated with *The Waves* from its earliest inception (*D3* 131) to its completion (*D4* 10): her argument here concerns not just the innovations of *Mrs Dalloway*, but others that Woolf sought throughout her career.

Heilbrun's essay concentrates on larger questions of Woolf's motivation and philosophy. By contrast, Harvena Richter's 'The *Ulysses* Connection: Clarissa Dalloway's Bloomsday' (1989) is more textually focused, and less explicitly feminist in its aims.[13] At times Richter's approach and her critical vocabulary owe something to the New Criticism: 'imagery' and 'leitmotif' are central to her account of the novel, and her argument is supported with abundant textual references; structure, and the unity of form and theme are also important. However, other features such as her quotation from extra-textual sources (Woolf's unpublished reading notes on *Ulysses*) might have been dismissed by the New Critics as 'scholarship' rather than 'criticism', and her interest in Woolf's feelings and motivations comes close to breaching the New Critical injunction against the 'intentional fallacy'.

Richter argues that the book publication of *Ulysses* in 1922 came at a propitious moment for Woolf: she had not felt as confident in her second novel, *Night and Day*, as she had in her first, and *Jacob's Room*, though well received by her friends, had been 'a critical disaster' (306). Like Heilbrun, Richter notes T. S. Eliot's admiration for *Ulysses*, and she suggests that it compounded Woolf's feelings of failure. More speculatively, she suggests that Woolf might have been irritated to find that one of the characters (Stephen Daedalus) had her maiden name as his forename, and that another (Leopold Bloom) was Jewish and had a name that recalled 'Leonard Woolf' (ingeniously, Richter points out that 'Woolf is almost Bloom spelled backwards'). She also notices that in early drafts, Septimus Smith is *Stephen* Smith, and that Sally Seton takes the name of Leopold Bloom's wife, Molly.

Richter itemizes the main areas of resemblance:

■ – the dual plot structure
  – three main characters
  – a contrast of two types of consciousness
  – emphasis on flowers / blooms
  – the date itself
  – relation of a symbolic number to the form / structure
  – man as microcosm
  – motif of heat
  – sexual humor
  – satire, irony
  – themes of impotence
  – the earth-mother figures of Molly Bloom, Sally Seton, and the beggar-woman[14] □

Richter suggests that Woolf's use of repeated imagery to bind together Clarissa and Septimus derived from her dissatisfaction with the coherence of *Ulysses*:

■ 'What is the connection between Bloom and Dedalus?' Woolf asked in her *Ulysses* notes. 'Connect, only connect', Septimus says in *Mrs Dalloway*.[15] And in an early manuscript version, 'They are always talking about making the connection, but they never do.' It would appear that Woolf's puzzlement over the separate stories of Bloom and Dedalus would spur her to design a series of connecting links between her own characters that would make her feel she had out-distanced Joyce – a private rebuttal for reasons of personal satisfaction. (307–8) □

Richter further argues that Woolf decided to make a virtue out of the split in the structure by emphasizing splits within the characters themselves: Septimus's 'split personality' is clear enough; that Clarissa was born under the sign of Gemini is something previously unnoticed by critics (we are told that she had 'just broken into her fifty-second year' [*MD* 31]). Clarissa is 'a typical woman Gemini: light and airy, "the perfect hostess" [*MD* 53], artistic [...], and composed of easily discerned twin selves: the outgoing social self, oriented toward life, and the inner emotional self, concerned with failure and death' (309). Richter gives a detailed account of the 'twinned imagery' through which Woolf dramatizes the bond between the two characters. The unifying effect of the imagery gives the novel a 'classical sense of balance' which Richter (following A. R. Reade) sees as a 'silent criticism' of the 'shapelessness' of *Ulysses*.

In her conclusion, Richter returns to Woolf's *Ulysses* notebook, where Woolf had characterized 'the big things' in Joyce's novel as 'love, death, jealousy and so on'; *Mrs Dalloway* likewise concentrates on these big themes. She also considers a passage where Woolf declares that reality lies in people's 'mind & feelings' and that it is therefore 'less necessary to dwell upon their bodies' (316). The vow to dwell on mind and feeling Richter sees as 'a revolt against Joyce's emphasis on the physical' (316). Although there are borrowings from *Ulysses* in *Mrs Dalloway*, 'they cannot be called imitation':

> ■ Rather, it is a question of transformation, of Woolf taking ideas from Joyce and adapting them to the particular needs of her novel. In so doing, she comments in an ironic manner on certain shortcomings of *Ulysses* and produces, at the same time, an original and indeed revolutionary work, its form related, as in all of Woolf's fiction, to the important symbolic themes. (316–17) □

Heilbrun attempts to make space for *Mrs Dalloway* by understanding Woolf's criticisms of *Ulysses* in their personal context. She makes large claims but does not engage in close reading of the novel. Richter makes a more specific reading, and transforms *Mrs Dalloway* from a passive copy of *Ulysses* to an active critique of it. If Richter makes some speculative leaps – there is no evidence that Woolf cared for astrology – they are not essential to her larger argument.

Recovering the Political

Woolf's account of *Mrs Dalloway* in her diary first entered the public domain in November 1953 with the publication of *A Writer's Diary*.

■ But now what do I feel about *my* writing? — this book, that is, The Hours, if thats its name? One must write from deep feeling, said Dostoevsky. And do I? Or do I fabricate with words, loving them as I do? No I think not. In this book I have almost too many ideas. I want to give life & death, sanity & insanity; I want to criticise the social system, & to show it at work, at its most intense. (*D2* 248)[16] □

Woolf's belief that she had 'too many ideas' was powerful though crude evidence with which to answer those critics who felt that she had too few, and that she was merely a novelist of sensibility; and her remarks about the 'social system' were useful evidence for those who recognized her political motivations.

One of the first critics to make use of this passage was Ralph Samuelson, whose 1958 article 'The Theme of *Mrs Dalloway*' expresses frustration with the then-dominant formalist analysis, or, as he terms it, the 'aesthetic approach'. It was not enough, wrote Samuelson, to say that *Mrs Dalloway* was 'a poem', as Leon Edel had claimed: one must ask whether it is a good or a bad poem. It was not enough to argue that it had a distinctive form: one must ask whether that form makes for a good novel. It was not enough 'to point to all the devices in *Mrs Dalloway* which Woolf gleaned from her reading of *Ulysses*'. The relationship of Clarissa and Septimus might echo that of Leopold Bloom and Stephen Dedalus in *Ulysses*, but Samuelson insisted that one must ask what the relationship meant 'in terms of the novel's theme.' For Samuelson, to read *Mrs Dalloway* as a novel is to ask 'what *Mrs Dalloway* is *about*'.[17] While such an approach could be reductive, in that it sees novels as nothing more than an embodiment of a theme, in its time it was a valuable redress, not only to formalists, but to critics such as D. S. Savage, who in 1950 had criticized Woolf for an absence of belief in her early novels. (Savage's approach was informed by his Christianity, but broadly resembled Leavisite arguments.)

Quoting Woolf's diary entry, Samuelson asserts that it contained 'all the major issues, the seeds of both the failures and the clear successes of the novel itself' (60). For Samuelson the entry particularly illuminates the relation of Clarissa to Septimus. Woolf does not wish simply to contrast the 'sane' society hostess and the 'insane' former soldier. The 'true "insanity" in the novel' is to be found in Sir William Bradshaw's idea of 'proportion' and Doris Kilman's idea of 'conversion' (61). Viewed from the perspective of Bradshaw, both Clarissa and Septimus are 'insane'. Bradshaw is 'the enemy of any tolerance which would allow the full expression of individual personality, and is thus the enemy of life itself' (66). For Samuelson, one of the novel's larger themes is the conflict between individual and society. Its prevailing attitude is one of sceptical questioning of accepted attitudes, leading to a tolerance of diversity.

■ Suicide, insanity, proportion: these are all terms which the novel forces us to use as we discuss it. But the very use to which the novel itself puts these terms, the ways in which the novel 'tests' them, as it were, should make us realize the impossibility of abstracting the terms and asking direct ethical questions about them: Is 'suicide' good? Is 'insanity' bad? Is 'proportion' desirable? Such questions obviously lead nowhere, and for the absolute moralist, *Mrs Dalloway* will remain a novel one might safely discuss only as an interesting display of technical virtuosity. Clearly Virginia Woolf insists that we ask: 'Suicide in what circumstances?' '*Whose* insanity?' '*What* kinds of proportion, dictated by whom?' (75–6) □

Samuelson concludes that the novel celebrates a 'very definite view of life': 'the worth of individual personality and the need for its expression, the affirmation of diversity itself'. His account of the novel emphasizes that Woolf's ideas tend to exist in her novels as interrogatives rather than declaratives: they prompt the reader's own critical thinking, rather than telling the reader what to think. And while his emphasis on the political is relatively muted, questions such as 'What kinds of proportion, dictated by whom?' recognize that, as later, Foucauldian critics would phrase it, discourse stands in a significant relationship to power.

The first book-length account of Woolf as a feminist writer was Herbert Marder's *Feminism and Art* (1968).[18] Between Samuelson's article and Marder's book, feminism had been revised through the influence of Simone de Beauvoir's *Le deuxième sexe* (1949, translated as *The Second Sex* [1953]) and Betty Friedan's *The Feminine Mystique* (1963). The Women's Liberation Movement, or 'second-wave' feminism, as it was later described, reflected that winning the vote had not been sufficient.[19] Wider legal and cultural transformations were necessary. As *Feminism and Art* is organized thematically rather than chronologically, it has little sustained discussion of *Mrs Dalloway*, but it marks a significant moment. Marder acknowledges from the outset that a portrait of Woolf as a feminist contradicts received opinion: she was more usually thought of 'as an experimental novelist who perfected a form of interior monologue', or as a member of 'some sort of esoteric cult: aestheticism, the Bloomsbury group' (1). Against this, drawing on *A Writer's Diary*, he sets her 1938 assessment of herself, echoing the *Times Literary Supplement*, as 'the most brilliant pamphleteer in England' (*D*5 148). It is notable that the context for her remark was the publication of *Three Guineas*, and by taking it as a key to Woolf's works, Marder inaugurates an important trend in Woolf criticism, particularly in North America. Unlike later critics, however, he does not find *Three Guineas* a successful work. The risk involved in granting interpretive centrality to *Three Guineas* is of projecting back the political situation of the mid- to late 1930s on to earlier works, and losing sight of the distinctive qualities of the 1920s. Marder's non-chronological approach facilitates the making of such connections across the decades, or, to put it more critically, the erasure of fine-grained historical differences.

Marder acknowledges that post-1945 critical distinction between art and propaganda when he begins to explain the relation of Woolf's politics to her art:

> ■ She was certainly committed to an aesthetic that stressed the purity of the work of art. She was also deeply interested in social problems. She combined these characteristics in her own highly individual way. Virginia Woolf never succumbed to the temptation to turn the novel into a vehicle for propaganda, as did, for instance, D. H. Lawrence. On the other hand, her novels are very far from being 'pure' works of art; there is, implicitly, a great deal of social criticism in them – a kind of latent propaganda. Virginia Woolf was perfectly capable of being doctrinaire, as her feminist essays show. Her desire to play the moralist was in conflict with her artistic conscience, and the conflict can be detected in almost everything she wrote. (2) □

Marder also warns that 'feminism' should be understood 'in its broadest sense', referring to Woolf's 'intense awareness of her identity as a woman, her interest in feminine problems', and should 'not be restricted to the advocacy of women's rights' (2). By 'women's rights' Marder means formal legal equality in matters of suffrage, employment rights or abortion rights. Marder's emphasis tends to be framed psychologically:

> ■ the subjugation of women is a central fact of history, a key to most of our social and psychological disorders. Western civilization has emphasized the (masculine) rational faculties to the exclusion of the (feminine) faculties of intuition. The Victorians – among them Virginia Woolf's father, Leslie Stephen – carried this one-sidedness to an extreme. Rejecting the feminine part of the psyche, they proved themselves to be barbarians in spite of their accomplishments. (2–3) □

The psychological emphasis can leave Marder sounding as if the ill effects of patriarchy were only felt psychologically, and as if they could be cured simply by individuals cultivating androgyny and achieving 'unity of being' (3). As Brenda Silver has noted, 'feminism' in Marder's account is subordinated to 'androgyny'.[20]

In his second chapter Marder turns to Woolf's treatment of the family as an institution which underwent dramatic changes during Woolf's lifetime. He compares the different presentations of domestic life found in *Night and Day, To the Lighthouse* and *The Years*. He touches on *Mrs Dalloway* when discussing different images of motherhood and the matriarch. In *To the Lighthouse* Mrs Ramsay is presented as a 'Great Mother', but she is also presented as an artist (39). Susan in *The Waves* is the 'pure mother' who 'lives in order to bear children', and who in consequence 'lives close to the ground of life' (39). Marder contrasts Susan with Clarissa Dalloway. Clarissa

■ is a hostess with a flair for giving parties, and a natural feeling for society and its conventions. She has a magnetism that draws people to her, but she is conspicuously unsuccessful as a mother. Whereas Susan is so close to the ground of life as almost to lose her individuality, Clarissa is so far removed from it as to lose touch with her basic instincts. (39). □

Marder sees Mrs Ramsay as combining the good qualities of both Susan and Clarissa: the move reflects the consensus of the time that *To the Lighthouse* was Woolf's greatest novel.

Later in the chapter Marder turns to Woolf's negative portrayals of home and married life, and he gives an extended consideration to Sir William and Lady Bradshaw. His starting point is the 'symbolic portrait' of the patriarchy that had appeared in Woolf's *The Voyage Out*. There, the minor character Evelyn Murgatroyd had paired photographs of her mother and father: the former appearing as someone with the life crushed out of her, the other a confident soldier.[21] The Bradshaws are another example of an 'unequal couple' (48). To achieve his professional success, Bradshaw has dehumanized himself, and in consequence, Lady Bradshaw, as pictured in his office, had 'gone under' (*MD* 85).

Marder remarks upon the irony in Woolf's portrayal of Bradshaw, arguing that she became 'the victim of her own indignation', and could not resist portraying the doctor in a caricatural mode. Her emptying him of 'human qualities' was exactly what she had accused Bradshaw of doing to himself. Marder notes that the language surrounding Bradshaw is often 'inflated', and that Woolf allowed herself to substitute 'rhetoric' for 'dramatic insight' (50): he quotes as evidence the description of Lady Bradshaw's subservience to her husband ('[the] slow sinking, waterlogged, of her will into his', *MD* 85), and the passage summarizing their married life ('[quick] to minister to the craving which lit her husband's eye so oilily for dominion, for power, she cramped, squeezed, pared, pruned', *MD* 85).

However, although he finds the two-dimensional quality of Bradshaw to be a 'flaw' in the novel, making it 'a shallower book than it might have been', it is not 'fatal', because *Mrs Dalloway* mostly focuses on the 'richer life' of Clarissa, Septimus and Peter Walsh. Moreover, Marder accepts that, despite the failing of the Bradshaw passages 'as fiction', they enable Woolf 'to convey a social message of real power':

> ■ The Bradshaw egoism is typical of the evils of modern life. In the home she [Woolf] saw it taking the form of paternal tyranny; in the mind it was pedantry; in the social code, convention emptied of human values; in politics, dictatorship. (50) □

While Marder's judgement that the Bradshaw passages are among the least successful in the novel is not unusual, the terms in which he frames it – that Woolf was 'a victim of her own indignation' – have in recent years come under critique, as feminist critics have attempted to rehabilitate the element of anger in Woolf's writing, freeing it from the implications that it is incompatible with art, and from the underlying residual idea that anger is 'unladylike'.[22]

Lee R. Edwards's 'War and Roses: The Politics of *Mrs Dalloway*' (1977) makes a conscious break with accounts of the novel that were interested only in its technique, style or form.[23] Its concerns are political, and in its closing paragraphs it anticipates the ethical turn in literary criticism of the 1980s and 1990s. Its break with older concerns is seen most clearly in its discussion of the grey motor car (*MD* 12–17). The car is important

> ■ not simply because it provides a convenient way for Virginia Woolf to move through time and space. It is important precisely because, unlike a conventional plot, the device is arbitrary, is not connected with human motivation, makes individuals feel, for the most part, insignificant, makes them feel that because the car is powerful whoever rides in it must be powerful as well. (166) □

Although Edwards might have accommodated her account of the car in a critical language of 'symbolism' (as had, for example Jean Love), that too is an approach she avoids.[24] For Edwards, the car is part of 'a web of references interweaving, mechanism, and human beings who have shifted their allegiance to some set of monumental abstractions' (166). She begins by asserting that two figures 'dominate' the novel, Clarissa and Septimus, and this, as she later makes clear, is a deliberate challenge to Avrom Fleishman's then-recent account of the novel as being '[d]espite its grounding in social and political life [...] the fictional biography of a single character'.[25] And although those two characters dominate the novel, their lives are not lived 'in a vacuum': 'To see the characters embedded in a social structure containing possibilities for both limitation and liberation is to discover the beginning of a new analysis, both feminist and social, not just of *Mrs Dalloway*, but of all the works of Virginia Woolf' (160). *Mrs Dalloway* is 'a serious, implicitly political investigation of the strengths and failures of middle-class society' (161).

To facilitate the recognition of *Mrs Dalloway* as a political novel, Edwards had explicitly to reject the narrow definition of politics as concerning 'the organisations of government, management, factions' and political parties (162–3). While the broader definition is now taken as read in most Woolf criticism, in 1977 it had to be argued for. For Woolf, Edwards argues, politics 'has first to do with people as individual entities rather than corporate masses'; there is a 'chasm' between politics understood in terms of 'human and humane value on one side and systems, bureaucracy, Acts of Parliament on the other' (163). As the glancing reference to Clarissa's musings on the alcoholic 'frumps' who can't be dealt with by Acts of Parliament implies (*MD* 4), this chasm is something Woolf herself had recognized.

Although Edwards is not a historicizing reader in the sense of one who contextualizes the work with reference to external events or texts, it is crucial to her argument that *Mrs Dalloway* is a novel of post-war London. She identifies the various ways that the war marks the present moment of 1923, noting, as a very obvious point, the army cadets who Peter Walsh finds marching (*MD* 43–4), and as a subtler one, the respect for authority embodied in the scene with the grey car. Her account of Septimus has at its heart the phrase about Septimus having 'developed manliness' in the trenches (*MD* 73). She also highlights the opposition of culture and masculinity, remarking as few critics do that Septimus's interest in culture and poetry had aroused suspicion and concern even before the war: his manager Mr Brewer had advised that he take up a manly pursuit like football. On 'develop[ing] manliness', Edwards remarks:

■ How odd that what a man is should not be sufficient to define him as a man, and that 'manliness' should be seen as a quality to be learned. We do not, after all, have to teach a horse to be horsely or a rose to be a rose. How odd, too, that for so long we have not noticed, much less condemned, this oddness. (168) □

She goes on to note the particular lesson that Septimus learned when he became a man: that 'he must not feel'. Edwards's innovation at this point is not so much in her argument as in her tone, committed to a political position and mocking the exclusion of such political considerations from critical and social discourse.

Edwards attempts to defend Woolf's one-dimensional portraits of the doctors, Holmes and Bradshaw, as being 'neither accidental nor a flaw' in Woolf's technique. They emerge 'harshly and without shadows because Virginia Woolf wishes us to see them literally as vampires who feast "most subtly on the human will" (*MD* 85)' (171). They embody the 'social imperatives' that force men and women to abandon their individuality. Edwards explains that Woolf uses them

> ■ to show in fictional terms the linkage she treats more abstractly in *Three Guineas*, a network that ties all forms of oppression to each other, that has at its roots a love of power, an egotistic craving to stamp the world out according to the pattern that exists in one's own head or, failing that capacity, simply to stamp out the other patterns in the world. (171) □

If Edwards's defence is not wholly successful, it is because her political justification starts from different premises to the aesthetic objections to Holmes and Bradshaw. She does not address the unwritten rules of literary aesthetics that state when a 'one-dimensional' or 'flat' character is admissible in a novel, or the larger question of when worthy political ends might justify aesthetically crude means.

Elsewhere in the essay, Edwards sees the complexity of Woolf's characters, her willingness to given them self-contradictory traits, as a virtue of the novel, its way of blocking the impression that it is 'asserting the innate superiority of women over men' (173). Thus, for example, several of the female characters subscribe to the values of 'Proportion and Conversion', and neither Peter Walsh nor Richard Dalloway are, by the standards of their society, 'quite "manly" or "successful"' (174). Edwards's explanation is that Woolf wishes to avoid imprisoning the world 'in a code of feminism', and thus to avoid being guilty of a crime of imposing her values similar to that perpetrated by Holmes and Bradshaw. However, another more important virtue emerges from contradiction in characterization. Woolf's focus, Edwards argues, is not on the ultimate causes of our actions and social structures, but

> ■ on the ways in which individuals respond to the roles assigned them by the world, and on the nature and significance of the roles themselves. Freedom in her books is measured by the degree to which individuals can manipulate their socially assigned and defined roles. Clarissa and Sally Seton survive in Mrs Richard Dalloway and Lady Rosseter. [...] Finally, in those situations where a choice must be made, we can endorse the heart rather than the brain, choose roses and not war. Such freedom, Virginia Woolf suggests, is more easily available to women precisely because they have less power in society and therefore less of a vested interest in either society or power. (174–5) □

Although Edwards does not return to her argument about Holmes and Bradshaw at this point, the implication is that the price they pay for their power is a lack of freedom to respond to the roles assigned to them; their selves have become identical with their roles to the point of ossification. However, the argument that a novel can depict one-dimensional people because there are such people in the real world does not address the issue of whether such depictions are aesthetically satisfying.

In a coda to her main argument, Edwards admits to being unable to overcome doubts about the novel that she had felt on first reading it, and more particularly, doubts about the portrayal of Clarissa. She implicitly engages with Fleishman's idea of Clarissa as Flora:

> ■ Had we – women, that is – come so far, I asked, merely to be confronted with a vision of woman as goddess, an endorsement, however complex or ambiguous, or our sex as maintainers of some ineffable 'life', a vision of the world which suggested hostess as an honorable profession? Hadn't women been goddesses and hostesses long enough? (175) □

Moreover, such status seems inadequate to the problems the novel poses: in its own terms, roses are inadequate to help the persecuted Armenians. Edwards's response is to suggest that we change the terms of the question, and ask what else might help the Armenians. She does not deny that the conventional responses ('money, letters, and other signs of support') have achieved something, but also presents conventional politics as too pessimistic and narrow in its outlook. Is there not another way? she asks:

> ■ Could we create an alternative motion and set of social patterns based neither on systems nor on power but deriving instead more directly from individuals, from a notion that people are quite various and variable and that therefore we must learn to live leaving the ideas of others alone, learn to live with their solitude and our own as well? (176) □

There should be, she asserts in conclusion, a connection between 'politics' on the one hand, and 'feelings' and 'values' on the other (177). If this final phase of Edwards's essay reminds us of one of its frustrating features – that she sometimes answers her own questions obliquely, changing the terms rather than tackling them directly – it also speaks to the strength of the essay: its ability to pose new and difficult questions, and to speak in a voice that extends the range of literary criticism and that makes it possible to discuss such questions with passion and with precision.

Woolf critics in the late 1960s and in the 1970s worked to rescue Woolf from the condescending attitudes typified by Holroyd, from those modernist critics who placed James Joyce at the centre of the canon and allowed *Ulysses* to dictate the terms of inclusion, and from the narrow formalism of the New Criticism. The last part of this chapter has focused on the recovery of the political, and has noted that there were precedents for such work as far back as the 1950s. There were, of course, other currents. Some critics reacted against New Critical formalism not by concentrating on political content, but by arguing that Woolf wrote novels, and that critics needed to concentrate on the characters: Mitchell Leaska's *The Novels of Virginia Woolf* (1977) is the prime example, but there is a similar tendency in Jean Alexander's *The Venture of Form in the Novels of Virginia Woolf* (1974), while, as we shall see in the next chapter, Roger Poole's *The Unknown Virginia Woolf* (1978) related Woolf's characters to biography in a way that the New Criticism had completely outlawed. Some critics expressed antipathy to politicized readings on the grounds that they were reductive,[26] but a search for aesthetic 'pattern', 'form' or 'structure' can be just as reductive as a search for political intent. An awareness of Woolf's politics has become a given in almost all Woolf criticism, though there has been lively disagreement about what exactly her politics consisted of, and of how it related to her fiction.

CHAPTER THREE

Woolf and Philosophy

Early Reviews

Even during Woolf's lifetime, critics disagreed about whether her works could or should be fruitfully related to a 'philosophy', either one of her own devising, or one derived from other thinkers. The unconventionality of her novels, and in particular their avoidance of conventional portrayals of character and action, led some critics to detect a philosophical atmosphere to them. However, to connect her works to a philosophy is potentially to reduce them to it, and to fail to engage with their qualities as works of art. Relating her works to a philosophical background may have the benefit of bestowing an intellectual seriousness upon them that counteracts the myth of an unintellectual and aesthetic Virginia Woolf, but it potentially makes her dependent upon a canon of philosophers whose ways of thinking were alien to her.

Critics who wished to separate Woolf from a morally earnest tradition of English fiction often underplayed the extent to which she had a philosophy: this was E. M. Forster's rationale in writing about her early experimental fiction, 'The Mark on the Wall' (1917): her art, he wrote, 'has no moral, no philosophy, nor has it what is usually understood by Form'.[1] Here, 'philosophy' is more or less equivalent to moral outlook. If we understand philosophy differently, it is possible to see Woolf's unconventionality as 'philosophical'. For example, the *New Statesman*'s review of *Mrs Dalloway* remarked that Woolf had extraordinary gifts, but questioned whether they were the gifts of a novelist. It noted particularly that she excels in the description of a mood, but qualified this praise: 'the mood might be anybody's'. The reviewer went on to say that, in the whole novel, 'there are no people. It is like that ghostly world of Mr Bertrand Russell's philosophy, in which there are lots of sensations but no one to have them.'[2] The reviewer may well have been aware that the philosopher Russell (1872–1970) was on the fringes of Woolf's circle, and thereby suggests a line of inquiry for later, more scholarly critics. Other critics, without using the word 'philosophy', hinted that it was helpful to approach *Mrs Dalloway* from a philosophical perspective. Concluding his review in 1925, Gerald Bullett remarked:

> ■ One part of this method's general effect on the reader is to make him feel that he is observing, from a great height, a world of disembodied spirits. It is not so much that the picture lacks definition as that it lacks stability; its outlines are incessantly flowing into new, bright patterns. Nothing for a moment stands still; [...]. To those who desire a static universe, in which they can examine things at their leisure, this speed, this insubstantiality, this exhilarating deluge of impressions, will be perhaps unpleasing.[3] □

Talk of a 'static universe' and its opposite, and of 'insubstantiality' and sense 'impressions' derives from philosophical discussion, even if the terms are not used with the precision that one would find in formal works of philosophy.

In the early reviews of *Mrs Dalloway*, the fullest consideration of Woolf's philosophical inclination was Richard Hughes's. Hughes praised Woolf for the vividness of her portrayal of London, and her 'sense of form', but went on to suggest that Woolf had other, greater strengths:

> ■ Philosophy as much as smell of violets is grist to the artist's mill: in actual practice it is generally more so. Here, Mrs Woolf touches all the time the verge of the problem of reality: not directly, like Pirandello, but by implication.[4] □

As we saw in Chapter One, Hughes goes on to place Woolf's understanding of the world in relation to philosophical relativism, and the idea that what the mind finds in the external world is merely the reflection of itself. Luigi Pirandello's play *Six Characters in Search of an Author* had been performed in English in 1922, and the games it plays with identity and reality had been widely discussed. Hughes's praise, however, suggests that philosophy in Woolf is at its strongest when it is least direct, and that the solipsistic position – the belief that we can have no real knowledge of anything outside ourselves – is present in the novel not so much in speeches or explicit thoughts, but in the atmosphere of anxiety, keyed to the repetition of the phrase from Shakespeare's *Cymbeline*, 'Fear no more the heat of the sun.'

Reviewers of her later novels were more inclined to praise Woolf, as E. M. Forster had done, for not insisting on a philosophy. In his review of *The Years* (1937), David Garnett praised Woolf for not having brought philosophy into the novel.[5] Garnett may well have had in mind Woolf's essay 'The Novels of George Meredith' (1928), in which she had remarked that Meredith's teaching 'obtrudes': 'and when philosophy is not consumed in a novel, when we can underline this phrase with a pencil, and cut out that exhortation with a pair of scissors and paste the whole into a system, it is safe to say that there is something wrong with the philosophy or with the novel or with both' (*E*5 550). Garnett also contrasts Woolf's contemporary D. H. Lawrence in this regard. For Garnett, philosophizing and vivid immediacy are mutually exclusive. By avoiding intrusive philosophy, Woolf frees herself to give the 'unsophisticated directness of sense impression': 'The only realities are the things she has seen that touched her imagination and that are lighted up in her mind.'[6] Shortly after Woolf's death, another reviewer, perhaps also with Lawrence in mind as a contrast, praised her for having 'kept her immediate "material", sensual or conceptual, constantly in mind', and for having 'shut out all that vague mass of cheap idealism and subjective emotionalism which masqueraded under the loose name of philosophy'.[7]

Philosophies of Perception and Form

After Woolf's death, several attempts to identify a philosophy in her work drew analogies with the ideas of figures who influenced or were members of the Bloomsbury group, notably the Cambridge philosopher G. E. Moore (1873–1958) and Woolf's friend Roger Fry, an art historian and art theorist.

In some cases, the attempt to identify a philosophy is barely distinguishable from an attempt to clarify Woolf's aesthetics. One of the earliest articles to consider *Mrs Dalloway* in this light, John Hawley Roberts's '"Vision and Design" in Virginia Woolf' (1946), argues that the novel 'incorporated' Fry's critical ideas in its form.[8] Citing Woolf's 'Mr Bennett and Mrs Brown' (1924), Roberts sharply contrasts the 'sociological' realism of Bennett, Galsworthy and Wells with Fry's vision of art, in which 'art differs from life in that it requires no responsive deeds' (835). Woolf's literary art has this 'self-contained quality': in other words, her philosophy of art is a formalist one. Such a philosophy was expounded in Fry's collections of critical essays *Vision and Design* (1920) and *Transformations* (1926). In the words of a later art critic, Fry's study of the artists he called the Post-Impressionists led him to understand art as 'depending for its effect solely on the relations of forms and colours, irrespective of what the forms and colours might represent' (K. Clarke, quoted Roberts 836). Our pleasure in looking at art derives not from recognizing the objects or people represented, but from 'the recognition of order, of inevitability in relations' (Fry, quoted by Roberts 836–7). Roberts goes on to identify several such 'relations' in the structure of *Mrs Dalloway*, and to assert that these are the source of our readerly pleasure. His first and most significant instance is the relation of the characters of Clarissa and Septimus. Citing in support Woolf's introduction to the American (Modern Library) edition of the novel (*E4* 548–50), in which she had noted that originally that the two were 'one and the same person', Roberts says that 'They are not separate and individualized characters, but opposite phases of an idea of life itself. Their reality consists not of themselves as persons, but of their relationship to each other as forms' (837). Our pleasure in reading the novel 'consists in our recognition of the rightness of this basic design, that is, of the way in which Clarissa and Septimus complement each other, Clarissa's elementary love of life matching Septimus's repudiation of it' (837). Roberts cannot readily find evidence to support such an assertion, and assumes that we will not find any conventional pleasure of identification with the characters; secondarily, it might be remarked that by foregrounding Clarissa's 'love of life', Roberts both underplays her melancholy and underestimates the satirical aspect of the novel.

The argument that the novel relies on patterns of contrasts is easier to support; Roberts equates such contrasts with relations between pictorial lines and masses. He considers in particular the image of a coin flung away, which is first announced in Clarissa's memory of 'throwing a shilling into the Serpentine' (*MD* 8), and partly echoed when Septimus flings himself on to the railings (*MD* 127); the connection is secured when his death recalls to Clarissa her having thrown away a shilling (*MD* 156). The other pattern of relations considered by Roberts lies in the parallels between the scene in which Clarissa sees the old lady opposite climbing the stairs, and the scene in which Septimus, shortly before his suicide, sees an old gentleman opposite descending the stairs (*MD* 107, 127). Again Roberts has to assert something about the reader's reaction:

> ■ The reader's response to the whole is very much like that of one who standing before a painting begins to see, as Fry would see, how this mass necessarily balances that, how this line repeats, with a difference, that one, how a high-light here inevitably answers a shadow there, how, in other words, the meaning of the picture lies in our discovery of the fact that the forms agree. (839) □

Roberts goes on to find more complex instances of patterning involving events such as the chiming of Big Ben, the mysterious motor car, or the skywriting aeroplane. In these instances there is a greater dynamism than in the earlier instances, and this draws comparison with Fry's remarks about the Post-Impressionist painter Paul Cézanne: Roberts asserts that *Mrs Dalloway* embodies 'the vivid sense of life and the vibration and movement that Fry found in Cézanne' (842). While Roberts's focus on the form and technique of Woolf's novels ensures that the philosophy he finds meets Woolf's criterion of not obtruding, the focus on the 'self-contained' quality of her art means that it is a 'philosophy' of no relevance to anything other than the novel in question.

Anna Benjamin's 1965 article 'Towards an Understanding of the Meaning of Virginia Woolf's *Mrs Dalloway*' has some characteristics in common with Roberts's.[9] At its core is an analysis of the novel's structure, and this essentially formalist analysis is used to support a larger claim about the novel expressing 'a view of reality' (214). Benjamin's analysis focuses on the novel's time-framework, and aims to show 'how Woolf dealt with the problem of representing in words a time within which a moment cannot be isolated' (216). The underlying view of reality in the novel is an 'organic' one, in which every location and every moment in time is interconnected with every other. Though Benjamin keeps specific philosophical references in the background, her notes cite the mathematician and philosopher A. N. Whitehead in particular, and her phrase 'simple locations' echoes one used in his *Science and the Modern World* (1925), where it describes a commonly held but ultimately oversimplified notion of space.[10] While Benjamin's account does not ignore Septimus, and indeed makes much of Septimus having been born at about the time that Clarissa rejected Peter at Bourton, it does not emphasize the difference in social class; nor does it make reference to Woolf's remarks about wanting to show the 'social system' at its most intense, though these had appeared in *A Writer's Diary* (1953). Thus Benjamin sees the novel as one in which philosophical concerns are more prominent than social ones:

> ■ In searching for meaning in *Mrs Dalloway*, we find a reassertion of the value of living life in its fullest as part of the universe, just where we might expect to find life at its most trivial, insignificant level: among the restricted privileged class in London. The very rejection of social issues and the placing of the problem of the meaning of life amid the privileged class make the basic issues presented in the novel clearer. (223) □

In Benjamin's view, the novel ends with an 'affirmation' that 'the very living of life fully, together with the feeling of being part of the universe' is more important than the question of 'whether or not life is good' (223). In this regard, Benjamin's reading anticipates some slightly later readings of the novel that see its philosophy as existentialist.

In her 1970 book, Harvena Richter was cautious of 'linking any writer's method with a specific philosophy or doctrine', but in proposing that Woolf's fiction attempted to embody a distinctive idea of consciousness, Richter noted philosophical parallels, particularly the phenomenological tradition of Edmund Husserl as mediated by G. E. Moore.[11] Richter argues that consciousness is not merely mental, nor even composed of ideas and feelings, but is 'part of a complex synthesis of the individual's total response to life' (p. vii). Woolf 'seeks to approximate the actual ways in which man sees, feels, thinks, and experiences time and change' (p. vii). While wary of associating Bloomsbury with a 'fixed doctrine', Richter suggests that we can identify 'a mental atmosphere or "climate"' (19).

> ■ Governed by G. E. Moore's 'scientific method', the Bloomsbury attitude was outwardly rational and questioning, but also inward-turning, examining philosophical and aesthetic questions from an intuitive or neo-mystical standpoint. Maynard Keynes in his memoirs has described it as a religion. This term is misleading, but it does suggest the pervasiveness of certain ideas which became not dry doctrine but a mode of living and perceiving reality. What applied to art and philosophy could apply to life. Questions of inward and outward reality, subject and object, conscious and unconscious, or problems of the relationship between the self, art, and the world, were strong Bloomsbury concerns, and they find their echo in the works of Virginia Woolf. A more specific example, perhaps, is that of G. E. Moore's principle of organic unity which widened, especially for Virginia Woolf, and to some extent for E. M. Forster and Roger Fry, into a recognition of the unity between the self and the preceptual [sic] world. (19–20)[12] □

While J. K. Johnstone had emphasized G. E. Moore's *Principia Ethica* as an influence on Bloomsbury, Richter turns to his later collection of essays, *Philosophical Studies* (1922), noting particularly papers in which he examines 'the different varieties of sensory experience and the separation of that experience, or consciousness of it, from the object itself', arguing that Woolf incorporated Moore's ideas about sensory experience into her own 'subjective modes' (20–1).

Richter's study is organized thematically, and as such is of greatest value to readers familiar with the entirety of Woolf's oeuvre; she is less concerned to reach conclusions about individual novels than she is to present the large picture. Nevertheless, the study has many important insights into Woolf's presentation of consciousness in *Mrs Dalloway*. Richter brings out how Woolf's desire to express the fullest conception of consciousness shapes the syntax of her prose. In a passage in *To the Lighthouse*, the narrator remarks of a central character that 'to follow her thought was like following a voice which speaks too quickly to be taken down by one's pencil' (*TL* 23), and Richter remarks that Woolf was conscious of 'the impossibility of actually recording in words what occurs simultaneously [...] in the mind' (45). One of Woolf's solutions is to use parenthetical phrases to record moments when a thought and action occur simultaneously, sometimes literally using a parenthesis sign, on other occasions using subordinate clauses. For example:

> ■ But she could remember going cold with excitement and doing her hair in a kind of ecstasy (now the old feeling began to come back to her, as she took out her hairpins, laid them on the dressing-table, began to do her hair), with the rooks flaunting up and down in the pink evening light. (*MD* 20–30) □

Richter remarks that the passage combines simultaneous thought and feeling, and, in addition, present action with past memory and action (46). Another of her examples concerns Clarissa's reaction to Hugh Whitbread:

> ■ For Hugh always made her feel, as he bustled on, raising his hat rather extravagantly and assuring here that she might be a girl of eighteen, [...]; she always felt a little skimpy beside Hugh; schoolgirlish; but attached to him [...]. (*MD* 5) □

Here Woolf combines thought and action in a single sentence.

In Richter's account, Woolf is aware that the 'angle of vision' affects the presentation of experience, the 'angle' here standing for both the physical and psychological position from which a person sees the world. Septimus Warren Smith serves as a key example of 'visual distortion caused by abnormal perception' (88). Septimus

> ■ not only thinks in metaphor, he experiences it, projecting his inner vision onto outward reality. He literally sees Rezia as a flowering tree, or the sound of music as 'smooth columns'. Instead of feeling emotionally one with nature, he images red flowers growing through him, communicates with leaves, and hears birds speak Greek. (88) □

While Richter is firm that we are supposed to recognize Septimus as a schizophrenic – in footnotes she draws on the then-current medical literature to confirm this diagnosis – she does not wish to reduce Septimus to his illness: 'In showing the world through Septimus's disordered vision, Virginia Woolf helps the reader to discover the rich resources of human perception' (89).

Later chapters in Richter's study consider the multiplicity of personality (with Clarissa sitting at her mirror [*MD* 31] as the typical case), and the technical problem of finding a voice that can articulate this complex sense of being, and, going beyond the individual, a sense of being that 'is at once conscious and unconscious, personal and impersonal, individual and collective' (129). Richter gives as an example the opening pages of *Mrs Dalloway*, and invites us to trace how 'voice follows voice' (131):

> ■ We see how the morning 'seemed' to Clarissa herself, how 'one' feels at night hearing Big Ben (the implied 'I' is exchanged for a more universal pronoun), how time and motion (the third voice, concretized in the 'whirling young men, and laughing girls' in transparent muslin, 'unwound' by the morning) form part of the world surrounding Clarissa. The result is a whole Clarissa, an emotional tonality not limited by confinement to her thoughts. The use of 'I' (stated or implied by 'she') would shrink Clarissa to the mere observing, inactive self. The reverie, on the other hand, is a reflection of Clarissa's total participation in life. (131). □

Particularly intriguing is Richter's suggestion that one of the voices in Woolf's novels is impersonal: 'the voice of history, myth, legend' (140), which she illustrates in *Mrs Dalloway* by reference to the passage about the sound made by the 'rusty pump', the 'battered old woman' (*MD* 69). Richter asks: 'Is it a woman, or a spring?' and responds: 'It hardly matters, for it is the voice of water, of time', and suggests that it anticipates the voice of Anna Livia Plurabelle in Joyce's *Finnegans Wake*.

In concluding her study Richter returns to her ambivalence about associating Woolf with a particular philosophical school. First, there is the problem that, as much as reminding us of her forebears such as Henri Bergson or William James, Woolf seems to anticipate later developments: 'Virginia Woolf belongs to the moment of now' (245). Moreover, in so far as Richter's study attempts to associate Woolf with a particular philosophy, it is one that emphasizes the importance of the non-rational components of experience – the emotional and the bodily, or 'lived experience' (245), rather than rationalized experience – and so it seems to exceed philosophy as it is normally understood.

Woolf and Bergsonism

That the French philosopher Henri Bergson was influential in the English-speaking world from 1909 onwards has never been in doubt; whether he influenced Virginia Woolf's works has been a far more contentious question. If he did, then *Mrs Dalloway* is the most relevant text, because at the heart of Bergson's philosophy was a claim about time: that the true nature of time was something indivisible (which Bergson called *la durée*, 'duration'), but that the intellect falsely spatialized duration into the segments of *le temps*. The constant chiming of Big Ben in

Mrs Dalloway seems to speak to one side of this division, while the interweaving of present and past through personal memory seems to speak to the other. The passage about the clocks of Harley Street 'Shredding and slicing, dividing and subdividing' the June day (*MD* 87) seems particularly in tune with the idea that *le temps* performs an act of violence on *la durée*.

A version of the Bergsonian reading of the novel had been suggested by Floris Delattre in his French study (1932), discussed in Chapter One, but in the Anglophone world, the most influential early account came in James Hafley's *The Glass Roof* (1954):

> ■ *Mrs Dalloway* represents the conflict, not between person and person, but between duration and false time. On twenty occasions during the course of the novel, clocks strike [he quotes the 'clocks of Harley Street' passage] and against the materiality of this spatialized day in London is placed the spirituality, the true duration, of Mrs Dalloway's consciousness, the continuity of which denies that 'dividing and subdividing.' (62) □

Shiv Kumar's *Bergson and the Stream of Consciousness Novel* (1962), while making a wide survey of novels by Dorothy Richardson, Woolf and James Joyce in relation to Bergson, examines *Mrs Dalloway* in only two pages. Kumar remarks upon Woolf's ability to accommodate extensive memories of the past (for example, Clarissa's recollections of Bourton) in a relatively narrow portion of clock time (the half-hour from 11am to 11.30am). He recognizes the contrast between the central characters (Septimus and Clarissa), who live in *la durée*, and the doctors, who 'uphold the tyranny of external time over the inner stream of experience', but limitations of space, or of his analytical framework, prevent him from developing any more complex account.[13]

Arguments against the Bergsonian reading came in two forms. One, the more scholarly argument, raised sceptical questions about whether Woolf knew (or was interested in) Bergson's philosophy. Woolf herself had written to an academic inquirer in 1932 to say that she had 'never read Bergson' (*L5* 91).[14] Such denials may be countered in several ways. We may treat them as outright untruths, intended to direct critics to attend to Woolf's art rather than the portentous philosophies they might find behind it. We may treat them as literally true, but note that while Woolf may never have read Bergson's own works, his ideas and his characteristic vocabulary were available in many secondary accounts published in 1910–13.

The other form of argument, seen in J. W. Graham's 'A Negative Note on Bergson and Virginia Woolf' (1956), is to argue that regardless of whether Woolf had read Bergson or Bergsonian works, her own works are not in themselves Bergsonian. Such an argument has the merit of attending to the works themselves, but can take the form of a sweeping rejection of all forms of non-literary influence: it sets an impossibly high standard for being 'Bergsonian', and when the author fails to meet the standard, it asserts that Bergson is an irrelevance. As novels are not works of philosophy, they can never attain the right level.

Mary Ann Gillies's account of the problem, in her study *Henri Bergson and British Modernism* (1996), took advantage of the great wealth of additional information that had emerged since Graham's article and Kumar's book.[15] Woolf's late memoir 'A Sketch of the Past' is important to Gillies for the distinction it makes between 'moments of non-being' and 'moments of being' (109). The latter are rarer: they are moments when 'one becomes alive: aware of one's immediate surroundings and also of one's place in history' (109). They seem to 'arrest the flow of time', but should not be seen as moments 'out of time': rather, in Bergsonian terms, they are 'moments of pure duration, moments during which past and present time not only literally coexist, but during which one is aware of their coexistence' (109). Gillies sees Woolf's experimentalism as an attempt to create 'new narrative strategies' that would capture the quality of moments of being (110). *Jacob's Room* partially succeeds, but is compromised by contradictory impulses. It demonstrates Woolf's Bergsonian understanding of memory as a faculty that links 'current and past experiences in such a fashion that the two reflect upon each other: the present experience is rendered comprehensible by comparison with a previous experience and the past is renewed and altered by its contact with the present' (114).

The Bergsonian idea of memory becomes important in Gillies's account of *Mrs Dalloway*, as does Woolf's account of her digging 'beautiful caves' behind her characters, her 'tunnelling process' (*D2* 263, 272). The novel contains a conventional chronological narrative; it is transformed by 'the inclusion of the novel's second level, its *durée*':

> ■ An incident sparks off a memory of the past which, in turns brings about a fresh understanding of the present. [...] The 'tunneling process' does not just provide background information; it knits together present actions and choices with the elements that led the character up to the moment of action. (115–16) □

Gillies's first illustration is taken from the closing scenes of the novel, where Clarissa's past, present and future come together 'in one single, prolonged moment of insight into herself' (116). Gillies reads Clarissa's sympathetic re-experiencing of Septimus's death in terms of Bergsonian intuition, a faculty that enables one to discern 'what is unique and inexpressible in another' (116). Moreover, she sees Clarissa as acting on her intuition when she returns to the party: for Bergson, the self-knowledge that comes from intuition is 'useless' unless we act on it (118). Gillies's argument also considers the place of memory in *Mrs Dalloway*, contrasting Peter Walsh's properly functioning memory with Septimus's damaged mind. She examines the way that Peter Walsh, waking in Regent's Park, is transported back to Bourton by the involuntary recollection of the phrase 'The death of the soul' (*MD* 50). Septimus, by contrast, cannot make his memories join with his present life, resulting in 'a fragmented existence' (119): 'Memory unassimilated with present life is seen as the source of madness' (120). By bringing Peter and Septimus together in Regent's Park, Woolf 'underlines the power of memory and its role in forming the present life' (120).

Gillies's account of Bergson in *Mrs Dalloway* goes beyond a commentary on time, taking in aspects of his philosophy such as his ideas about memory and intuition. Though Gillies sidesteps the scholarly question concerning how Woolf might have come to learn Bergsonian ideas, her exploration of the novels is persuasive as to their relevance.

Existentialism

Existentialism came to prominence as a movement in philosophy and literature in the years immediately after the Second World War, though it could trace its roots back to the first half of the twentieth century, and to the Danish philosopher Søren Kierkegaard (1813–55); Kierkegaard's writings were themselves significantly rediscovered after 1945. The noun 'existentialism' first appears in English in 1941; 'existentialist' in 1945. *Existence and Being*, a collection of essays by the German existentialist philosopher Martin Heidegger (1889–1976), including his 'What is Metaphysics?', appeared in English in 1949; *Being and Nothingness* (*L'Être et le néant*, 1943), by the French existentialist Jean-Paul Sartre (1905–80), was published in an English translation in 1956. Among the influential works on the literary side of the movement were *The Outsider* (*L'étranger*, 1941), translated in 1946, by Albert Camus (1913–60), and Sartre's *Nausea* (*La nausée*, 1938), translated in 1965.

Existentialist approaches to *Mrs Dalloway* have never claimed that Woolf was influenced by thinkers or works that were either unpublished or relatively unknown; rather, they imply that Woolf reached her own existentialist position independently, and that it may be clarified by reference to the more formal statements of existentialist philosophy. One of the most important concepts in relation to Woolf's work is that of *inauthenticity*. A person leading an inauthentic existence allows him- or herself to be bound by conventional expectations of human nature, and lacks a sense of their own uniqueness. The prospect of death sharply divides the authentic from the inauthentic: the inauthentic concedes that 'one dies', where the authentic person recognizes the possibility of his or her *own* death.[16] While existentialist philosophy is usually articulated in terms of such timeless notions as life and death, there are also respects in which it is historically situated: the implication that inauthenticity is a kind of social conformity was particularly relevant in the years after the Second World War, with the expectations that society would return to normality. In this the post-1945 period echoed the post-1918, in which conservative forces had also been concerned to see a 'return to normality', meaning a return to conventional gender roles.[17] One obvious implication is that existentialism has particular relevance to feminism.

Lucio Ruotolo's *Six Existential Heroes* (1973) includes Clarissa Dalloway among its existentialists.[18] Ruotolo takes a thematic approach, reading the novel as embodying a certain philosophy; he is only marginally interested in Woolf's sources for this philosophy. Although there is extensive reference to Heidegger, Ruotolo does not imply that Woolf was familiar with Heidegger's work; rather it serves to clarify her philosophy. He provides little in the way of formal definition of existentialism, nor does he attempt to differentiate its various strands, but in his treatment of *Mrs Dalloway*, much rests on the moments of dread, emptiness and loneliness, and, related to these, the feeling that one's existence is inauthentic. Clarissa feels early on in the novel that 'something awful was about to happen' (*MD* 3). While Ruotolo's reading does not depend on biographical background, he draws our attention to the similarity to a moment of 'inner loneliness' recorded in Woolf's diary in October 1929 (13; see *D3* 260). Ruotolo paraphrases Heidegger's lecture 'What is Metaphysics?' as saying that 'man must face nothing in order to be something': in each of these moments of existential anxiety, Woolf and her characters are facing nothingness.

Like many critics, Ruotolo prefaces his analysis of *Mrs Dalloway* with a consideration of the essay 'Mr Bennett and Mrs Brown' (14–18), which in his account becomes an exploration of the question 'What is Being?' rather than of the more literary and more limited question of how a novelist might convey a sense of another person's being. Woolf's account of the complacency of Edwardian life resembles the inauthentic existence identified by existentialism: 'Virginia Woolf suggests that her contemporaries have largely ignored the particularity of human existence' (16).

Ruotolo presents *Mrs Dalloway* as Woolf's attempt to 'establish a perspective for the novel outside the realm of manners' (18) ('manners' being inauthentic), and sees it as an exploration of 'nothingness within the context of Being and time' (18). In this reading, Septimus's

Dr Holmes becomes typical of the inauthenticity that pervades many characters in the novel. His recommended cure, that Septimus must take notice of 'real things' (*MD* 22), is interesting to Ruotolo because of its failure to recognize the problematical nature of reality. Such an attitude also affects Rezia, for example, who is 'forever concerned with what other people will think of her husband's odd behavior' (20). It affects the crowds, who are distracted by passing royalty or by advertising, and who miss the big questions that bother Septimus: 'About these central characters float a chorus of sleepwalkers, the countless passersby shaken into a momentary consciousness by the backfiring of an automobile, merging with a crowd of onlookers before an airplane skywriting advertisements, seeking self-distraction in every object' (20). It affects Peter Walsh and Sally Seton, who 'have chosen to live largely in retrospect, preserving autonomy against the unexpected intrusion of foreign ideas and unsettling passions' (33).

Ruotolo sees Clarissa and Septimus as closer to authenticity than the other characters. Of Clarissa's early reflections about London ('Heaven only knows why one loves it so', *MD* 4), Ruotolo remarks that Clarissa loves 'London on this particular moment of a June morning' (22): in other words, she is seeing it authentically for itself at that particular moment. The key claim of existentialism, that 'existence precedes essence', to which Ruotolo alludes elsewhere (16), is relevant here: there is no 'essential' quality of London, no definition of 'Londonness' from which the moment-by-moment existence of London derives; rather London *exists* first of all, and any 'essential' characteristics are inferred from the particular moments of its existence. Clarissa has a quality of independence: she 'allows things to reveal themselves in new ways once she has classified them within their familiar context. Her openness to innovation reflects her own independence. She does not require others to supply the meaning of her life' (22). Reading Clarissa's appreciation of London this way requires Ruotolo to downplay the element of satire in Woolf's portrayal: one might argue that Clarissa's socially and materially privileged vision of London is inauthentic because it is too dependent on a reductive idea of its liveliness.

Death – the news of Septimus's death – brings a crisis. Ruotolo examines the scene where Clarissa, 'alone in her finery', compares her throwing of a shilling into the Serpentine with Septimus's flinging his life away, and where the pronoun 'it' shifts ambiguously from representing the scene of Septimus's suicide to his life (*MD* 156). The conflation of life and death in this scene suggests Heidegger's presupposition that Being and non-Being are inseparable. Ruotolo remarks particularly on Clarissa's 'terror' at having been given a life, 'this life, to be lived to the end' (*MD* 157), and suggests that her terror is essentially similar to Heidegger's notion of 'dread'. 'Dread' (German *Angst*) is absolutely different from fear (German *Furcht*): fear is usually fear 'of' or 'about' something, whereas the object of dread is indefinite.[19] Unlike Septimus, however, Clarissa 'accepts' the dread, and this is part of what makes her heroic for Ruotolo. Moreover, although Clarissa recognizes that she 'has led an inauthentic life' (30), her moment of triumph comes when she decides to return to her party: 'her resolve to share with her friends the life she has experienced in solitude marks her existential triumph' (32). In the closing paragraphs of his chapter, Ruotolo contrasts less favourably the reactions of Sally and Peter to Clarissa, arguing that they are so steeped in 'the values of the age' that they cannot see Clarissa's authenticity for what it is. Thus the novel's concluding words, Peter's 'For there she was' (*MD* 165), although 'messianic' (34), may be ironic, because they reflect Peter's need for 'a presence that sustains his melancholy', living, as he does, in the past; but they may also affirm the 'miraculous' (34) and 'mysterious' (35) qualities of Clarissa. In his conclusion, as in the body of the essay, Ruotolo makes as strong a case as can be made for the admirable qualities in Clarissa, but does so at the cost of underplaying the novel's satirical attitude towards her.

Published in the same year as Ruotolo's book, James Naremore's *The World Without a Self* is less concerned to associate Woolf with a particular named philosophy, and has in common with several of articles and books in this section a debt to an established approach of close reading.[20] However, Naremore's stated purpose is to escape from discussions of style and form, and from 'familiar critical themes' such as time and psychology, and to consider 'the erotic and visionary character of her novels, and her fascination with death' (3). The first part of his chapter on *Mrs Dalloway* considers Woolf's technique of indirect interior monologue, and pays particular attention to the transitions from one character to another. Naremore is not afraid to differentiate the more and less successful passages in the novel, and in particular singles out one phrase for being 'too literary', too self-consciously an effect (84). But his larger purpose is to ask why Woolf developed the style that she used in *Mrs Dalloway*. She felt a need

> ■ to develop a style that sometimes suggests consciousness but never directly reports it, that can give the feeling of both the particular and the general, moving easily between the thoughts of several characters and the ruminations of the author without changing its quality; in sum, a style that makes us feel both the individuality of the character and his relation to the whole of life. (101–2) □

More importantly, he wishes to ask about the 'vision of life' that 'determined this style' (102). Clarissa, like so many of Woolf's characters, 'is beset by the problem of aloneness and separateness in life' (102). Naremore quotes the passage in which Clarissa ponders 'the supreme mystery': 'here was one room, there another' (*MD* 108). He comments that it is 'the central problem' in all of Woolf's fiction: 'It is intimately related, of course, to the problem of death, the ultimate separation and from one point of view the ultimate confirmation of the separateness of things' (102). The passage in which Peter recalls Clarissa's 'transcendental theory' (*MD* 129–30) suggests a

■ view of life which is confirmed by the tale and the whole manner of telling it. This view implies that there is no clear boundary between the 'inside' and the 'outside', just as there is no clear boundary between Virginia Woolf's characters or between the author and her materials. The self, in this view, is not simply an ego bound by space and time, but the total context of the physical world that the self creates and/or embraces in its movement through life, a context that helps define the self and remains after the individual 'appearance' has gone. (103) □

The scene of the aeroplane 'soaring over Greenwich' and particularly its final descriptions of thrushes snatching snails (*MD* 24) is 'characteristic' of Woolf, if not of *Mrs Dalloway*:

■ All of Virginia Woolf's fiction attempts to indicate a universal, timeless sense of life which may be called truth or reality. Very often this truth is expressed through descriptions of nature – vast perspectives where we sense a beautiful but impersonal force that is destructive to individuals but seems to live in all things. In a more indirect sense, this vision of reality is expressed in the stylistic peculiarities of Mrs. Woolf's novels – in her fluid transitions, for example, or in her explorations of her characters' ostensibly trivial thoughts and memories, which link them in a community. (105) □

Septimus's death 'has symbolic overtones' (106) which Naremore finds most prominent in the passage where Clarissa reflects that 'Death was an attempt to communicate' (*MD* 156). 'Death, in this view, is transformed from the ultimate separation into the ultimate union, the most complete form of that embrace that Mrs Woolf said she wanted her novels to show' (107).

Both Ruotolo and Naremore turn to existentialist philosophy to break with narrowly formalist interests in Woolf's style, form and method. In Ruotolo's case, existentialism provides a way of judging Clarissa in relation to the other characters. In Naremore's, questions of style are not entirely left behind, but existentialism provides a larger explanation for Woolf's stylistic experiments.

Woolf and Phenomenology

Harvena Richter's emphasis on lived, bodily experience was taken further in two influential studies of Woolf, Roger Poole's *The Unknown Virginia Woolf* (1978) and Mark Hussey's *The Singing of the Real World* (1986).[21] Both took their cue from the philosophical movement of phenomenology, though both are at pains to emphasize that they attempt to understand Woolf on her own terms. The key text for later twentieth-century phenomenology was *Phenomenology of Perception* (translated 1962) by the French philosopher Maurice Merleau-Ponty (1908–1961). Since at least the eighteenth century, philosophy had understood perception in terms of a self or 'subject' perceiving external 'objects', but this dualistic way of understanding the world ran into difficulties when it considered the body: is the body part of the external world which the subject perceives? If so, the 'subject' would seem to be simply a version of the Christian soul or spirit. The dualistic approach cannot overcome the paradox that the body both enables perception and is an object of perception. Traditional philosophy had also seen the body in a relatively passive relation to perceived objects: light falls on the retina, for example, and the mind recognizes the object. Phenomenology sees the subject as necessarily embodied, and as having an active intentionality towards the world; in consequence, one cannot think of that world as 'external'.

Roger Poole's study is partly biographical in orientation, and deliberately aims to break down the barrier created by the New Criticism between the author and the work. Poole began from a biographical question and a feeling of dissatisfaction with the labelling of Virginia Woolf as 'insane' or 'mad', terms that appear in Leonard Woolf's autobiography (1960–69) and Quentin Bell's biography (1972). The book starts from 'this failure to regard Virginia Woolf as a subjectivity. She was the author of some of the most remarkable analyses of intersubjectivity in the language: why had no-one done her the compliment of examining her own subjectivity in a way which attempted to come up to her own very high standards?' (2). The novels become 'records of a life' (2), and other biographical documents, such as Woolf's memoirs first published in *Moments of Being* (1976), become valid as materials. Poole's method, however, is not narrowly tied to representation: he is not interested in whether a given scene or incident related to a similar scene in Woolf's life; rather, characters' modes of being throw a light on Woolf's own.

Poole is particularly concerned with the idea of embodiment, both as it relates to Woolf, and in *Mrs Dalloway*, as it relates to Septimus. By embodiment he means 'the way the "lived body" perceives the world.

Embodiment in this sense is an activity, not a passive process. It is everything that [eighteenth-century philosopher John Locke] ignored in his theory of the passivity of the experiential atoms breaking into an empty mental space [...]' (198). Poole prefers 'the view which Merleau-Ponty has of our perceptual process, a view which emphasises the manner in which the "lived body" takes an active part in conferring the meanings we wish to confer upon the world through our "intentionality"'. He sees Merleau-Ponty's view as 'an exact parallel, in the realm of philosophy, to what Virginia Woolf attempted in her novels. [...] The ways the body is "lived", is active in creating, and participating in, a world of meanings, is her theme throughout her fictional career' (198).

Poole is interested in understanding Septimus in his own terms, and through him understanding Woolf's subjectivity in ways that avoid prematurely evaluative labels like 'mad'. However, he does not argue that Septimus's way of seeing the world is any more true than those of other characters, Septimus's 'counter-subjects' in the novel. The way that the world seems to Septimus is given to us, 'in all its flickering oscillation between control and panic', in many places in the novel where 'perception becomes active in bringing a world of meaning into being'. But, importantly, that world of meaning is 'inter-subjectively disconfirmed': Poole acknowledges the provenance of the concept in the work of the German philosopher Edmund Husserl (1859–1938). It is, for Poole, 'part of the genius of the novel' that we can see simultaneously 'how a world could appear like that to someone in Smith's embodied state, and also how the world is not in fact, for his embodied counter-subjects, like that'. By giving Septimus 'such a carefully graduated series of embodiments', Woolf 'opens up the whole question of how the world is perceived through and by means of the fact that we inhabit bodies which are themselves creators of meaning in the world of created meanings' (199).

Elsewhere in the book, Poole outlines a case for Septimus being 'an extremely subtle and cogent symbol for what was really wrong with [Virginia Woolf] in 1912–13', the period leading up to and including one of her most serious nervous breakdowns. Septimus's 'root problem' is 'that "he could not feel"', a phrase repeated six times in two pages (185–6; see *MD* 74–5). For Poole, the central lines of *Mrs Dalloway*, 'philosophically and humanly', are those where Septimus speculates that 'the world itself is without meaning' (*MD* 75). Poole notes that 'they are given to us immediately after the eight-fold repetition of "he could not feel" and only two pages after the death of Evans (*MD* 73).[22] The death of Evans leads to the inability to feel. This in its turn leads to a philosophical conclusion: the world might well be without meaning' (187). Poole considers the failings of Sir William Bradshaw in examining Septimus. First, Bradshaw 'makes no attempt to investigate, or understand, how the world in fact appears to his patient'; second, 'he ignores the embodiment of his patient, which would doubtless be highly significant: extreme nervousness, absence of attention, a sense of his being bodily absent, being bodily "somewhere else"'; and third, 'he ignores the most important kind of evidence of all – the verbal associations and puns that Smith makes, his inversion of values, his tone of muddled contempt' (191). It might be objected that, prior to the advent of modern phenomenology and its application to psychiatry, Bradshaw could not be expected to pay attention to the 'embodiment' of his patient. Poole remarks that Woolf is particularly careful 'to emphasise the significance of Smith's embodiment, that is to say, the way he "lives" his body and the way the world appears to him "through" his body' (191–2). He gives as instances Septimus's account of the backfiring motor car and of Regent's Park, and comments that 'Smith experiences the world as a perpetual bombardment of intolerably loud noises, sharp feelings, bright light, clear insights – in other words, his body has ceased to act as a buffer between him and the world. [...] Everything has become present mentally in an intolerable way' (192–3). But Bradshaw reduces this information to the diagnosis of 'shell-shock' (193). Understanding Septimus is, for Poole, ultimately a preliminary to understanding Virginia Woolf's subjectivity, and at this point in this discussion he turns back to the question of what happened to her when she was in the care of doctors in 1913.

Hussey's book, while acknowledging a debt to Poole's work, differs in that it is less concerned with the biographical question about Woolf's subjectivity. It is concerned to establish the philosophy of the novels, but not as a matter of intellectual history in which Woolf's debts are traced to one philosopher or another. The 'deep concerns of Woolf's art' are themselves 'implicitly philosophical' (p. xi). Unlike writers in the realist tradition, Woolf aims not to tell us 'about an external, objective Reality', but rather 'about our *experience* of the world' (p. xiii). In this regard, phenomenology becomes a useful analogy; as well as citing the work of Merleau-Ponty, Hussey references 'existential psychoanalysis', particularly the work of Ludwig Binswanger and R. D. Laing, which is concerned with 'an embodied self, in *relation* to others' (p. xv). For Hussey, 'Virginia Woolf's novels are concerned with knowledge: knowledge of others, and knowledge of the world. The question of the nature of self is at the heart of her thinking, and, I believe, is the dynamic of her fiction' (p. xv).

Hussey deliberately avoids taking a 'novel-by-novel' approach to Woolf's work, arguing that this tends to towards a literary criticism of definitive readings and a false idea of interpretative closure, inimical to the approach that he takes. Although, in consequence, there is no extended discussion of *Mrs Dalloway*, because the question of embodiment and perception is so central to his approach, his first chapter on 'The Body' considers Septimus in some detail. Hussey contrasts two characters from Woolf's *The Waves*, Jinny and Susan, who tend towards complete embodiment, with another character from *The Waves*, Rhoda, and Septimus, who live the body in a way that tends towards 'unembodiment'. For the latter pair, 'the self's position in the world is altogether more precarious' (12).

In Hussey's analysis, Septimus's problems begin with Evans's death and with a presumption that it is 'masculine' to show no feelings of grief (13); Hussey himself treats emotions and their expression as requiring embodiment. Hussey comments that 'Throughout the novel, Septimus is largely unaware of his body as it appears to others in the actual world' (14). Hussey quotes a passage in the aeroplane scenes ('Happily Rezia put her hand down with a tremendous weight on his knee so that he was weighted down, transfixed' [*MD* 19]), and comments that to Septimus:

> ■ his body is one more object in that world, bobbing up and down in the breeze along with the trees, feathers, and birds. Septimus's unembodiment causes a serious disjunction between his perceptions and those of others around him. In order to stave off the madness that Septimus feels this disjunction threatens him with, he translates his sensations into an inexpressible 'religion' of which he is the prophet, and gives meaning to a world that he sees might well be meaningless. (14) □

Being unembodied means that Septimus can avoid facing up to Evans's death, and can create a fantasy world where 'there is no death' (*MD* 21).

The people who oppress Septimus, primarily Holmes and Bradshaw, but also his employer Mr Brewer, and even to some extent Rezia, take a different view of 'reality'. The crucial passage, in this regard, is the one where Rezia recalls how Dr Holmes has told her to make Septimus 'notice real things, go to a music hall, play cricket' (*MD* 22). Hussey is less concerned by Holmes's pitifully inadequate measures of reality (leisure activities) than by the consequences of perception. 'Such attention', he comments, 'would necessitate embodiment for [Septimus], and thus feeling and recognizing death. The insistence of the actual world drives Septimus further into unembodiment. Holmes and Bradshaw treat the body, but Septimus, as *he lives* his body, cannot be touched by them' (15).

Concluding his discussion of Septimus, Hussey considers the passage in which Septimus, shortly before his death, lies on the sofa in his sitting room and contemplates the patterns made by light on the walls (*MD* 118). 'Carefully, Septimus, drawing calm and courage both from the sights and sounds of nature, and from Rezia's stability, begins to take stock of his surroundings.' He looks at 'real things', though he is cautious, as they are 'too exciting', and he does not wish to 'go mad' (*MD* 120). Hussey comments that Septimus 'begins to move away from unembodiment, to "re-embody" himself through vision (primarily). When he closes his eyes, however, the world he has been carefully approaching, one item at a time, disappears. Alone, he feels that his world (that is, the world of his unembodied self) has gone forever – he is stuck with the sideboard and the bananas, which undermine his vision by their mundaneness, deny what he considers the truth' (15–16).

Hussey argues that Septimus and Rhoda represent one extreme of the ways that 'the body is lived' in Woolf's works, and that for the majority of her characters, the actuality lies somewhere between this extreme and the other defined by Susan and Jinny. In the succeeding chapter, he goes on to consider Clarissa Dalloway and the question of how identity is shaped by naming and through an uneasy tension with others. He notes in particular the constraints created by her having a name that is not her own: 'this being Mrs Dalloway; not even Clarissa any more; this being Mrs Richard Dalloway' (*MD* 9). Hussey illuminates Clarissa's awareness that she has multiple names and thus multiple identities by considering a passage from the episode in which Peter Walsh follows the young woman. To Peter, it seems that the woman has 'singled him out', 'as if the random uproar of the traffic had whispered through hollowed hands his name, not Peter, but *his private name* which he called himself in his own thoughts' (*MD* 45, emphasis added). There are satirical echoes here of the idea, in Judaeo-Christian tradition, that God's true name is unutterable; Peter is far from God-like. Hussey remarks that 'Names may serve to fix an identity, but they may not reflect what a person feels is his or her "true" self' (25). In Clarissa's case, a glimpse of that true self is to be found in her past. Though Clarissa feels 'an emptiness' (*MD* 26) on learning that her husband has been invited to Lady Bruton's without her, Hussey reminds us that her sense of self is replenished by her recollections of Bourton and in particular of Sally Seton (*MD* 27–30). In the following chapter (48), Hussey also draws attention to the diamond, the image for Clarissa's sense of firm identity in the scene before the mirror (*MD* 32), also being the image for the 'infinitely precious' present given to Clarissa by Sally (*MD* 30). Although identity depends on the body – and one of the biggest contributions of Hussey's book is to legitimize the body as a topic within Woolf studies – it also depends on relationships.

Works in the phenomenological mode have not gone uncriticized, with Poole's book having proved particularly controversial. Some of the objections related to biographical matters rather than their literary critical consequences: Frank Kermode judged that Poole had been excessively harsh on Leonard Woolf, and had in consequence misread Virginia's suicide letter to him. He also questioned whether Poole's insistence that

Woolf was not 'mad' was not a matter of semantics, given that Poole concedes that she suffered 'very distressed periods' or that her 'nerves gave out'. Mark Spilka objected that the entire work was 'thesis-ridden and grossly-misleading'. In particular, he suggested that Poole judged Leonard Woolf and Virginia's doctors by standards which were only just beginning to gain acceptance in her time (Freudian psychoanalysis) or which were yet to emerge (R. D. Laing's existential psychoanalysis). Hermione Lee objected that Poole's 'post-phenomenological' approach, far from being a 'new departure in literary studies', looked like 'an old-fashioned blurring of biography and criticism'. The problem is, that '[if] the fiction is to be used as a testimony to the life, equivalents have perpetually to be found', and these are often reductive: 'Leonard "is" Rezia, who is frightened of Septimus's madness', but at the same time, Leonard 'is' Richard Dalloway, a 'good, naïve, trusting soul'.[23] That Hussey's book escaped such criticisms is due in part to Poole's having prepared the ground, but also due to Hussey's focus being on Woolf's philosophy and not her biography.

Woolf and Bertrand Russell

The attempt to locate the value of Woolf's work in a 'philosophy' diminished in importance in the mid- to late 1970s as critics increasingly identified the value of her work with its politics. (Of course Woolf could reasonably be described as having a political 'philosophy', but the world-changing orientation of any such philosophy distinguishes it from the kinds considered in this chapter.) In more recent years some critics have returned to considering Woolf in terms set down by philosophy, not as an alternative to her political commitments, but as a recognition that she articulates her ideas in a register that is as much philosophical as it is political. The return to philosophical themes is less concerned to claim that Woolf 'had' a philosophy and more concerned to identify the philosophical roots of her literary work.

The most substantial such study is Ann Banfield's *The Phantom Table: Woolf, Fry, Russell, and the Epistemology of Modernism* (2000), which argues that Woolf's modes of representation are indebted to the Cambridge philosopher Bertrand Russell, mediated through the aesthetic theory of Roger Fry. In the theory of knowledge underlying Woolf's work, she writes:

■ Objects are reduced to 'sense data' separable from sensations and observing subjects to 'perspectives'. Atomism multiplies these perspectives. Objects familiar because seen, heard, sensed, observed, tucked cosily into the observer's viewpoint, lose their familiarity once rendered unseen, unheard, unobserved, revealed to have a sensible existence independent of an observer. A perspectivized style records the vision mutely, imparting its strangeness to the vision. The first conclusion of this logic is the idea of death as the separation of subject and object. The second starts from that conclusion, deriving from it an elegiac form that is an adequate response to the world revealed by science. (1–2) □

Banfield's organization of her material means that she does not make a sustained analysis of *Mrs Dalloway*, or of any single novel. Nevertheless, there is much in the novel that is immediately relevant to her theme of reality and how we perceive it. Septimus's distorted perceptions and interpretations are of particular importance: Banfield focuses particularly on the passage in which he, in effect, undertakes a philosopher's thought experiment into the question of whether objects of perception can be said to exist when the perceiving subject does not perceive them: 'open[ing] his eyes to see whether a gramophone was really there' (*MD* 120) (62). (In *To the Lighthouse*, the philosopher's son Andrew Ramsay attempts to summarize his father's work by saying, 'Think of a kitchen table [...] when you're not there' [*TL* 22].) Banfield also notes two points in which characters let go of sensory perceptions by falling asleep: Lady Bruton and Peter Walsh. Commenting on the passage in which Lady Bruton falls asleep ('Lady Bruton went ponderously, majestically ... ; snored' [*MD* 94–5]) and lets 'the thread' that connects her to Richard Dalloway 'snap', Banfield comments that the thread 'is consciousness itself' (221). When Peter Walsh takes his nap in Regent's Park (*MD* 48–50), he undergoes 'a similar severance from a world which continues around his inert body. The tablet of his mind, receiver of sense impressions, is erased by sleep. In the moment of erasure, the collection of sense-data flashes by' (221).

The world of *Mrs Dalloway* is also an atomized one, in which individuals live in relative isolation. Banfield notes that the image of the lighted window recurs throughout Woolf's novels as a symbol of the individual self in a greater darkness, and *Mrs Dalloway* is no exception: 'the lights of human habitations, like that of the old lady in *Mrs Dalloway* [*MD* 157–8], indicate here and there occupied perspectives' (109). The isolation of person from person can be seen also in the varying estimates of time offered by the clocks of Big Ben and St Margaret's: 'Both are accurate from their point of view' (144). Language, the distinguishing feature of human beings that might be hoped to overcome isolation, is presented in Woolf's works as being 'at a ghostly remove' from reality: in support of this claim, Banfield draws our attention to the words of the skywriting aeroplane in *Mrs Dalloway*, 'languishing and melting in the sky' (157).

Although firm evidence about Woolf's reading of philosophy is difficult to come by, her work often raises philosophical questions which are best answered in a philosophical discourse. As Banfield's discussion of isolation reminds us, philosophical approaches to Woolf's novels need not be purely intellectual: they very often lead back to potentially emotional questions of a distinctively modern loneliness and alienation. The best of such readings recognize that Woolf addresses philosophical questions through the medium of the novel, but there is always the risk that they value her more as a thinker than as a writer. The next chapter considers a different intellectual current in the late 1970s and 1980s, deriving from structuralist linguistics and anthropology, which directed attention to the linguistic sign as a medium of communication, and which necessarily directed attention to Woolf as a writer, at the same time as it illuminated unrecognized subtleties in her thought.

CHAPTER FOUR

Structuralism and Post-Structuralism

From Linguistics to Criticism

The readings of *Mrs Dalloway* seen in the previous two chapters based their claims to its value on it, or its author, possessing a politics or a philosophy. While many of these readings display sensitive attention to the fine details of the text, their primary focus is on what the novel means rather than how it makes meaning; they are interested in hermeneutics rather than poetics.[1] Moreover, they assume that a coherent singular meaning or philosophy can be found. The rise of structuralist literary criticism, and, immediately succeeding it, post-structuralism, created alternative emphases. Literary structuralism begins in the structuralist linguistics of Ferdinand de Saussure (1857–1913); it also drew on the later structuralist anthropology (notably the work of Claude Lévi-Strauss [1908–2009]) that had taken inspiration from Saussure's notion of a science of signs.

Saussure had argued that linguistic signs were arbitrary, relational and constitutive. They were *arbitrary* in that there is nothing, for example, inherently foot-like about the English word 'foot' realized either as sound or writing. They are *relational* in that the meaning of the sign depended on its relation to other signs: what we call a (bodily) foot is defined by its relation to other body parts. The sounds of a language (its phonemes) are also defined relationally: in English the contrast between /b/ and /v/ signifies ('bat' and 'vat' mean different things), whereas in other languages, /v/ would simply sound like a badly pronounced /b/. Finally, and most controversially, signs are *constitutive*: the kinds of distinction that a language draws will shape reality for speakers of that language. Meaning is created only within a culturally agreed framework. When we use a language, we tend to forget the arbitrariness of that framework; structuralism brings it back into focus. Saussure was interested more in the linguistic system (*langue*) that made individual utterances possible than he was in the utterances themselves (*parole*).[2]

It will be apparent from this very brief summary that the idea of *contrast* is important for structuralism. One strand within structuralist anthropology and literary criticism seeks to find the most profound contrasts within a literary culture or within an individual literary text. Anthropologists, for example, noted the profound distinction between nature and culture, expressed in everyday life as the distinction between raw food and cooked. Post-structuralist approaches question the stability of the oppositions and structures thus uncovered: they seek to *deconstruct*; the term is increasingly used as a synonym for 'analyse', but it can mean something more precise and specific. Whereas structuralism found relative stability in the system of signs, post-structuralism finds looseness ('play' in a technical sense), self-contradiction and movement.

Structuralism is a very flexible tool, the potentialities of which remain under-utilized. Wherever meaning is created through contrast – which is everywhere – structuralism has the potential to clarify how the process works. It might be used to clarify the meaning of individual words or utterances, as if the literary text were no different from ordinary uses of the language in which it is written. But it might also be used at a higher, more abstract level, seeing characters as signs and seeing how they become meaningful through contrasts with each other, and through contrasts with a culturally understood system of character types. (At times Woolf allows Clarissa herself to become conscious of the respects in which she signifies as an upper-middle-class 'hostess', or as a 'wife', 'Mrs Richard Dalloway'; but structuralist criticism does not depend on the text demonstrating self-consciousness about signification.) At the higher level, it might attempt to identify the fundamental units of narrative (*narratemes*) and their relations to each other, an approach that has been particularly productive in relation to folk tales.[3]

In 1956, the Czechoslovakian linguist Roman Jakobson (1896–1982) isolated the tropes of metaphor and metonymy as a fundamental linguistic and cognitive contrast, citing in evidence the two dominant types of linguistic disorder.[4] The distinction was the starting point for several papers by the British literary critic David Lodge. In *The Modes of Modern Writing* (1977), Lodge uses the contrast as a way of categorizing literary works, and finds both metonymy and metaphor (in extended senses of each word) at work in modernist writing.[5] When he considers Woolf, the contrast provides a way of narrating the trajectory of her writing. He finds in modernist writers 'a general tendency to develop (either within the individual work, or from one work to another) from a metonymic (realistic) to a metaphoric (symbolist or mythopoeic) representation of experience' (177). By reducing Woolf's literary development to five novels – *The Voyage Out*, *Jacob's Room*, *Mrs Dalloway*, *To the Lighthouse* and *The Waves* – and treating the others as 'diversions, digressions or regressions', Lodge is able to argue that the 'essential line' of Woolf's 'literary development' conforms to the typical modernist pattern. (Whether the sacrifice of half Woolf's oeuvre is a price worth paying for such an elegant pattern is something I will leave to the reader.) Within this pattern, *Mrs Dalloway* becomes a transitional work:

> ■ In our terms, the novel [*Mrs Dalloway*] marks the transition in Virginia Woolf's writing from the metonymic to the metaphoric mode. Instead of lineality, simultaneity ('If *Jacob's Room* shows cinematic cutting and fading, *Mrs Dalloway* borrows from montage and superimposed frames', Carl Woodring has shrewdly commented). (184–5)[6] □

Rather than presenting 'different people in the same place at the same time', as she had done in *The Voyage Out*, she presents 'different people in different places at the same time [...] perhaps looking at the same thing', such as the aeroplane.

> ■ Instead of a life, or a voyage, a single day. Instead of authorial narration, the stream of consciousness in which events (i.e. thoughts) follow each other on the principle of similarity as much as contiguity – a June morning in Westminster, for instance, reminding Clarissa of mornings in her youth because a simile of children on a beach seems to her equally applicable to both. (185) □

While Lodge's way of examining *Mrs Dalloway* brings certain features into sharp focus, like his treatment of her literary development, it risks leaving out other important features altogether. If we expect richness and complexity from literary text, the simplicity of the binary of metaphor/metonymy may feel reductive.

Structuralism and Close Reading

Nancy Armstrong's 1983 account of *Mrs Dalloway* is more attuned to the verbal particularities of a text.[7] Her article recognizes that part of the power of *Mrs Dalloway* lies in the way it renders conventional literary-critical terminology powerless: 'To read one of Woolf's novels, one has to formulate special rules and categories just for that fiction. We find that she has done away with the old rhetorical categories of character, plot, setting, and narration, and as if to compound this difficulty, she confronts the reader with 300 pages of chapterless prose in *Mrs Dalloway*' (343). Armstrong sees Woolf as a proto-structuralist: she 'tentatively played with the idea that words are arbitrary in relation to things in the world and thus meaningful in relation to one another' (344).

Armstrong's article builds on work by Yuri Lotman,[8] founder of the Tartu-Moscow School of semiotics, and particularly on his *The Structure of the Artistic Text* (1970, translated 1977). From Lotman she takes the idea that all acts of communication are poised between principles of equivalence and difference, between 'the collective and individual aspects of language'; and that 'any point in cultural history may be understood as a compromise between these two poles' (346). Whereas Saussure had spoken singularly of the linguistic system, *la langue*, Lotman recognizes that any culture contains a plurality of 'codes'. Armstrong argues that the early twentieth century was the moment when the literary consensus of the eighteenth and nineteenth centuries broke down, and there was a shift from general equivalence to difference. 'Such a situation arises, Lotman contends, with the increasing semiotic complexity of the culture. Not only is there more flexibility in the way that codes may be used and hence a proliferation of specialized languages, but there is also less ability to translate one use of language accurately into another' (346). Where nineteenth-century realism had employed a commonly understood 'rhetoric' of fiction, the modernist writers cultivated their own individual *styles*. The cultivation of style might seem a retreat into non-referential artistry, but Armstrong makes the case that Woolf's fiction 'tells us something rather basic about the communication situation' in which it arose (347).

Armstrong uses Woolf's dispute with Arnold Bennett and the novelists she classified as 'Edwardians' to situate her in relation to the novel-reading public of her time. She reminds us, though, that we need to be familiar with Bennett or at least the realist tradition in order 'to isolate Woolf's personalized style' (349). She also suggests that Woolf at times embeds the older style of fiction in her novel, pointing in particular to a passage where Peter Walsh recalls, at Bourton in the 1890s, a story being told of an upper-middle-class man who had married one of his housemaids; the housemaid, on being introduced to society, 'was absurdly overdressed, "like a cockatoo," Clarissa had said', and had talked too much. Peter also recalls how the young Clarissa had imitated her (*MD* 50). The scene is of interest because it is a moment of representation framed within the representation. Clarissa's imitation of the housemaid, though not itself represented, reminds us of an older tradition of mimesis in the novel. Armstrong comments that Woolf 'writes in a way we should not find too much out of place in Edwardian fiction' and notes that the scene also depicts consensus: everyone in the scene (other than the former housemaid) sees things 'in much the same way' (352).

In Armstrong's account of *Mrs Dalloway*, such moments of consensus are rare. Armstrong pursues moments in the novel where representational and interpretative codes clash. Septimus's reinterpretations of events – for example, of Rezia having removed her wedding ring (*MD* 57) – are 'the logical and frightening extreme' of the principle of difference coming to predominate (350). In opposition to Septimus's 'dysfunctional language' we have 'the standardizing codes of Bradshaw's psychiatry'; analogously, 'the scattered and arbitrary affairs of the Empire' prompt 'the diplomatic prose of Richard Dalloway and the rigid protocol of Hugh Whitbread' (351).

In the London of 1923, 'Univocality understandably gives way to a cacophony of urban voices, one untranslatable into another' (352). Armstrong sees Clarissa's parties as an attempt to counteract the slide into difference; Peter Walsh's account of how Clarissa 'made her drawing-room a sort of meeting-place' notes the 'odd unexpected people' who sometimes come, and who are integrated into Clarissa's society (*MD* 65–6). Armstrong cautions that Clarissa's 'network of polite exchanges' may be marginal to the male-dominated languages that control the political and economic worlds (353), but the process is of interest nevertheless. Armstrong senses a quality of 'suspense' in the exchanges in Clarissa's drawing room: a fear that the 'old codes' will not work (353). She takes as an example the scene where Clarissa interrupts Professor Brierly and Jim Hutton, whose conversation is struggling, and finds a 'bond' between then in Bach (*MD* 149–50). Armstrong comments that 'the speech of the hostess reconstructs the means by which a social exchange may take place' (353). However, such reconstructions come at a loss: 'The norms of the Dalloway parlor are oppressive to the degree that they cause personalities to collapse into the types of Edwardian fiction' (354): Jim Hutton becomes merely, in Armstrong's words, 'the arty young man with red socks who loves Bach' (354). 'The novel generates a terrible uncertainty as to whether the common ground between individuals may altogether disappear, but it also generates a contrary anxiety of equal magnitude', which is the anxiety about the loss of selfhood consequent on playing by Clarissa's rules (354).

The final phase of Armstrong's argument turns to the two moments of authorial intrusion in the text of *Mrs Dalloway* and their relation to the reader. The first is the passage about Sir William Bradshaw that associates him, through the figures of Proportion and Conversion, with imperialism (*MD* 85); the second, contrasting in style, the 'solitary traveller' passage (*MD* 48–50). In the 'Proportion' passage, Woolf implies that 'Social codes are the same thing as cultural imperialism' (355–6). In criticizing imperialism, Woolf renounces 'the commonplaces of her readership' and aligns 'her viewpoint with those of the suppressed minorities' (356):

■ By implication the author is a potential victim of colonization by way of the conventions that readers bring with them to the work of art. But Woolf alludes to British colonialism not to say something about the seamy side of political history, but to clarify her own perspective by marking its difference from the other paroles of the culture. The author's voice as manifest in her style is neither that of the ruling classes nor that of the silenced minorities. It is one removed from the social context altogether. Just by disengaging the context, however, Woolf's language still participates in the general dynamics of culture. We recognize this detached voice as that of an avant-garde or intellectual elite (356). □

The second of the passages inserts 'highly lyrical language into the text of a novel'; by doing so, Woolf's prose asserts '[its] freedom from the conditions governing communication in general' (356). And here Armstrong finds a paradox: Woolf's prose 'presents itself as a language unimpeded by convention, one giving free rein to individuality', but the reader is not free to use Woolf's words as he or she wishes. 'To the contrary, one's own linguistic and cultural competence must ultimately submit to other and presumably more adequate rules for conceiving and constructing experience in written form' (357).

In her concluding paragraph, Armstrong pursues the question of how the novel situates its reader. She notes that there is potentially a gulf between the 'ordinary reader' who prefers 'accessible' work and the reader who has 'accepted the modernist conditions for meaning' (357). If we treat the novel as if it spoke in an 'independent language,' we may be inclined to discount the things said in 'the most common cultural codes' as being 'too obvious or inaccurate to constitute a meaningful statement' (358). But Armstrong suggests that 'we' – readers comfortable with modernism – 'have something at stake in not looking too closely at what it means to become the model reader of Woolf's or, for that matter, of any modernist fiction' (358). In defining the novel as constituting 'a language of its own', she wonders whether we are drawing a dividing line between those who can read it this way and those who cannot, or prefer not to. Ultimately, however, Armstrong defends Woolf from the implication that she inscribes her readers 'as snobs or masochists' by making them endure difficulties that ordinary readers could not face. In spite of their difficulties, Woolf's novels subscribe to the 'basic condition' of all fiction; some sort of 'cultural exchange' still takes place.

■ By momentarily granting Woolf the power to control, if not create, the conditions for meaning, as middle-class readers we will receive in return a tangible sign that the individual is still intact in the culture, that there are still aspects of the self beyond language, and that there is still a realm of elite culture independent of the rules of the marketplace that encroach on ordinary life. (358) □

Implicit in the final phrase is the idea that the much-vaunted 'ordinary reader' and the processes of 'accessible reading' might not be as pure as their simplicity suggests; they are subject to the rules of the marketplace, in which cultural exchange is subordinated to, or at least tinctured by, monetary exchange.

Although Armstrong's analysis has its roots in structuralism, as this passage shows, hers is not a narrowly formalist structuralism. Like Lotman, Armstrong is interested in how literature differs from normal discourse; its difference can be both a strength, in that it creates a space for social criticism, and a weakness, in that it potentially isolates literature from society. By placing *Mrs Dalloway* in a larger narrative about the coherence or incoherence of society and of social codes, Armstrong relates it to social change, but keeps the textuality of the text in focus. In her concluding argument, by turning to the reader's dilemma, Armstrong identifies another respect in which *Mrs Dalloway* becomes something more than a formal, stylistic experiment.

Teresa L. Ebert's 1985 essay on the novel draws on Jakobson's idea of the binary divide between metaphor and metoynymy, but applies it to the stylistic detail of the novel and to the question of androgyny.[9] The centrality of the concept of androgyny in Woolf criticism derives from *A Room of One's Own* (1929), where Woolf had proposed that 'there are two sexes in the mind', and that in the 'normal and comfortable state of being', the two 'live in harmony together, spiritually co-operating' (*ROO* 127–8). Ebert argues that critics who have attended to androgyny in Woolf have often done so thematically, without recognizing that it is embedded in the 'verbal structure' of her novels, while critics like Lodge who have attended to metaphor and metonymy have missed the 'energizing relationship' between tropes and gender. Ebert also contends that Woolf's vision of androgyny is one in which male and female are in 'dynamic interplay' rather than 'fused' (153); she claims that a similar interplay may be found in the interaction of tropes in Woolf's work.

Ebert follows Nancy Bazin in stating that the 'male' mind is 'realistic and empirical', 'concerned with the factual and the evanescent', and tends towards a belief that life is meaningless; the female 'focuses on the timeless, eternal solidity underlying the flux' (153). Her use of 'male' and 'female' for qualities that are not strictly associated with sexual difference complicates her argument; later feminist critics might prefer the terms 'masculine' and 'feminine'. Ebert cautions that she does not claim there is 'a rigid one-to-one correspondence' between male and metonymy and female and metaphor (157). Taking the scene in which Clarissa contemplates her torn dress (*MD* 32), Ebert claims that Clarissa thinks metonymically and has thoughts that occur within a particular time and place. Ebert further claims that 'Whenever a character's perception begins to delve beyond the surface details', metonymic language 'moves increasingly towards metaphor' (157). For example, in the scene where Clarissa mends her dress, the 'green folds' of the dress become the metaphorical waves of the sea (*MD* 33–4).

What particularly interest Ebert are the moments where there is a 'complex and sophisticated contrapuntal movement of the two tropes' (160). She suggests that the novel contains what she calls 'metaphorized metonymy': 'a passage in which the associations of the narrative's content are largely contiguous, but the linguistic structure of the passage is composed of repetitions and limited similes that consist of relations of identity and substitution and therefore are metaphoric and poetic' (160). Examples tend to occur when Clarissa or Peter is walking through London, 'involved in the flux of life' but 'at the same time aware of the underlying "thread" of connection, of life, hidden in these details' (160). For sustained analysis, she takes Clarissa's celebratory reflections in the fifth paragraph of the novel ('For Heaven only knows ... this moment of June', *MD* 4). The passage contains thoughts and observations about the 'empirical details' of the street scene, in the metonymic tradition of the realist novel (160). But through grammatical patterning it creates 'relations of identity and substitution' (161):

> ■ The strings of participial phrases and nouns that make up the passage are literally relations of identity and substitution. The string of participial phrases: 'making it up', 'building it round one', 'tumbling it', 'creating it' all equally stand for 'seeing' and 'loving' this June day. Similarly, the long list of nouns substitutes one detail, one observation for the next: the people's 'swing' replaces the 'people's eyes'; the 'tramp' displaces the 'swing'; 'vans' and 'omnibuses' are equivalent replacements for 'carriages' and 'motor vans.' (161) □

The combination of the metaphorical and the metonymic 'undercut[s]' the 'empirical particularity' of the details, and suggests that what is being depicted is not the singular existence of this moment in June in this place, but 'any June moment, on any central London street in the city's long existence'. Ebert sees the opposition as gendered: a 'male and metonymic' surface contrasted to an 'underlying verbal pattern' that is 'metaphoric and female' (161).

Most readers would agree with Ebert's judgements about power of the passage to evoke the flux and bustle of London, but the more technical argument is less convincing. The weakness of Ebert's reading lies in its lack of definition as to what constitutes metaphor and metonymy, and its willingness to stretch or narrow the terms, or to overlook complicating instances, in order to make the novel fit the pattern. Certainly the lists in the passage imply relations of equivalence, but while equivalences are a necessarily preliminary to the making of metaphors, it is questionable whether they actually constitute metaphor.

Edward Bishop's 1986 article covers a wider territory: he is interested in the way in which the narratorial voice 'engages the reader, implicating him or her in the rhythms of the novel', and, in a reflexive turn characteristic of this period of structuralist and post-structuralist work, 'the related consideration of how the functions of language constitute a major theme of the novel'.[10] More speculatively, he relates to the novel to a debate initiated by the leading post-structuralist philosopher Jacques Derrida (1930–2004) on the relation of writing and speech. Both might be considered equivalent forms of sign-making (one graphic, the other phonic), but Derrida identified a deep-rooted assumption that speech was prior, which he related to the concepts of presence and origin; Bishop argues that the particular qualities of *Mrs Dalloway* may be defined by its oscillation between the qualities of speech and writing (397).

Bishop begins in a relatively conventional mode of close-reading when he identifies the ways that sentence rhythms contribute to the effect of *Mrs Dalloway*: throughout the novel, he says, Woolf explores the 'non-intellectual capabilities of language' (405). He takes a close interest in Nancy Armstrong's argument about the possibility that the 'common ground' between individuals may disappear, but reaches a more optimistic conclusion (406). While conceding that there is 'potential' for 'tension' about such collapse of a common code, he finds 'that rather than generating anxiety over whether or not the old codes will work, the novel records a quite marvellous lessening of tension and a slow-growing communion among the guests. And the instrument of this, which liberates rather than frustrates the expression of personality, is Clarissa's social language' (406). Armstrong had seen the 'triviality' of 'parlour language' as a weakness, but Bishop suggests this might be a virtue: both speaker and addressee are aware that the 'denotative meaning' of an utterance is 'irrelevant'; 'speech is being used as gesture' (406). In this regard, Bishop follows Walter J. Ong, who had argued for the primacy of orality. Bishop also notes that in several of Woolf's novels, a crucial moment is embodied in a person's cry, particularly of another's name: the exclamation is a fundamentally oral form of sign-making. At the same time, Woolf anticipates a post-structuralist awareness of language's tendency to become autonomous, governed less by the things to which it refers than by its own laws (410). Some of Bishop's most compelling evidence in this regard comes not from *Mrs Dalloway*, but from several essays in which Woolf contemplates forms of writing that seem to exceed the ordinary bounds of writing: '*Twelfth Night* at the Old Vic' (1933), 'Notes on an Elizabethan Play' (1925) and 'Poetry, Fiction and the Future' (also known as 'The Narrow Bridge of Art') (1927). In the *Twelfth Night* essay, Woolf comments on the way that 'the echo of one word' seems to lead to 'another word', so that the play seems 'to tremble perpetually on the brink of music' (*E6* 4). This might seem to resemble the 'play of the signifier' spoken of frequently in post-structuralist criticism,[11] but Bishop cautions that Woolf sees Shakespeare's referential language as going to 'the brink', but not over it (411).

Bishop's evidence in relation to *Mrs Dalloway* draws on a paradox observed by Norman Page in his *Speech in the English Novel* (1973). Woolf ostensibly aims to capture the quality of 'casual thought', and avoids 'the traditional sentence' with its 'hierarchical internal organization', preferring instead sentences with features such as 'repetition, self-interruption, and self-questioning' that more closely resemble speech. And yet the haphazardness is 'more apparent than real'; Woolf's prose is 'heavily patterned', and has a 'rhythmic quality'. Bishop argues the contradiction is deliberate, and that Woolf is deliberately aiming 'to locate her discourse between speech and writing' (413). Bishop concludes the article by arguing that, for Woolf 'the word is always striving towards orality'; her novels '[resolve] themselves into cries at the edge of silence. The word must be retrieved from writing in order to live' (419). Like realist novels, Woolf's fictions are 'grounded in a world beyond the text', but at the same time 'they are meditations on the curious way in which that world exists only in the text' (419). The power of Bishop's article lies in its ability economically to allude to larger concepts (such as Derrida's distinction between speech and writing) while presenting its argument in a relatively untechnical critical idiom, and while being careful not to reduce Woolf to a predetermined theoretical pattern.

Structures of Interpretation

A 1986 article by Herbert Marder, 'Split Perspective', though it does not cite structuralist or post-structuralist theory, shares with Bishop's a willingness to accept contradiction within *Mrs Dalloway*.[12] Like a number of pieces from the 1980s and early 1990s, perhaps because of the influence of reception-theory, it recognizes the need to look for larger patterns by examining critical responses. Beginning with Woolf's own ambivalence about the novel, 'between lyrical nostalgia and angry distaste' (51), Marder identifies two schools of thought about the novel: 'those who emphasize Woolf's mythical vision and those who emphasize her attitude as a social observer' (52). To the first, Clarissa is an 'existential heroine', an 'exemplary character', 'a proud, independent woman who resists tyranny'; the novel is mythical in that the action is set in, as Suzette Henke puts it, 'a larger symbolic context of ritual sacrifice and eucharistic communion', and Septimus's death is transfigured into a redemptive sacrifice. To the second group of critics, Woolf's portrait of Clarissa is 'a study in social decadence' (52): Marder finds an earlier example in Woolf's friend Lytton Strachey, and more recent one in Alex Zwerdling's '*Mrs Dalloway* and the Social System' (1977). Though some critics have attempted to mediate between the extremes – for example, Phyllis Rose in *Woman of Letters* (1978) – Marder aims in his article 'to display the contradictions rather than to resolve them' (53). Rather than incongruity being an accident, and therefore something to be apologized for or explained away, it is 'inherent in Woolf's art, and the key to an understanding of her narrative technique' (53). In the body of the article Marder adopts more traditional strategies, outlining biographical background from 'A Sketch of the Past' (54–5), and turning to Woolf's essay 'Modern Fiction' (1919/1925) (60–2). Marder comments that Woolf's mode of narration has a role to play in allowing contradiction to exist: the narrator 'tolerate[s]' the contradiction, 'as if it were the most natural thing in the world' (59).

Pamela Caughie's brief but incisive treatment of *Mrs Dalloway* in *Virginia Woolf and Postmodernism* (1991) takes a similarly analytical approach to the novel.[13] Earlier in her chapter, Caughie outlines her approach in relation to *Jacob's Room*. She argues that critics need to ask new questions: not whether it has a plot, but what it does with plotting; not what it is 'about', but what it brings about for the reader (70). In other words, the text, rather than being the passive repository of 'plot' or 'theme', is a dynamic entity that brings them into being (successfully or otherwise) for the reader. Although *Mrs Dalloway* is formally very different from *Jacob's Room*, Caughie notes that the two are often read 'in terms of the same thematic concern: the expression of a unifying vision of life' (73). Critics too often uncritically follow Woolf's 1928 Introduction, in which she wrote of Septimus as being Clarissa's double: 'they assume that what she [Woolf] says is what she does' (73). Such readings also imply an underlying formal unity to the novel, but Caughie suggests they do not account for those points where the narrator is clearly distinguished from the characters, for example the passage about Proportion and Conversion (*MD* 84–5) (73). Nor do they account for the 'strained transitions' (73) which Naremore calls 'arty' and others call 'contrived' (73), such as the little girl who approaches Peter and Rezia in Regent's Park and so unites the novel's two plot strands. Caughie reminds us that the novel contains many different outlooks on life, all of which claim to present a 'unified vision of experience': 'Sir William Bradshaw's sense of proportion, Miss Kilman's religious belief, Peter's possessive love, Lady Bruton's social conscience, and Clarissa's party'. Their mutually contradictory views of the world 'should caution us against employing the term unity too loosely, against celebrating it as a value in itself, and against positing a single unity where there are only different ways of effecting unity' (74). If *Mrs Dalloway* is 'about' anything – and Caughie appears cautious about the idea – it is 'how unity is perceived and contrived' (75). In order to recognize this quality, we need to 'attend to the didactic narrator as well as the modulating one, the fragmented structure as well as the continuous flow, and the narrative leaps as well as the subtle transitions' (75). Unity is not 'a theme' but 'one relation to the novel' (75). *Mrs Dalloway* contains many different rhetorical devices of unity; what is common to all of them 'is the desire to create meaningful orders, to impose some kind of unity on random life' (75). In Caughie's account, *Mrs Dalloway* is a novel that is self-conscious about the processes that bring aesthetic order, and is conscious about them in their socio-political dimensions. It brings to the surface the desire to create order, 'acknowledging the limitations of our own unifying systems. In doing so, it disturbs our orientation to the narrative, though not as flagrantly as *Jacob's Room* does. Just when we get comfortable in the minds of characters, we are made to acknowledge the "artificiality" of the narrative' (76).

The articles and chapters by Lodge, Armstrong, Ebert, Bishop, Marder and Caughie come from a relatively small interval of time. They by no means represent all the work on *Mrs Dalloway* in a structuralist and post-structuralist vein: one might also consider, for example, Gerald Doherty's deconstructive approach to death in *Mrs Dalloway*,[14] or Emily Dalgarno's account of the novel, which foregrounds communication, and the ways that characters and narrator 'may use the same word but in different codes'.[15]

Despite the brief interval, there are large changes in method: whereas for Lodge the contrast of metonymy and metaphor is a stable one, providing a tool for analysis, in Caughie's work it seems as if any binary contrast that we might use has been anticipated by the text itself. The rigorously self-reflexive turn of structuralist theory may have been one reason for its early dissolution. Additionally, it was open to the criticism that, for all its theoretical sophistication, it preserved old-fashioned ideas about the self-contained status of the text. As Armstrong's article demonstrates, this need not be the case, but in practice it seemed a limitation; historicism in various guises offered to open the text to a wider range of contexts. Moreover, in its more clinically detached modes, structuralist and post-structuralist analysis seemed removed from what is emotionally engaging in literature and what is politically insightful. The psychoanalytic criticism examined in the next chapter offered an account of Woolf's novels in which familiar human questions about relationships and identity were more central, even when psychoanalysis broke with conventional humanist beliefs about the self; in its later phases it absorbed structuralism's concerns with signs, and employed them in an account of human identity.

CHAPTER FIVE

Woolf and Psychoanalysis

Early Works (1953–1973)

Virginia Woolf and *Mrs Dalloway* have attracted psychoanalytic critics from early on: Woolf because of her history of mental illness and because of the role of the Hogarth Press in publishing the works of Sigmund Freud (1856–1939); *Mrs Dalloway* because of its concerns with madness, mourning and sexuality. Developments in the field have occurred as additional biographical information and previously unpublished texts have become available, and because of developments in the field of psychoanalytic literary criticism. There was a brief outburst of interest in the 1950s in the pages of the journal *Literature and Psychology*, preoccupied with the questions of whether Peter Walsh's pocket knife could be treated as a Freudian symbol.[1] The only lasting value of these articles lay in their uncovering a previously neglected letter from Woolf in which she had said that she was acquainted with psychoanalysis 'only in the ordinary way of conversation', and eliciting a further clarification from Leonard Woolf about Virginia's knowledge of Freud's work:

■ We only began to publish psycho-analytic books in 1924 and I don't think my wife had read any of Freud except perhaps the *Psycho-pathology of Everyday Life* before she wrote *Mrs Dalloway*. Also, I very much doubt whether my wife ever used symbols in quite the way that you think she used them in relation to the knife. She never read much of Freud and I don't think she ever read the *Interpretation of Dreams*.[2] □

Perhaps discouraged by Leonard Woolf's account of Virginia's knowledge of Freud, psychoanalytic work on *Mrs Dalloway* subsided in the later 1960s and the 1970s, though the idea of Septimus as Clarissa's double was connected to Freudian theory by Hollingsworth and Page.[3] Beverly Ann Schlack's 1973 article makes some predictable identifications of phallic symbols (Peter's knife; Clarissa's being like a knife; and the epithets 'straight' and 'rigid').[4] It encounters the usual difficulty about chronology when trying to claim the influence of Freud's 'Psycho-Analytic Notes upon an Autobiographical Account of a Case of Paranoia', a work in which he analysed Daniel Schreber on the basis of his memoir about his madness: the Hogarth Press did not publish the English translation until May 1925, long after the main composition of *Mrs Dalloway*.

Later Freudian Approaches

Mark Spilka's *Virginia Woolf's Quarrel with Grieving* (1980) came at the beginning of a new era for Woolf criticism, newly enabled and invigorated by the publication of Quentin Bell's biography, *Moments of Being*, the letters, and some of the volumes of the diaries.[5] Spilka's account of *Mrs Dalloway* makes great play of its derivation from the short story 'Mrs Dalloway in Bond Street', first published in *Mrs Dalloway's Party* (1973). It also comes at the end of an era for psychoanalytic criticism, the point at which the dominant influence of Freud was modified by the linguistic turn of post-structuralist psychoanalysis and theory, particularly feminist theory. Spilka's argument has a biographical starting point, but is attentive to the novels as novels and as writing. For Spilka, the key event in Woolf's life is the moment at her mother's deathbed in 1895: as Woolf recalled in 1924, 'I laughed ... behind the hand which was meant to hide my tears' (*D2* 300–1). Spilka asserts that Woolf had a 'difficulty with grieving', and that the 'elegiac impulse' in many of her books was 'delayed, disguised, or thwarted', at least until she wrote *To the Lighthouse*, in which the presentation of Mrs Ramsay (based on her mother) brought her a measure of consolation.

Spilka's account of *Mrs Dalloway* makes frequent use of two early versions of the novel: one, the never-written version that Woolf described in her 1928 Introduction, in which Clarissa rather than Septimus was to have killed herself; the other, the version of the opening found in 'Mrs Dalloway in Bond Street'. Although Spilka does not articulate his method explicitly, the earlier versions become repressed memories that intermittently erupt into the published text and that point to its 'secret causes' (62). Spilka begins with the feeling that there is something missing in the presentation of Clarissa Dalloway, which results in what Woolf termed her 'tinselly' quality. He argues that by displacing the burden of mourning on to Septimus, Woolf lost some of the depth she might have given Clarissa.

Spilka makes particularly subtle use of the presence in 'Mrs Dalloway in Bond Street' of 'Adonaïs' (1821) by Percy Bysshe Shelley (1792–1822), an elegiac poem about the death of John Keats, and of the absence of the poem in *Mrs Dalloway*. Keats, the doomed poet, Spilka associates with Septimus. It is particularly important to Spilka that the earlier version of Clarissa remembers Shelley's lines in which one of the consolations of death is the escape from the need to mourn waste, neglect and old age: 'He is secure and now can never mourn / A heart grown cold, a head grown grey in vain' (Shelley, quoted 55). By removing the lines from 'Adonaïs' from the novel, and using instead the lines from Shakespeare's *Cymbeline*, Woolf alters the nature of Clarissa's fears about death and ageing, which in the story originate in 'a desire to escape from mourning' (56). Spilka also notes that Jim Hutton, the radical poet in red socks who attends Clarissa's party (*MD* 149–50), is a displaced version of Keats, because in 'Mrs Dalloway in Bond Street', Clarissa had speculated 'Would one have liked Keats if he had worn red socks?' (*CSF* 157). By association, the poet at the party is a version of Septimus.

In the novel, all that remains of a mourning Clarissa is the passage concerning the death of her sister Sylvia (*MD* 66). Spilka is interested both in the brevity of the account (which suggests that something is being repressed) and in the 'stoic atheism' (59) given to Clarissa (her desire, for example, to 'mitigate the sufferings of our fellow-prisoners' [*MD* 66]), because her stoicism has something in common with the outlook of Woolf's mother, Julia Stephen. Moreover, Spilka detects something inconsistent in the characterization of Clarissa. She asserts that 'she enjoyed life immensely' and no longer felt any 'bitterness' (*MD* 66), and yet she is beset by anxiety at the approach of death.

Spilka also finds contradictions in the causes of Septimus's madness and his mourning of Evans. The novel's insistence on the intimacy of the relationship with Evans suggests that shell-shock in itself is not a sufficient explanation. Spilka considers Bazin's explanation that, because he felt guilty about his sexual attraction to Evans, Septimus wanted him to die, and now feels guilty about having achieved his wish. For Spilka the argument is ultimately unpersuasive because there is no evidence that Septimus feels guilt (62–3); the guilt is a consequence of Septimus's failure to mourn, not a cause of it. Although Spilka does not reductively identify Woolf with Septimus, he notes that in a draft version he was called 'Stephen' (Woolf's maiden name), and that 'Stephen' survives as a 'hidden anagram' in 'Septimus Warren Smith'. Less persuasively, he suggests that the full name has 'nearly sufficient lettering' to match what he calls her 'present name', 'Virginia Stephen Woolf'; the problem is that after marriage Woolf never incorporated her father's surname into her full name.

One way of treating the absent motivations in *Mrs Dalloway* would be to refer them back to unresolved issues in its author, but Spilka also suggests that, if we examine the novel on its own terms, something is being mourned, namely 'the death of romantic love' (67). Clarissa's mourning for love is focused on the figure of Peter: he is someone who violates her privacy just as Holmes and Bradshaw do Septimus's, and yet 'she opens up his deepest feelings, understands him as no one else does, communicates with him without words' (66). The death of romantic love is the cost of maintaining 'the privacy of the soul' (*MD* 107). Within this theme, Spilka makes sense of the appearance of Mrs Hilbery at Clarissa's party, because Mrs Hilbery's fairy-godmother intercession in Woolf's *Night and Day* is crucial to resolving the love story, and *Night and Day* is the last novel by Woolf in which romantic love seemed to be a viable basis for a plot. It is revealing that Mrs Hilbery tells Clarissa that she 'looked tonight ... so like her mother as she first saw her walking in a garden in a grey hat' (*MD* 149). It is a recollection that brings tears to Clarissa's eyes, and it seems as if Woolf, through the medium of Clarissa, has briefly mourned her mother.

One persistent problem with psychoanalytic analyses of characters is that they tend to treat the novelistic medium as transparent, forgetting that they are dealing with constructs made from language and the conventions of fiction, and not a real patient on the analyst's couch. Suzette Henke's 1981 article 'Virginia Woolf's Septimus Smith', although essentially a character analysis, is more than usually alert to the linguistic dimension, and as such anticipates the linguistic turn in literary psychoanalysis that came in the later 1980s.[6] Henke's article also shows the benefit of the publication of the diaries and other works mentioned earlier, and of scholarly thoroughness about the composition of *Mrs Dalloway*. Henke's basic argument is that Woolf's portrait of Septimus is strikingly close to a Freudian case history: 'Not only does she explore the narcissistic and homosexual resonances of Smith's behavior; but she also succeeds in re-creating, with startling verisimilitude, particular patterns in the schizophrenic use of language' (14). For the first points, Henke draws on Freud's essay 'On Narcissism' (1914; English translation 1925); her sources for the point about language are the later Freudians Harry Stack Sullivan, J. S. Kasanin and Norman Cameron.

Septimus conforms to Freud's diagnosis of paraphrenia: he suffers from megalomania, and has withdrawn his interest from people and things in the external world. Henke also suggests that Septimus is suffering from '*paranoia persecutoria*' because of his sexuality. She notes the passage of Septimus and Evans depicted as two dogs playfully fighting, and remarks that the phrase 'share with each other' (*MD* 73) was used in homosexual contexts to indicate cohabitation or being sexual partners.[7] That Evans returns 'from the fields of Thessaly' (*MD* 59) further hints that theirs was 'Greek love'.

Sir William Bradshaw's remark that Septimus was 'attaching meanings to words of a symbolical kind' (*MD* 81) opens the discussion of Septimus's schizophrenic language. Henke summarizes the main features:

'He devises a discourse that is autotelic and self-referential. Trees are alive; birds sing to him in Greek; dogs and men become interchangeable; and real objects assume a frightening, horrific and guilt-laden symbolism' (15). At times the symbolism is impenetrable. Why do a sideboard and bananas (*MD* 123) lead to a memory of Evans? The phallic symbolism of the bananas is explicable enough, but the sideboard is incomprehensible. 'At some level of perception, Septimus knows that the value he attaches to certain terms is highly private and idiosyncratic. But he does not care' (16). In her conclusion Henke gives detailed consideration to Septimus's final words, 'I'll give it you' (*MD* 127), noting in particular that there is no obvious syntactic referent for 'it':

■ It seems appropriate that in his final 'message' to society, Septimus lapses into a 'paralogical' discourse that invests language with symbolic value. Smith's utterance has private, autistic connotations that necessarily remain opaque. One can sense, intuitively, an illusory note of triumph in Smith's challenge to the insensitive Holmes. But the actual 'meaning' of his statement depends on a schizophrenic process of condensation, displacement, and symbolism. Through a series of disconnected and paralogical associations, Smith has come to believe that he must sacrifice his life in order to defeat the 'enemy', and to save himself from authoritarian institutions that could destroy him; but the meaning of his gesture is contingent on an 'utterly novel, perfectly magical' use of autistic symbolism. (21) □

While Henke treats character as real to the extent that she diagnoses Septimus's illness, by simultaneously foregrounding the linguistic qualities of *Mrs Dalloway*, she never allows us to forget that we are dealing with a literary text. However, by scrupulously referencing psychoanalytic case histories, Henke risks leaving Woolf in their shadow, valuing her only for her ability to intuit the ideas of later experts, and not for her ability to formulate her own ideas.

Psychoanalysis after Freudianism

Several critical works, translations and anthologies in the late 1970s introduced the Anglophone world to developments in psychoanalysis in France after Freud and to the literary theories that engaged (sometimes critically) with them. These included the *Écrits: A Selection* (translated 1977) by Jacques Lacan (1901–81); Sherry Turkle's *Psychoanalytic Politics: Freud's French Revolution* (1979); *New French Feminisms*, edited by Elaine Marks and Isabelle de Courtivron (1980), which included essays by Julia Kristeva (b. 1941), Hélène Cixous (b. 1937), Luce Irigaray (b. 1930) and many others; and Kristeva's *Desire in Language* (translated

1980). While this wave of psychoanalytic work was indebted to the linguistic turn of structuralism and post-structuralism, it was as interested in the nature of the mind before it acquires language and in the ways that such 'irrational' elements persist into mature consciousness.

Lacan's re-reading of Freud emphasized the prominence of language in his case histories and his theories. Lacan replaced the two crucial elements in the Freudian dream work, condensation and displacement, with linguistic equivalents, metaphor and metonymy. He argued that there were two essential stages to the development of a sense of self. In the first, the mirror stage, the helpless infant, incapable of speech or co-ordinated motion, sees its reflection in a mirror (or sees another being) and imagines its own potential to be a co-ordinated being. In the second stage, Lacan's rewriting of the Oedipal stage, the child, still strongly attached to its mother, encounters the jealousy of the father, which Lacan punningly terms the *'nom-du-père'* (in French this sounds like both the 'name of the father' and the '"no" of the father'). At the same time, the child begins to acquire language. Lacan's theory of the human subject develops the anti-humanist potential of the Freudian unconscious, undermining the coherent humanist subject to the point where it is merely a convenient fiction.

Feminist psychoanalysis and literary theory criticized Lacan's tendency to treat female development as a deviation from a male norm, and sought to reconceptualize the pre-linguistic phase in a way that would see it as valuable to the subject, not as a feared irrational element. In her 1974 doctoral thesis, Julia Kristeva reconceived the pre-Oedipal phase as 'the semiotic'. The semiotic is characterized by the rhythmic pulsions of what Kristeva terms the *chora*. The chora 'constitutes [...] the heterogeneous, disruptive dimension of language, that which can never be caught up in the closure of traditional linguistic theory'.[8] Saussure's emphasis on fixed structure, introduced with his concept of *langue*, is displaced in favour of a more dynamic conception of language. The pulsions of the *chora* are readily associated with the aspects of literary writing that escape rational explanation, particularly rhythmic effects both in poetry and prose. Kristeva's work achieved wide distribution in the English-speaking world in 1980 in Marks and de Courtivron's *New French Feminisms* and *Desire in Language*, a selection of her essays.

While Elizabeth Abel's 1983 essay 'Narrative Structure(s) and Female Development: The Case of *Mrs Dalloway*' does not explicitly root its analysis in post-Freudian materials, it specifically cites *New French Feminisms*, and its use of Freud has much in common with French theory.[9] Crucially, it shifts attention away from relationships between the sexes and onto relations between women. It is psychoanalytic in its theorization of relations between women, and also in its method of reading:

Abel argues that women's writing in the twentieth century consists of layered plots and 'clandestine' stories; her method of uncovering the concealed stories and finding significance in gaps and margins implicitly resembles the analyst finding the latent content in the patient's dreams and utterances. Excavations into women's writing have often revealed 'an enduring ... narrative concern with the story of mothers and daughters', and with what Freud termed the 'pre-Oedipal' relationship, 'the early symbiotic female bond that predates and coexists with the heterosexual orientation toward the father and his substitutes' (163). Such plots are often relegated to the background of a courtship or marriage plot. It is important to Abel's analysis that Clarissa's life is presented in two major portions: Bourton in the past and London in the present; we learn almost nothing of Clarissa's life before the Bourton scenes, or of the years between that period and the novel's present. Clarissa's development 'proceeds from an emotionally pre-Oedipal female-centred natural world to the heterosexual male-dominated social world' (164); in a classically structuralist moment, Abel presents Clarissa's development as 'a stark binary opposition between past and present, nature and culture, feminine and masculine dispensations' (166). One curious effect of the absence of any true childhood scenes, Abel argues, is that 'the earliest remembered scenes become homologous to a conventional narrative point of departure: the description of formative childhood years' (167). Although Abel largely eschews biographical parallels, she takes as one epigraph for the essay a remark Woolf made to Violet Dickinson (1865–1948), a woman who became something of a mother-substitute following the death of Julia Stephen in 1895 – 'I wish you were a Kangaroo and had a pouch for small Kangaroos to creep to' (*L1* 79) – and she suggests that Clarissa's feelings for Sally Seton at Bourton are similar. Peter Walsh is then the substitute father-figure who shatters the pre-Oedipal bond. She quotes Clarissa's account of Peter's motives: 'she felt his hostility; his jealousy; his determination to break into their companionship' (*MD* 31).[10] To Abel this suggests 'an Oedipal configuration: the jealous male attempting to rupture the exclusive female bond, insisting on the transference of attachment to the man, demanding heterosexuality' (169). It is also notable that Clarissa sees Peter as resembling a 'granite wall' encountered in the dark: Peter constructs barriers. Abel also dwells on the violent death of the marginal figure Sylvia, killed by a falling tree, and the way that Clarissa attributes blame to her father, Justin Parry, in a parenthetical remark '(all Justin Parry's fault—all his carelessness)' (*MD* 66).

■ The violence of Sylvia's death ... and the very incongruity between the magnitude of the charge against her father and its parenthetical presentation suggest a story intentionally withheld, forcibly deprived of its legitimate proportions, deliberately excised from the narrative yet provocatively implied in it, written both into and out of the text. (170) □

Again, Abel's method is to look for almost-occluded moments and to tease out the concealed narrative.

The closing part of Abel's essay turns to the ways that other female characters 'subtly reflect Clarissa's experience' (175) and so encode the plot of female development. Abel argues that Rezia, like Clarissa, goes from a female-dominated Milan to a male-dominated London, and notes how in her final appearance, under the influence of sedatives, Rezia feels she is 'opening long windows, stepping out into some garden' (*MD* 127), a phrase that recalls Clarissa's opening scene and that suggests that in the novel Bourton, gardens and nature represent a shared pre-Oedipal world. Abel also brings something new to the well-worn territory of Septimus as Clarissa's double, noting that by displacing the suicide onto Septimus, Woolf avoids the tradition of 'violently thwarted development' common in female-centred novels of development, such as Maggie Tulliver's death in George Eliot's *The Mill on the Floss* (1860) (177). She also notices how phrases in Clarissa's reflections on Septimus's death echo phrases in her earlier reminiscences of Sally at Bourton: most crucially, the 'thing that mattered' (*MD* 156) that Septimus's death has preserved echoes the 'something central which permeated' (*MD* 27); Septimus's 'treasure' echoes the 'present' that Sally had given Clarissa (*MD* 156, 30). Abel concludes that Clarissa's grief 'is not for Septimus, but for herself' (178).

In the conclusion to her essay, Abel gives particular attention to the Elizabeth Dalloway scenes, which take as their subject female development 'in the altered contemporary world'. The transition from child to woman that had been so traumatic for Clarissa has apparently been straightforward for Elizabeth (183). However, Woolf figures Elizabeth as 'inscrutable' and as an 'unopened bud', and so 'encloses in her text the unwritten text of the next developmental narrative'. Woolf 'does not evaluate this new developmental course, does not tally losses and gains' (184).

Jean Wyatt's 1986 article 'Avoiding Self-Definition' explicitly relates *Mrs Dalloway* to a Kristevan framework.[11] It concentrates on Clarissa, but is less concerned with analysing individual characters than with recovering Woolf's implicit model of the self and comparing it to late twentieth-century feminist theory. Wyatt begins by noting that in many twentieth-century novels by women, the protagonists 'affirm a sense of self in flux'; they do not 'rush to define what is inchoate and amorphous in themselves, but welcome the chaos of a diffuse self for its promise of change and celebrate the possibilities for renewal in the experience of merging'. Some Freudians had seen 'a return to an undifferentiated state of being' as regressive, but Wyatt argues that, 'viewed in a context of female experience, the capacity for opening up to identification and fusion reveals revolutionary and renewing powers' (115). In *Civilization and its Discontents* (1930), Freud had described the 'infant at the breast' as one who does not differentiate ego from external world; it has feelings 'of limitlessness and of a bond with the universe' which he characterized as 'oceanic' (Freud, quoted 116). Some later Freudians had treated the 'oceanic' state as inferior to having a clearly defined self, but Wyatt wishes to partially redeem it for feminist criticism. Nancy Chodorow's *The Reproduction of Mothering* (1978) offers Wyatt an important account of how mothers' relations to sons and daughters differ. In short, 'women are more comfortable vaulting over ego boundaries to fuse with what is outside than are men', because the 'oceanic feeling' is 'built into their primary definition of self' (119). Kristeva is useful to Wyatt because she 'thinks of the mature human being as embodying a dialectic between the semiotic self and the symbolic self – more process than progress' (119). The 'I' is a fiction and an abstraction.

Mrs Dalloway 'implies that alone, without the social scaffolding of discourse, we are diffuse, not just internally – subject to the changing currents of impulse and feeling – but externally as well: without firm boundaries, the self merges with its surroundings' (120). Wyatt notes Clarissa's morning walk, in which she feels herself part 'of the trees at home; of the house there' (*MD* 8). Merging does not cause Clarissa a loss of self – far from it: 'Clarissa loses life when she can't merge' (121).

The problem with this aspect of Wyatt's argument is that it apparently aims to make Woolf a precocious Kristevan; the novel is valued for its theoretical anticipations, and not as a novel. Wyatt's account of Clarissa's scene at the mirror, in which she collects 'the whole of her at one point' (*MD* 31), has a similar tendency. Wyatt notes the respects in which Woolf's account of identity anticipates psychoanalytic work: 'The discrete entity "herself" is not an intuitive certainty, but a laborious reconstruction of her "point" in the network of family names and social roles' (123). Such readings were not uncommon in theoretically informed work in the 1980s: while they can be criticized for reducing literary texts to theory, they also demonstrate that theory is not so very alien to literature, and that many of its insights had been anticipated by well-known works.

In any case, as well as establishing the basic theoretical similarities between *Mrs Dalloway* and psychoanalytic theory, Wyatt goes on to develop a reader-response position. She claims that the rhythms of Woolf's prose work on 'the reader's susceptibility to rhythm', and persuade the reader 'to give up the burden of the structured symbolic self who decodes abstract words for the sensual self who lets the words' rhythms play across her/his body' like waves (122). In saying this, Wyatt draws on Kristeva's 'The Novel as Polylogue' in *Desire in Language*:

'a text can precipitate a takeover by the semiotic in the reader' (122). Rhythmic pattern wins over grammatical order. The reader of *Mrs Dalloway* is 'encouraged to imitate the dissolution of Clarissa's social self into a rhythmical space played on by oceanic patterns of alliteration and repetition' (122). While such an idea cannot be definitively proved, it brings the formal properties of Woolf's texts into play, and moreover suggests a route whereby psychoanalytic ideas might be used for analysis that is focused neither on the author nor on her characters, but on texts and their interactions with readers.

Makiko Minow-Pinkney's *Virginia Woolf and the Problem of the Subject* (1987) was the first book-length exploration of Woolf's work using recent French psychoanalytic thought.[12] It has remained influential, and, unusually for a scholarly book, was reissued in 2010. Minow-Pinkney's larger argument is that Woolf's modernist experimentalism and her feminism are not mutually exclusive. One critical tradition held that her experimental works (with *The Waves* as the pinnacle) represented a retreat from the world and from facts about the world. Minow-Pinkney argues that Woolf's feminist aesthetic and her modernist aesthetic are 'two faces of a single project' (14); the search for new fictional modes is a rejection of the existing patriarchal symbolic order. Woolf engages in 'feminine writing': for Minow-Pinkney, 'feminine' does not connote any essential relation to biological sex; rather, it is an 'an attempt to inscribe positions against or alternative to those of the dominant male order' (16). This raises a problem though, within Lacanian psychoanalytic terms: how is a feminine writing possible, if 'the repression of the feminine is the very condition of the human subject's speech'? (17). The answer lies in a Kristevan definition of the subject as being never permanently settled, but perpetually 'en procès' (both 'in process' but also, in legal terminology, 'on trial'). Kristeva's 'semiotic' is crucial to Minow-Pinkney's account but she recognizes that the woman writer cannot remain in the semiotic: as in Jean Wyatt's account, the self is a dialectic between the semiotic and the symbolic. The androgyny which Woolf saw (in *A Room of One's Own*) as essential to the great writer, Minow-Pinkney argues is an inevitable part of women's subjectivity. This, at least in part, is the titular 'problem of the subject':

■ woman cannot but be androgynous. Even if she identifies herself with the mother in the position of the repressed and marginal, she must have a certain identification with the father in order to sustain a place in the symbolic order and avoid psychosis. On the other hand, if she identifies herself with the father, denying the woman in herself, she is none the less biologically female: the father-identification remains precarious, stands always in need of defence. Here arises the tragic difficulty for women artists who try to situate their work over the interplay of the symbolic and the semiotic. (22) □

For the male, a return to the pre-Oedipal brings pleasure, but for the female it (in Kristeva's words) 'destroys the symbolic armour'. However, a woman's 'precarious, double position' is also a kind of privilege, because she can access both worlds (22).

Minow-Pinkney's chapter on *Mrs Dalloway* begins with a careful technical analysis of the effects wrought by Woolf's use of free indirect discourse, and its wider ramifications. For example, in a passage recalling Septimus's earlier interactions with Dr Holmes, we see the following:

> ■ When the damned fool came again, Septimus refused to see him. Did he indeed? said Dr Holmes, smiling agreeably. Really he had to give that charming little lady, Mrs Smith, a friendly push before he could get past her into her husband's bedroom. (*MD* 78) □

Minow-Pinkney notes how in a single passage that is formally the narratorial voice we find a phrase that derives from Septimus's perspective ('damned fool') and another ('charming little lady') from Holmes's (58). Woolf's use of free indirect discourse creates 'an effect of subjective haziness ... across the whole text' (54). Such ideas have antecedents in older styles of criticism: Minow-Pinkney quotes approvingly Auerbach's analysis of *To the Lighthouse* (in his *Mimesis* [1953]), and in particular his conclusion that the narratorial voice of that novel consists of 'spirits between heaven and earth, nameless spirits capable of penetrating the depth of the human soul' (quoted 58). However, she also wishes to see Woolf's achievement in terms of post-Lacanian psychoanalysis:

> ■ what Woolf's writing effects is a denial of the unified subject which supports all discourse and is necessarily 'masculine', since the symbolic order is established with the phallus as its fundamental signifier. The narrative consciousness in her writing, if indeed there is one, has stopped judging, interpreting, explaining; it has no single identity or position. (58–9) □

Minow-Pinkney identifies similarities between the formal procedures of the novel and its content at the level of character. For example, the movement of the narrator from character to character, particularly when it abandons one character and turns to a newcomer, and its 'nimble manoeuvring between individuals and groups' (57) resembles the movements of a hostess at a party. 'There is a parallel between the mode of subjectivity that constitutes the stylistic principle of the book, and the state of being of Clarissa and the other characters' (62). There are several passages in which this parallel becomes particularly clear: the scene of Clarissa before the mirror, 'collecting the whole of her at one point' (*MD* 31); Peter's recollection of Clarissa's 'transcendental theory' (*MD* 129); Clarissa's morning walk (*MD* 8); and Clarissa saying that she would not say of anyone 'they were this or were that' nor 'I am this, I am that' (*MD* 7). It is worth noting that this approach tends to take Clarissa at her word, and it is worth asking whether she really never attributes a fixed identity to anyone, or whether it is rather a belief that she likes to hold about herself, no more trustworthy than Peter Walsh's self-image as a buccaneer (*MD* 46).

In finding consistency between levels in the novel, Minow-Pinkney might appear to be engaged in a relatively traditional critical activity: her approach resembles the New Critical search for a unified work of art or an 'organic unity'. However, she does not take the novel's unity entirely uncritically. In particular, she notes what one might see as a failure of nerve on Woolf's part about 'the utopian value of the semiotic' (63). Having formally asserted it, the novel tries to tame the energies it has released, through what the Russian formalists called a 'motivation of the device' (64). First by setting the novel in the post-war period, Woolf allows the 'disruptive intensity of the novel's sensory perceptions' to be 'rationalised as the simple expression of relief at national survival'. Secondly, 'semiotic intensities are naturalised by being implicitly presented as the effects of a summer heat wave' (64). In other words, rather than allowing her formal devices to work their effects on the reader, Woolf finds 'naturalistic motivation[s]' for them.

Having considered the larger form of the novel, the chapter presents detailed analyses of characters from a Kristevan perspective. Minow-Pinkney's primary interest is Clarissa, and although there are insightful remarks on other characters, both major and minor, it is to Clarissa that the argument returns. Like Abel, Minow-Pinkney sees many of the minor characters as existing to amplify qualities presented fleetingly in Clarissa, or to clarify them by contrast. One of Minow-Pinkney's central points about Clarissa is that her character involves a 'dialectic' between a 'cold contracting of the self' and a 'schizophrenic dispersal' (68). One side of that character is seen in her retreat to her attic room; the other in the significant passage where Clarissa considers her sexual feelings (without directly naming them as sexual) and compares them to 'a match burning in a crocus' (*MD* 27). The minor character Mr Bowley, who is said to be 'sealed with wax' and yet capable of being 'unsealed' unexpectedly echoes this tendency in Clarissa (68). Minow-Pinkney links the unsealing to Clarissa's refrain of 'Fear no more the heat of the sun.' The old woman who Clarissa sees descending the stairs in a house opposite also provides 'a mirror image' of Clarissa in her attic, 'a symbol of both independence and isolation in patriarchal society' (69). The novel recognizes a kind of 'feminine comradeship which went beneath masculine lunch parties' (*MD* 90).

'Comradeship' is a concept which is entirely compatible with a humanist idea of a unified human subject, and which, moreover, is associated with a different philosophy of feminism from the one Minow-Pinkney explores. Minow-Pinkney argues that 'comradeship' is not sufficient:

> ■ The problem for women is to assert a female specificity as difference and to open up a space for this difference in the masculine structure of society. This is not to be achieved simply by the assertion of women's comradeship; it involves, rather, the question of the subject. Having remained close to the maternal body in spite of its enforced repression, the girl or woman inscribes herself naturally within the semiotic, in touch with what Kristeva terms the 'spasmodic force' of the repressed. (70) □

However, to associate exclusively with the semiotic is not possible. 'Women must somehow keep a hold on the symbolic, and thus as if in reinforcement of the mirror phase [...] Clarissa needs her own reflection' (70). Minow-Pinkney returns to the scene of Clarissa at the mirror, but also notes the phrase about Clarissa feeling that she lacks 'something central which permeated'; she sees this lack as being 'the maternal body which she must repress to become a subject in the symbolic' (70).

The problem of the subject's relation to the maternal is focused in two scenes within the Regent's Park section of the novel. The essential tension lies between 'The pain of severance from the maternal' and 'the risk of fusing with the mother' (72). The risk of fusion is illustrated by the scene of Peter Walsh falling asleep next to a female nurse. That the nurse is knitting associates her with the earlier scene of Clarissa mending her dress (*MD* 33–4), an action that Minow-Pinkney had read as invoking Penelope in *The Odyssey*, weaving by day and unweaving by night in order to delay the suitors who wished to claim her in Odysseus's absence. Peter imagines he could be blown 'to nothingness' (*MD* 49) by the woman, and Minow-Pinkney comments that he invokes 'an ideology of femininity in order to avoid contact with the real woman' (72). The other scene is that of the beggar woman, whose voice 'is precisely the voice of the mother' (73). Minow-Pinkney comments that 'The woman or mother is always a void, a hole in the discourse – as the unconscious, the unrepresentable: "so rude a mouth [...] tangled grasses" [*MD* 69], an image irresistibly suggesting the female genitals' (73). Within the larger Kristevan schema, her song, 'A mere rhythmic babble of phonemes', is easily identifiable with the 'pre-symbolic' (73).

Minow-Pinkney's treatment of Septimus's madness and death has attracted criticism for too readily recuperating them as a sort of victory over patriarchy. Minow-Pinkney begins her account of Septimus by describing him as another 'victim of patriarchy' (77), and she understands his losing the 'capacity for communication' and his hearing voices in essentially Lacanian terms: he has left the symbolic order; for him 'the division between signifier and signified is no longer clear' (78). Glossing the phrase 'He was not Septimus now' (*MD* 20), she remarks: 'he can no longer sustain a stable self, and body, world, word fuse, intersect and traverse each other. Inner meaning seems about to emerge from the world at any moment. The word is no longer an empty sign but an absolute reality through which the truth shines with no dividing bar between signifier and signified' (78). (The 'dividing bar' between the two is a crucial part of Lacan's adoption of Saussurean structuralism.) In her account, Septimus is 'released from the constraints of the symbolic order', and becomes (in his way of perceiving the world, at least) the poet he had always wanted to be. Minow-Pinkney examines a passage about Septimus's feelings in Regent's Park ('To watch a leaf quivering in the rush of air was an exquisite joy. [...] Beauty was everywhere' (MD 59)). She comments: 'In this state, Septimus enjoys colours, rhythms, sounds with extreme intensity as the thetic subject is dissolved into the semiotic *chora* it had formerly so severely repressed' (79). Judy Little has remarked that what looks like a kind of liberation may not be so: 'I am not convinced that the visions of Septimus free him into a pre-oedipal and liberated subjectivity; indeed, he is floundering in the still very manly, but garbled, symbolic order.'[13]

Minow-Pinkney's account of Septimus's death rests heavily on Clarissa's phrases about 'the impossibility of reaching the centre' and there being 'an embrace in death' (*MD* 156) and the novel's images of absent sons and grieving mothers: Mrs Foxcroft, Lady Bexborough, the 'elderly woman' (*MD* 49) in Peter Walsh's dreams. Minow-Pinkney comments: 'In psychoanalytic terms, the 'embrace' which Septimus aims at in death may be regarded as an embrace with the Mother. It is impossible to reach the 'centre', since the subject is split in its very constitution.' By trying to 'decipher' Septimus's death, Clarissa establishes a relation with him: 'If Septimus does indeed "embrace" the Mother in death, it is because he now in a sense has a 'mother' who acknowledges him: "She felt very like him"' (*MD* 158) (79). Trudi Tate notes that this interpretation treats Clarissa as a primarily 'sympathetic' figure whose insights may be trusted, whereas the novel 'constructs her quite explicitly as someone with whom we identify *and* whom we are forced to judge'. The passage about death as an embrace 'draws too much comfort from the imagined familial structure'.[14]

Although she has been criticized for, in effect, idealizing Septimus's mental illness, Minow-Pinkney's book has remained influential. It has survived because it offered a politicized account of subjectivity that made it more than a narrow application of psychoanalytic theory.

Death and Mourning

Many critics have followed Spilka's lead in considering the theme of mourning in Woolf's work, and not only in *Mrs Dalloway*. *To the Lighthouse* has been a focal text, because Woolf felt that in writing it she had completed the grieving process for her mother: 'I did for myself what psychoanalysts do for their patients. I expressed some very long felt and deeply felt emotion. And in expressing it I explained it and then laid it to rest.'[15]

John Mepham's 'Mourning and Modernism' (1983) deals principally with *Jacob's Room*, *To the Lighthouse* and *The Waves*, but makes some valuable general points about mourning as well as commenting on *Mrs Dalloway*.[16] Mepham begins with the question of why Woolf felt it necessary to experiment formally, and, while he acknowledges many motivations, he argues that Woolf was dissatisfied with the inability of conventional fictional form to deal with the contradictory emotions involved in mourning. Conventional fiction 'encourages rapid judgement as to the meaning of an experience' (137), and cannot deal with what Woolf called 'tumultuous and contradictory emotions' ('Poetry, Fiction and the Future', *E4* 438). In Woolf's novels, he claims, 'death is never incorporated into plot and never functions as the termination of a story' (149); while Rachel Vinrace's death in *The Voyage Out* might be cited as a partial exception, his point is certainly true of *Mrs Dalloway*. It is not Evans's death that is the subject, but Septimus's response. (149). Septimus is 'incapacitated' by Evans's death 'because he cannot assimilate it into any stable system of meaning' (150). The problem of mourning is a problem of distance. 'Recovering from grief involves recovering, calling back again, the dead. It is necessary to feel their presence within you before it is possible to release them to the earth. But it is also necessary to establish a distance from them, to externalize them and to say farewell to them. If the dead remain too close they stay to haunt us as Evans haunts Septimus, speaking to him from behind the bushes, walking towards him across the park' (151). Mepham establishes with clarity some of the basic paradoxes involved in mourning.

Susan Bennett Smith's 'Reinventing Grief Work' (1995) begins within a biographical frame, asking why the family doctor was called when Virginia Woolf's mother died in 1895.[17] She contrasts Virginia's and Leslie Stephen's reactions to Julia Stephen's death: Leslie's reaction was excessive and theatrical; Virginia, on the other hand, seemed to register the death only in suppressed laughter. The contrast is to do with gender, but also generational differences. Leslie Stephen's reaction continues Victorian conventions of mourning; by contrast, Virginia was believed to require medical attention. The 'rest cure' recommended for Woolf may be understood as a medicalized version of an older style of mourning: the seclusion that it involved, in 'the company of sympathetic women' (312), resembled the rituals that a middle-class woman would have undertaken earlier in the nineteenth century. Smith suggests that Virginia's treatment registers a transitional moment in the history of grief, and she argues that Woolf's writings made a critique of the changing assumptions. The article covers both *Mrs Dalloway* and *To the Lighthouse*. In the former, Woolf 'tells a cautionary tale of the fatal results of the feminization and medicalization of grief, but offers no viable alternative'; in the latter, she provides a viable model for 'grief work' (310).

In *Mrs Dalloway*, Woolf 'explores the debilitating effects of feminizing and medicalizing grief that leave Septimus without any legitimate means to express his sorrow' (313). Relative to other interpreters, Smith downplays the importance of Septimus's sexuality in his breakdown, and she emphasizes the unprecedented scale of the loss in the war. Septimus's relationship 'complicates his bereavement', but sexuality is 'secondary' to bereavement as a cause (317). She notes in particular the passage where Septimus believes he sees Evans walking towards him:

> ■ But no mud was on him; no wounds; he was not changed. I must tell the whole world, Septimus cried, raising his hand (as the dead man in the grey suit came nearer), raising his hand like some colossal figure who has lamented the fate of man for ages in the desert alone ... and with legions of men prostrate behind him he, the giant mourner, receives for one moment on his face the whole. (*MD* 59–60) □

Smith remarks that, as a 'colossal figure' in the desert, Septimus resembles the statue in Shelley's 'Ozymandias' (1818). The strangeness of the figure not only 'conveys Septimus's mental imbalance', but also 'suggests the absence of models for male mourning in Western culture' (314). The legions of men 'prostrate' behind him she interprets not as Septimus's imagined worshippers, but as the innumerable, unmournable dead. Smith places Septimus's inability to mourn in a historical context where stoicism and fortitude were prized. She notes in particular that Rezia explains Septimus's illness by saying that he had been working too hard (*MD* 20): where men were prescribed the rest cure, it was usually because of 'overwork' rather than mourning or mental illness. Septimus's mental state appears to be a classic case of what Freud called 'melancholia', particularly in Septimus having undergone such a fall in self-esteem that he believes himself to have committed crimes and feels suicidal.

Smith interprets Clarissa as providing a contrast to Septimus in matters of grief work: 'Clarissa represents sane bereavement, whereas Septimus's mourning is pathological' (313). Like Minow-Pinkney, Smith believes in Clarissa's empathy for Septimus, and suggests that it has its roots in her experience of the rest cure, in consequence of which she is wary of Sir William Bradshaw's power. Clarissa appears to have successfully mourned, and yet Smith notes that she has not done so on Freud's terms. Freud had argued that the purpose of mourning was to 'detach the survivor's memories and hopes from the dead' (quoted 325); Clarissa, by contrast, seeks to maintain connections with her friends. Smith says very little about Clarissa's dead sister Sylvia in this regard, concentrating instead on Peter and Sally as people who have left Clarissa's life. Clarissa has 'shared her past' with them (*MD* 154), and sees it as one of the rewards of having cared for someone that 'they came back in the middle of St James's Park on a fine morning' (*MD* 6), reappearing not literally but in memory. This is Clarissa's 'sane version' (313) of Evans's reappearance before Septimus in Regent's Park. However, because Peter and Sally are not literally dead, the model that Clarissa provides of 'sane bereavement' is not adequate as a counterpart to Septimus. It is only in *To the Lighthouse* that Smith finds an adequate account of 'grief practices', one that is 'defeminized and demedicalized'. In the earlier novel, though Woolf had critiqued the medical establishment for its insensitivity, she had fundamentally accepted its diagnosis of grief 'as a disease'; in the later novel 'Woolf expresses grief without conventions, without doctors and without therapists' (323).

Christine Froula's '*Mrs Dalloway*'s Postwar Elegy: Women, War, and the Art of Mourning' (2002) places the process of mourning in the historical context of the post-war period: the novel joins Woolf's Bloomsbury friend John Maynard Keynes in a debate about the future of post-war Europe.[18] Sigmund Freud is present as much for his post-war writings *The Future of an Illusion* (1928) and *Civilization and Its Discontents* (1929) as for his writings on mourning and melancholia. However, Freud is also present in Froula's method, which is psychoanalytic in that it seeks to uncover that which the text censors. In doing so, she makes use of Woolf's manuscript draft of the novel, published in 1997 under its working title *The Hours*. As she says in conclusion, with reference to Woolf's idea that the novel was to contain the truth and the insane truth side by side (*Hours* 412), '*The Hours* preserves smouldering "truths" that even *Mrs Dalloway* cannot openly explore' (157).

Woolf's remark in June 1925 that she needed 'a new name' for her novels, perhaps 'elegy' (*D3* 34), has usually been taken by critics to refer forward to *To the Lighthouse*, which she had begun to plan in the previous month; Froula, however, uses it as a way of opening up the elegiac aspects of *Mrs Dalloway*. Froula argues that Woolf discovers the genre's resources 'for dramatizing and mediating violence both psychic and social' (126). She follows Peter Sacks's 'psychosocial analysis' of poetic elegy: it is not a private genre, but one with work to do for the whole community. She identifies three key features. First, the classical elegy

■ figures the work of mourning through ceremonies surrounding the death and rebirth of a vegetation god such as Adonis, and its dialectical movement towards consolation (always necessarily symbolic) recalls the funeral games and contests through which a community of mourners negotiates its inheritance from dead father-figures or paternal deities. Mourning, then, has an oedipal dimension as the immediate loss reawakens old crises of loss and brokenness... To mourn is to relive every loss back to the first loss of the mother and to suffer again the anguish of submitting to the reality principle figured as the law of the father. (126) □

Second, the elegy has as its 'bad other' the genre of revenge tragedy. The formal mechanisms of classical elegy aim to restrain 'the mourner's chaos of feelings'. The mourner is threatened by melancholia on one side, and on the other by a rage 'that may veer from symbolic expression to actual murder or suicide' (127). Froula finds traces of formal poetry in the novel's 'structures of repetition and refrain', and notes the rage of Miss Kilman, the madness of Septimus, and Clarissa's near annihilation in 'existential doubt' as signs of the chaos of feelings.

Third, Froula suggests that *Mrs Dalloway* takes classical elegy's polyvocal 'singing matches', which 'channel grief into skilled performances that contest and carry on those virtues of the dead "deemed important for the community's survival"', and turns them into 'urgent social critique and contestation of the future' (127). In the contrasts of, for example, Clarissa's atheism and Miss Kilman's evangelicism, or Septimus's clash with his doctors, Woolf is asking questions about the future direction of European civilization. The idea of 'singing matches' allows Froula to open out the article into a consideration of the political contexts for the novel, not all of which can be summarized in the present account.

Froula notes that in her previous appearance in *The Voyage Out*, Clarissa Dalloway had been associated closely with Shelley's elegiac 'Adonaïs', and that the association had continued into 'Mrs Dalloway in Bond Street' (128–30). In the Bond Street shop in the short story, Clarissa ponders how Lady Bexborough can 'go on' in the face of her loss, and in doing so, 'expresses a communal grief and desolation and a longing for solace' which is assuaged neither by Shakespeare nor by Shelley (129). Froula focuses on Shelley's phrase about the 'sad Hour' at which Keats died, and his exhortation to the personified hour to rouse its 'obscure compeers' and teach them its sorrow. This, Froula suggests, is imitated by Woolf in the interlinked psyches of the novel, which create 'a polyphony of private griefs' (130). (She does not consider the French *unanimiste* school, and particularly Jules Romains's *Mort de quelqu'un* (1911), which seem an equally likely source for this aspect of the novel.)[19]

Froula traces what Woolf does with one biographical source, the death in 1922 of society hostess Kitty Maxse in a mysterious fall. Maxse had been a friend or mother-substitute to Woolf from 1895 to 1908; it was unclear whether her fall was an accident or suicide. Froula argues that her death, which came as Woolf wrote 'Mrs Dalloway in Bond Street', changed the course of the work:

> ■ in keeping with Sacks's point that the death the elegy mourns is always the elegist's own, [Woolf's] fantasy casts Kitty – hence Clarissa and Septimus – as her doubles. Kitty stands to Woolf [...] in much the same specular and sacrificial relation as Septimus stands to Clarissa; 'S.' substitutes for Kitty, Clarissa, and not least, Woolf – the seventh/septimus of eight Duckworth/Stephen children. (131) □

The passage early in the novel in which Clarissa contemplates how 'she survived' and 'Peter survived' in 'the streets of London' (*MD* 8) becomes uncanny if we identify Clarissa with Kitty: 'In bringing Kitty back to "life" on a radiant June day that in fact she never lived, Woolf flaunts the elegist's power, invisibly flourishing Clarissa herself in Escherlike proof of Clarissa's own vision of life-after-death' (132).

Unlike Susan Bennett Smith, Froula makes Sylvia central to her account of *Mrs Dalloway*. Crucial to Froula's argument is the derivation of Sylvia's name from the Latin *silvanus* ('forest'), and the connection this makes with the novel's various trees and fruit-bearing branches: not only the tree that killed Sylvia, but the image of Clarissa surviving like a mist hanging in the branches of trees (*MD* 8). Sylvia is not so much a character as 'Death itself': 'the specter of Clarissa's, the harbinger of Septimus's, and ghost of Kitty's' (134). Froula traces the logic that connects Clarissa's recollection of mist-laden trees to *Cymbeline* in Hatchard's shop window:

> ■ The posthumous Kitty/Clarissa evokes the Posthumus [...] of *Cymbeline* – the play that inducted the nineteen-year-old scoffer Virginia into the bard's 'company of worshippers.' What she thought the 'best lines' in this or perhaps any play, 'Imogen says – Think that you are upon a rock, and now throw me again! and Posthumus answers – Hang there like fruit, my Soul, till the tree die', find echo in Clarissa's mist-laden branches and Woolf's tree of life hung with flowers/fruit/books [*L1* 45–6]. (135) □

Clarissa's 'transcendental theory' (*MD* 129) 'extends Posthumus's tree [...] into a vast arboreal metaphor that augments conscious and/or bodily presence with unconscious experience, memory, and perception' (136). The narrative method of the novel allows characters to haunt each other: Clarissa's theory is described not directly by her, but in Peter's recollection of it.

Froula's psychoanalytic method is also illuminating when she considers Sir William Bradshaw, Hugh Whitbread, and the novel's suppressed hints of sexual violence. Considering Clarissa's description of Bradshaw as 'obscurely evil, without sex or lust, extremely polite to women, but capable of some indescribable outrage' (*MD* 157), Froula questions 'her specific exclusion of "sex or lust" in a context that has not raised any such issue' (153). The denial, she argues, implies that Bradshaw in some way represents sexual violence against women. Froula notes that in the manuscripts, Clarissa's 'owning' of Septimus's death leads her to vow to 'fight Sir William Bradshaw' (*The Hours* 398). Froula also suggests that Hugh Whitbread is a 'freehand portrait' of Woolf's half-brother George Duckworth, on the grounds of his age (55), his smugness, and his connections in high places. In the manuscript, Hugh meets Lady Bruton's secretary, Milly Brush, and inquires after her brother: in the somewhat garbled draft, 'she was almost inclined to tell him about her brother, except that she was almost killed her brother [denied once that she] told a lie once about her brother'; in the margin Woolf wrote 'never let on that her brother was not' (*Hours* 157). In the *Mrs Dalloway* version, Milly resents the question, and says that he is 'doing very well in South Africa' when in fact he is 'doing badly in Portsmouth' (*MD* 88). Froula comments that 'As the narrative screws down the lid over a site of near-fatal sibling violence, Milly Brush silently mocks her interlocutor with the subaltern's lie' (154).

'*Mrs Dalloway*'s Postwar Elegy' is a rich exploration of the novel's dialogues with its contemporary context, presenting elegy and mourning not as private matters, but as public ones. Although (as we shall see in Chapter 7) it has been criticized for not attending sufficiently to the division between private religion and public mourning, it has many strengths. It demonstrates that a psychoanalytic method of attending to displaced and suppressed clues may be applied not only to individual characters, but also to the network of allusions and associations that constitute the text. While Smith's focus on grief work is biographical, Froula's approach leads the question of mourning from psychoanalytic territory into a socio-historical context, while retaining a psychoanalytical method of reading between the lines.

Mrs Dalloway and Trauma

Woolf's fiction has continued to attract psychoanalytic approaches, with the question of trauma having risen to prominence in recent years. Investigations into the nature of traumatic experience and its relation to memory, narrative and testimony have drawn on the experiences of war veterans, Holocaust survivors, survivors of sexual abuse and others. The field of trauma studies was brought into focus in the early 1990s by the publication of two collections of articles – Shoshana Felman and Dori Laub's *Testimony: Crises of Witnessing in Literature,*

Psychoanalysis, and History (1992) and Cathy Caruth's *Trauma: Explorations in Memory* (1995) – and one book, Judith Herman's *Trauma and Recovery* (1992). In the field of Woolf studies, David Eberly and Suzette Henke have traced a critical lineage back to Roger Poole's *The Unknown Virginia Woolf* (1978). By challenging conventional labels such as 'madness' and 'lunacy', Poole opened a space in which Woolf's mental condition could be understood in terms of post-traumatic stress disorder. Crucial to the theory of trauma is the idea that memories of traumatic incidents cannot be integrated into a narrative of self, and so exist separately from conventional memory, returning uncontrollably with a disturbing vividness. 'Although he does not invoke trauma theory as such, Poole implies that Woolf, throughout her life, made use of fiction as a means of re-scripting and mastering traumatic experiences by means of a therapeutic process of narrative reformulation.'[20] Another important influence, according to Eberly and Henke, has been Louise DeSalvo's *Virginia Woolf: The Impact of Childhood Sexual Abuse on her Life and Work* (1989), which identifies the abuse at the hands of her halfbrothers as the primary set of traumatic incidents. Other critics, including Eberly and Henke, have also noted the deaths of her mother, her brother Thoby and her half-sister Stella, and the mental illness of her half-sister Laura.

Critics attending to trauma in *Mrs Dalloway* have also been alive to the fact that a society and culture can be collectively traumatized, and that such traumatization affects its attitudes towards damaged individuals. Just as the traumatized individual needs to reintegrate traumatic memories, so the traumatized society needs to reintegrate traumatized individuals, and in both cases the process can be painful. Critics considering *Mrs Dalloway* have also had to take into account the ways that the fractured, disjointed qualities of modernist narrative resemble the nonlinear narratives of traumatized individuals, as if modernist fiction were bearing witness to some sort of cultural trauma.

Marlene Briggs's short and pioneering article 'Veterans and Civilians: The Mediation of Traumatic Knowledge in *Mrs Dalloway*' (1999) takes as its starting point the problem of the lack of connection between Septimus and Clarissa: they are widely separate in terms of social class, and never meet.[21] Critics have too readily used Woolf's account of Septimus as Clarissa's 'double' (*E4* 548–50) as a means of smoothing over the problem, making them, for example, both victims of war. Briggs insists on the wide distance between the Western Front and London society, and, borrowing a term from Shoshana Felman, suggests that Clarissa is at best a 'belated witness' to Septimus's trauma.

In Briggs's account, Septimus's problem is one of 'traumatic temporality': his consciousness is 'a timeless present, proliferating with dense imagery, metaphor, repetition and hallucination' (44). Trauma

> ■ overwhelms the frameworks of narrative, and the knowledge it produces is disjunctive, non-narrative and temporally dislocated; trauma resists emplotment [...]. By representing Septimus through the 'unassimilable forms' [...] of traumatic knowledge, the text acknowledges the exceptional challenge to narrative assimilation embodied by the combat veteran. (44) □

Yet at the same time as it presents a plausibly fractured account of Septimus's consciousness, *Mrs Dalloway* demonstrates an awareness of the cultural mechanisms whereby trauma is interpreted and assimilated. The reader is able to construct 'a chronological narrative of Septimus's life' (45); moreover, Briggs quotes Peter Knox-Shaw as saying that 'At every point his symptoms coincide [...] with those listed prominently in contemporary writing on shell-shock' (Knox-Shaw, quoted 104). Septimus's '"madness" is constructed from composite narratives'; he is both an individual and a type (45). This is important because *Mrs Dalloway* 'explicitly probes those institutions which have the capacity to tyrannize through the imposition of narrative' (45). Those institutions are embodied as Holmes and Bradshaw, and Briggs is particularly insightful on Septimus's last words:

> ■ His last words before suicide, 'I'll give it you!' ensure his location within a narrative which defines his disordered state as 'cowardice' and 'lack of proportion': 'It was their idea of tragedy, not his or Rezia's [...] Holmes and Bradshaw liked that sort of thing' (*MD* 126–7). The veteran, however, defies any imposed norms of integration and Holmes's response to the suicide is couched in terms of narrative betrayal: 'Who could have foretold it? A sudden impulse, no one was in the least to blame [....]'. (*MD* 127) (46) □

For most readers, Clarissa seems far removed from the brutal doctors, but Briggs argues that her willingness to identify with Septimus ('She felt somehow very like him', *MD* 158) is 'an act of appropriation' not so very different from theirs (47). Her witnessing of his testimony is tainted by egotism. Although short, Briggs's paper packs in a great deal through economical allusion to foundational works on literature and trauma, and remains alive both to theoretical discourses and to the literariness of *Mrs Dalloway*; it has been an influential article for later critics.

The year 1998 also saw the publication of Karen DeMeester's 'Trauma and Recovery in Virginia Woolf's *Mrs. Dalloway*', a piece that takes its starting point from Judith Herman's work on trauma.[22] DeMeester begins with a general statement about modernist literature: it is 'a literature of trauma' that 'gave form and representation' to a 'psychological condition' not sufficiently understood at that time (649).

The form of *Mrs Dalloway* 'brilliantly mirrors the mind of a trauma survivor' (650). Whereas Briggs's paper had emphasized the power of the novel to interrogate discourses and representations, DeMeester gives more to its power to represent. DeMeester's account tends to emphasize the respects in which Woolf's account agrees with 'recent discoveries in trauma psychology' (649) and so accurately reflects the world. This gives DeMeester some authority when she declares that Suzette Henke's diagnosis of Septimus as a schizophrenic is wrong (653–5), but it means that the article has less scope than Briggs's for understanding Septimus as a representation (or a discursive construct) rather than a real man. Septimus is spoken of as an illustration of the scientifically correct truth. However, DeMeester gives a fuller account of the theory of trauma than Briggs has space for, drawing attention to the 'shattered sense of identity' of the war veteran and the difficulty of integrating an identity as a warrior into 'pre- and postwar civilian identities' (656). She draws on the work of the psychotherapist and Holocaust survivor Viktor Frankl (1905–1997) in emphasizing that the veteran's problem is 'not the suffering he experienced during the war, but his inability to give meaning to that suffering after the war' (658). She praises Woolf for recognizing that, 'for the trauma survivor, telling the story of his trauma or what he learned from that experience is [in the words of Kalí Tal] "a personally reconstitutive act"' (660). However, the community is not always willing to hear that story: 'In its effort to protect and preserve itself from this secondary trauma, the community jeopardizes the veteran's recovery from his own trauma by forcing him to deny or repress what he learned in the war [...]. The community wants him to be the man he was before the war' (661). In this regard, DeMeester agrees with the criticisms of Holmes and Bradshaw that are strongly signalled in the novel: they wish him to 'revise and repress' the understanding he has reached during the war (661). By attempting to silence Septimus, Bradshaw destroys his chance to recover, and 'destroys his own culture's meaningful recovery from the war' (662). DeMeester also questions whether Clarissa's 'reaffirmation of the meaning of her life' is as positive as it seems. Like Briggs, DeMeester identifies similarities between Clarissa and Sir William: her parties are instruments of social conformity; by 'reaffirming her commitment to a flawed culture' she 'obstructs meaningful recovery' (665). DeMeester ends by arguing that the modernist achievement is a mixed one: modernist writers 'brilliantly portrayed the effects of trauma', but contributed little to the healing of their traumatized culture (667).

From an early focus on symbolism, psychoanalytic criticism has grown wider in its scope and critically aware of the failings of psychoanalytic works that take the male as their norm. It has taken in a political notion of subject-formation in the work of Abel and Minow-Pinkney, and, in work on mourning and trauma, has acknowledged wider social forces at work in the mind and in the literary text. The political account of subjectivity in later psychoanalytic criticism was an important enabling factor in the works considered in the next chapter, in which sexuality and the body are foregrounded.

CHAPTER SIX

Sexuality and the Body

Origins: Lorde and Rich

In the late 1970s and 1980s a number of critics began to find a space in criticism for the idea that seemingly natural categories such as 'the body' and heterosexuality were in fact culturally produced and embedded in their history of their times. Feminist critics sought to reclaim and revise the notions of eroticism and of lesbianism itself. The work of Audre Lorde and Adrienne Rich was particularly influential, and is often cited by Woolf critics in the 1980s and 1990s. Lorde's lecture 'The Erotic as Power' (1979) is central to Blanche Wiesen Cook's pioneering article on Woolf, 'Women Alone Stir My Imagination' (1979).[1] For Cook, Lorde returns the erotic to its roots in 'love', and distinguishes between 'the truly unnatural separation of love from physical sensation as that which distinguishes the erotic interests of women from the pornographic queries of men' (733). Properly understood, the erotic should be a source of power for women, one which displaces patriarchal power: 'once women experience that power we will connect with the basic source of our strength, and it will be clear that we derive it from ourselves, not from men, not from any outside place' (739).

Adrienne Rich's often-cited 'Compulsory Heterosexuality and Lesbian Existence' (1980) took issue with a feminism that had merely tolerated lesbianism.[2] Rich critiqued the idea that lesbian attraction is an immature phase of sexuality with its roots in mother–daughter bonding, and likewise the idea that it is a deviation from a norm that needs to be 'explained' (636–7). Rather than being 'natural', heterosexuality is a political institution. Rich introduces the term 'lesbian continuum' in order to redefine lesbianism: she uses the term

> ■ to include a range [...] of woman-identified experience; not simply the fact that a woman has had or consciously desired genital sexual experience with another woman. If we expand it to embrace many more forms or primary intensity between and among women, including the sharing of a

rich inner life, the bonding against male tyranny, the giving and receiving of practical and political support; if we can also hear in it such associations as marriage resistance and the 'haggard' behavior identified by Mary Daly [...] we begin to grasp breadths of female history and psychology which have lain out of reach as a consequence of limited, mostly clinical, definitions of 'lesbianism'. (648–9) □

Rich also opposes the inclusion of lesbianism as a subset of male homosexuality, as a falsification of female history; for this reason she objects to the use of 'gay' as an inclusive term for male and female homosexuals. (Though Rich occasionally uses the term 'homosexual', the term is so closely associated with a medicalization of 'deviant' sexuality, as well as a failure to distinguish male and female experience, as to be of little value.) The translation of *Histoire de la sexualité* by Michel Foucault (1926–1984), the first volume of which appeared in French in 1976 and in English in 1978, brought further support to the historicization of sexuality; but it is noticeable that the earliest critics on Woolf drew primarily on Lorde and Rich for their theoretical grounding.

One of the struggles for Woolf critics in the 1970s and even in the 1980s was to win recognition of Woolf's lesbianism. In the authorized biography (1972), Woolf's nephew Quentin Bell had largely downplayed her attraction to other women and had treated her as sexually 'retarded' or 'frigid'. Articles such as Cook's, and others by Ellen Hawkes Rogat and Jane Marcus, drew on the letters and diaries to challenge Bell's view; Cook singles out John Lehmann's *Virginia Woolf and Her World* (1975) for criticism in this regard.[3] Cook quotes at length from Woolf's diaries about Vita Sackville-West (1892–1962) in order thoroughly to dispel the myth of 'frigidness' (726–8): Woolf and Sackville-West were lovers around 1925–26. She also remarks that in Woolf's relationship in the 1930s with the veteran suffragist and composer Dame Ethyl Smyth (1858–1944), Woolf's lesbianism was closely associated with a sharpening of her political radicalism, with the pacifist book-length essay *Three Guineas* one of the fruits.

Lesbianism

Emily Jensen's 'Clarissa Dalloway's Respectable Suicide' (1983) does not highlight sexuality in its title, but Clarissa's 'suicide' is her acceptance of heterosexual convention and her suppression of her lesbian self.[4] Jensen outlines her basic argument early in the essay:

■ It is my thesis that Clarissa Dalloway's fear of interruption is the most important feature of her personality and, concomitantly, that the event that is the source of that fear is the most important fact of her life. In that historic interruption of 'the most exquisite moment of her whole life' (*MD* 30), Clarissa agrees to deny her love for Sally Seton, decides marriage to Peter Walsh is impossible, and chooses instead to marry Richard Dalloway and become respectable. No simple girlhood crush, Clarissa's love for Sally is a profound reality that permeates her adult life. (162) □

Jensen goes on to outline her argument that the novel's 'metaphoric structure' reveals that the only 'real love' Clarissa has ever felt was for Sally. 'Crippled' by the conventions of heterosexual marriage, she feels herself to be punished for having denied her love for Sally. Clarissa's identification with Septimus – 'she felt somehow very like him – the young man who had killed himself' (*MD* 158) – is because she sees him as someone who committed suicide rather than give away the 'treasure' of his 'homosexual feelings'; his 'madness' expresses explicitly Clarissa's 'more guarded emotional life' (162). Clarissa's fundamental self-denial is, in effect, a form of suicide.

Jensen's essay repurposes the critical tools of the New Criticism for political ends that would have been anathema to the New Critics; she places great emphasis on what might in earlier work have been called patterns of imagery. She uncovers Clarissa's feeling of similarity to Septimus by examining 'the verbal network in the novel – phrases and images that by repetition take on the nature of a metaphor' (163). For example, the third paragraph of the novel ('What a lark! What a plunge!', *MD* 3) 'initiates a number of verbal strains, each of which is played upon later on' (163); she later refers to this as a 'sequence of imagery' (169). Jensen's attention to what might also be called leitmotifs, by analogy with classical opera, again borrows from New Critical practice. For her the novel is one 'of delicate weavings, tiny stitches overlaying other stitches to form a textured pattern' (164). While such patient teasing-out of implications can be summarized, the original article rewards reading in full.

In Jensen's reading the novel's third paragraph establishes oppositions between Bourton in the past and the here and now of London, and between '"plunging" into life versus the "solemn" fear "that something awful was about to happen"' (163). Clarissa's reflections after she learns that Lady Bruton had invited Richard to lunch without her (*MD* 25-7), leading to the 'crocus' passage (*MD* 27), Jensen takes to demonstrate that Bourton 'represents both Sally and Clarissa's love for women' (163). Clarissa and Sally's most intense moment, their kiss on the terrace, was interrupted by Peter Walsh; Jensen foregrounds the simile, 'It was like running one's face against a granite wall in the darkness' (*MD* 30).

The verbal strain of the 'plunge' connects Septimus's suicide to Clarissa's remembered plunge, and Jensen identifies many other points of contact. Septimus's love for Evans parallels Clarissa's for Sally; the interruption of that love by Evans's death parallels Peter's interruption on the terrace. Jensen brings together the parallels in Clarissa's reflections on Septimus's suicide. In her reflections (*MD* 156), Clarissa returns to the line from *Othello*, 'If it were now to die 'twere now to be most happy', that she had earlier associated with 'coming down to dinner in a white frock to meet Sally Seton' (*MD* 30). Thinking of Septimus's 'treasure' 'immediately calls up Clarissa's moment with Sally, inherent both in the line from Shakespeare and in the partial repetition of that intense moment' (167). In Clarissa's reflections, Woolf's text is vague, perhaps even evasive, about the 'thing' that mattered that Septimus has preserved. Such vagueness at such a crucial point allows for a host of different readings. Jensen is unequivocal that the 'thing' is sexuality:

■ Clarissa's assessment of her denial of that moment and therefore denial of her love for Sally Seton is bitter in its self-revelation: to admit that that love was 'defaced, obscured in her own life, let drop every day in corruption, lies, chatter' is devastating, given that the life Clarissa chose to live out, to make up, to build up, was that of a hostess creating the perfect environment for her invited guests; with the blinders off, she sees it for what it is: banal chatter, a life of corruption and lies. (167) □

The use of 'plunge' to describe Septimus's suicide, Jensen claims, implies 'that there is no difference between [Septimus's] leap into death and [Clarissa's] into the life she has chosen; both are suicidal' (168).

One problem for any account of the novel with lesbian identity at its centre is the largely unsympathetic account it gives of the most obviously lesbian character, Miss Kilman. In '*Mrs Dalloway*: The Communion of Saints' (1981), Suzette Henke had considered the problem and argued that Miss Kilman was 'one of Mrs Dalloway's alter egos'; she suggests, not wholly convincingly given differences of class and background, that 'Had the dice of the gods been cast differently, Clarissa might have loved Doris and befriended her.'[5] The claim paraphrases Clarissa's own account, but leaves out her conclusion: 'But not in this world. No' (*MD* 10). More plausibly, Henke notes that Woolf 'has a certain amount of sympathy' for her; she has been 'cheated by fate'. We are given enough of her background and story to recognise that she 'suffers from the spiritual constrictions that grow out of poverty'.[6]

Jensen also pays close attention to the passage in which Miss Kilman first appears, noting her status as 'one of those spectres with which one battles in the night' (*MD* 10). 'As such, Kilman reminds Clarissa of the choice she made to deny her love for women.'[7] Jensen's way of explaining Clarissa's hostility to Miss Kilman (and hence the novel's) is that she reminds Clarissa of what she might have been. Jensen does consider the phrase 'not in this world', and notes that 'The most salient characteristic of "this world" as it is presented throughout the novel is its determined confirmation of heterosexuality' (174): she notes, among other things, Richard's disapproval of implicit homosexuality in Shakespeare's sonnets, and his dismissal of Elizabeth's relationship with Miss Kilman as a schoolgirl crush. She also notes that Miss Kilman's feelings for Elizabeth echo the sentiments of Clarissa's phrase from *Othello*: 'If she could grasp her, if she could clasp her, if she could make her hers absolutely forever and then die; that was all she wanted' (*MD* 112).

There is much to learn from Jensen's perceptive account of *Mrs Dalloway*'s echoes, both internal and external, and from the centrality that she gives to repressed sexuality. However, her approach to parallels of phrasing and imagery can be reductive: she tends to treat parallels as indicating equivalence. Thus, at the largest scale, Septimus's sexuality becomes equivalent to Clarissa's. The possibility that verbal parallels pose questions about difference is rarely pursued; Jensen's reading assumes an organic unity to the novel's patterns of imagery. Moreover, Jensen tends to treat Clarissa's account of the world and herself as a reliable one; more recent critics have tended to be more sceptical. Relatedly, Jensen treats Clarissa's identification with Septimus as ultimately true; more recent critics have been more willing to see it as an act of appropriation.

The Body

The turn towards 'the body' as an object of critical debate has many aspects. The body can be a desiring, sexual body; a perceiving body; a physical apparatus conceived of as distinct from the self, and prone to degeneration and illness; or a phenomenological body inseparable from an embodied self. The connection to the theme of sexuality comes when the body is conceived of in terms of sexual desire: an alienation from one's sexuality then leads to an alienation from 'the body'.

George Ella Lyon's 'Virginia Woolf and the Problem of the Body' (1983) takes its lead in part from Roger Poole's phenomenological work in *The Unknown Virginia Woolf* (1978; see chapter 4), but also from Adrienne Rich's critical work: Lyon's article has an epigraph from Rich: 'I know of no woman ... for whom her body is not a fundamental problem.'[8] In Lyon's account, which deals only briefly with *Mrs Dalloway*, the problem of the body is a problem of embodiment, and Woolf's retreat from the body as a response to sexual abuse (here Lyon draws on Woolf's memoir 'A Sketch of the Past') and bereavement. Lyon notes that the death of Woolf's mother was, on Woolf's account, due to exhaustion from childbearing and child-rearing, and the death of her half-sister was associated with her pregnancy; she asks rhetorically how much these deaths must 'have given her forebodings about sexuality, about marriage, about the ability of her body to change and her inability to control that change' (112). For Lyon, Woolf's body is connected to her sense of autonomy, of 'ownness' (113). When Lyon turns to examining *The Voyage Out*, the feeling of disembodiment felt by Rachel Vinrace and Terence Hewet is a metaphor, at least in part, for their sense of detachment from social conventions. In Lyon's account of *Mrs Dalloway*, Clarissa's relation to her body is understood in terms of the imagery of nun-like retreat from 'freedom and sexuality' (118), while Septimus's is understood in the more severe terms of a loss of autonomy: 'he becomes an object; his body is not his own' (119).

Teresa Fulker's 'Virginia Woolf's Daily Drama of the Body' (1995)[9] also draws on the phenomenological tradition, as represented by Mark Hussey's *The Singing of the Real World* (1986), but notes a specific point of divergence from Hussey: 'for Woolf, having too much body is as dangerous as having too little' (5, n.2). As this suggests, one of the strengths of Fulker's article is its ability to detach itself from the various positions in relation to the body and to acknowledge the extent to which they are contingent on other factors. Even within *Mrs Dalloway*, she suggests, characters do not agree on what is meant by 'body' or 'flesh'.

Fulker begins by tracing the critical debate back to Woolf's own lifetime. In her more polemical essays 'Modern Novels' (1919) and 'Mr Bennett and Mrs Brown' (1924), Woolf had criticized the 'materialist' novelists (Bennett, Galsworthy and Wells) for their excessive attention to the material surroundings of their characters, and had contrasted the more 'spiritual' account of things found in the work of her contemporary James Joyce, and by implication, in her own work. In the hostile hands of her antagonist Wyndham Lewis, the opposition of the spiritual to the material was twisted to become a contrast of the spiritual to the bodily, and Lewis derided Woolf for focusing on 'the *private* values of the half-lighted places of the mind' (quoted 3); in his view, a full account of a human being needed to take account of 'his five senses' and to understand 'what a great part physical action plays' in the self (quoted 4). Fulker argues that, despite Lewis's protestations, Woolf believed that 'an accurate and satisfying novelistic representation of people' (4) required a consideration of their physical life. In this she disagrees with Harvena Richter, who had argued that Woolf was 'anti-sensual, transforming sensory contact with the object into an intellectualized image or concept of it rendered in abstract or visual terms' (Richter, quoted 6).

Although Clarissa contrasts her physical presence to the 'slow and stately' Lady Bexborough, feeling herself to have 'a narrow pea-stick figure' (*MD* 9), 'the fact that her body appears to be approaching the vanishing point is not evidence that the novel refuses her a physical existence, but that it portrays her as having a very specific relation to her body indeed' (10). Fulker argues that Woolf's reading of Joyce's *Ulysses* 'resulted in an increased attention in her own work to the influence of the physical on the contents of consciousness' (9), although Woolf's way of representing the body is very different in tone and content from Joyce's. She draws attention to the book review 'Body and Brain' (1920), in which Woolf expresses regret that biographies of cabinet ministers are focused entirely on their minds; and to 'On Being Ill' (1925), an essay in which Woolf writes lyrically about 'the influence of the body on the processes of the mind' (8). (It is from this essay that Fulker takes her title.) Fulker's account of the influence of *Ulysses* is most persuasive when she is dealing with 'Mrs Dalloway in Bond Street', in which Woolf 'records Clarissa's thoughts about the female body with unusual explicitness' (11). The story comprehends sexuality 'not in terms of female attractiveness or attraction to men but in terms of women's relations to their own ever-changing flesh, especially with regard to their reproductive capacity' (11). Hugh Whitbread's wife Milly is, Clarissa infers, seeing doctors because of the menopause; Clarissa gives consideration to the possibility that the shopgirl may be having her period. The lines from Shelley's 'Adonaïs' are associated with the death of a male friend, while the 'world's slow stain' seems literally embodied in 'little brown spots' on Clarissa's arm (*CSF* 158). In the novel, the nature of Hugh's wife's ailment is not specified, but, Fulker notes, the novel adds the detail of Clarissa's recent recovery from influenza. In Fulker's view, the illness has 'exacerbated' Clarissa's already limited interest in active sexuality: because of it, she sleeps alone in her narrow bed. 'The conjunction of menopause and disease at once establishes one aspect of female experience as a sickness, even as it portrays that sickness as a way to escape the pressures of sexuality which has never, apparently, been very attractive' (14–15). If there is a weakness in this section of the article, it is that Fulker does not explore why the novel is less explicit than the story about the body, and whether Woolf's revisions might be a kind of self-censorship.

The second part of the article considers social class as a factor influencing the presentation of physicality, with particular attention to the minor character Carrie Dempster and a more extended treatment of Miss Kilman. Fulker notes that Woolf saw Joyce's treatment of the body in terms of social class: he was 'underbred'; 'a self taught working man' (*D2* 189). In Woolf's essay 'Memories of a Working Women's Guild' (1930), which provides Fulker with crucial guidance, Woolf recalls her involvement with the Women's Co-operative Guild, and reflects on the obstacles to imaginative empathy with women whose lives seemed to be lived so much more physically than hers. In Fulker's words, the working-class woman becomes 'defined as flesh' to Woolf (18).

In *Mrs Dalloway*, Carrie Dempster is defined in terms of her physicality: her 'stout' body and the 'knobbed lumps' of her feet, and her enjoyment of the sea at Margate (*MD* 23). Her account of the aeroplane is contrasted with that of Mr Bentley, who dwells on theories (Einstein, Mendel) that allow the mind to move beyond the corporeal: Fulker comments that the contrast emphasizes the fact that Mrs Dempster's reflections 'can only briefly be lifted out of their biologically-bound condition' (19).

Miss Kilman is 'only too insistently embodied' (19). Clarissa and Miss Kilman 'assess each other's bodies in class terms': Miss Kilman sees luxuriousness and laziness in Clarissa; Clarissa sees ugliness, clumsiness and sweat (19–20). The 'sheer undeniability' of Miss Kilman's body recalls Woolf's account of Joyce's *Ulysses* as something 'distressing.... egotistic, insistent, raw, striking, and ultimately nauseating' (*D2* 189). While this quality is partly due to Miss Kilman's social class, she also 'represents an attitude to the body which Woolf sees as mistaken and unproductive: on the one hand, she treats the body as an end in itself [...]; on the other hand, she attempts to deny that body entirely' (20). Miss Kilman's excessive focus on the body is seen in her comfort eating; in the scene with the pink cake, we learn that 'eating was the only pure pleasure left her' (*MD* 110). In this context, the phrase about Miss Kilman wanting to grasp and clasp Elizabeth suggests her desire to incorporate her too. The pink cake passage 'demonstrates both a greed and a capitulation to the flesh that (for Woolf) marks not the artificial distinctions of class, but those of intrinsic quality' (21). On the other hand, after meeting Clarissa, Miss Kilman feels that she 'must control' her 'flesh' (*MD* 109). Fulker analyses what Miss Kilman means by the flesh, arguing that it is 'that within her which defies her will'; she makes her own body 'alien to herself' (22).

Through its interest in the body, Fulker's article adjusts the internal balance of *Mrs Dalloway*: the majority of critics have seen it either as a novel with two major characters (Septimus and Clarissa) or with three (Septimus, Clarissa and Peter). Fulker brings Miss Kilman further to the fore, seeing her and Clarissa as representing 'two extremes of corporeality' (22). Fulker's final move is to pair Clarissa with the old lady in the house across the road: her preparing for bed and turning out her light echoes Clarissa's ascent to her attic room, but with a more positive tone; Fulker suggests the scene sounds a note of optimism, suggesting that Clarissa 'may well find a way to accept, even to welcome, the passage of time and the changes it brings to her body' (24).

Medicine, Eugenics and Degeneration

The late 1980s and early 1990s saw a revival of interest in late nineteenth-century theories of eugenics and degeneration as a context for the literature and culture of the period. The period seemed to confirm Michel Foucault's theories about the cultural policing of normality through medical and psychiatric discourses and practices. While some works focused closely on the *fin de siècle*, the afterlife of such theories in Nazi Germany served as a reminder that, though they began in the nineteenth century, they did not end with it. Indeed, in Britain, the discovery during the Boer War (1899–1902) that many working-class men were unfit for military service had amplified anxieties about fitness and masculinity.

In *Degeneration, Culture and the Novel, 1880–1940* (1994), William Greenslade explores how writers incorporated and challenged the ideas and tropes of degeneration in fictional works.[10] A brief discussion of *Mrs Dalloway* forms the conclusion to his chapter 'Masculinity, Morbidity and Medicine'. Greenslade sees *Mrs Dalloway* as building on Woolf's personal suffering at the hands of her doctors, but as doing so with an intelligence that recognized the role played by medical discourses: she provides an objective presentation of the 'interpenetration of the conceptual with the personal' (228). Greenslade briefly sketches the opinions and cultural outlooks of two of the doctors who attended to Woolf, T. B. Hyslop and George Savage. Hyslop subscribed to the mid-Victorian idea that humans possessed a limited supply of energy which should be, in the case of women, preserved for the function of childbearing. 'The more our women aspire to exercising their nervous and mental function,' Greenslade quotes him as saying, 'so they become not only less virile, but also less capable of generating healthy stock' (Hyslop, quoted 229). Savage shared many of Hyslop's views, and was particularly concerned about young women taking school and university examinations: 'If a girl, he said, "is allowed to educate herself at home, the danger of solitary work may be seen in conceit developing into insanity"' (299). Like other doctors, he was reluctant to address psychological pain directly, preferring instead to treat its physical symptoms.

■ In the manuscript of *Mrs Dalloway* Woolf writes sarcastically about this treatment, here meted out by the general practitioner, Dr Holmes. 'Milk is the great standby, with raw eggs beaten up in it taken every hour, oftener if possible.' This was the still fashionable Weir Mitchell 'rest cure', prescribed for patients suffering nervous disorders; their treatment consisted of 'isolation, immobility, prohibition of all intellectual activity' and [...] overfeeding. (229–30) □

The concern with feeding survives in the published text, both in Holmes's advice (*MD* 77–8) and Bradshaw's (*MD* 84–5). Greenslade describes the doctors' response to Septimus in distinctly Foucauldian terms: 'the mentally disturbed man presents a spectacle of unpardonable deviancy which requires a counter-assertion of order, a redrawing of the boundaries of normality by which that behaviour can be fixed as transgressive' (230). Greenslade quotes the paragraphs describing Sir William's recommendation of proportion (*MD* 84–5), and comments:

> ■ In this pillar of the medical establishment, Woolf condenses her profound understanding of the sources of authority he exerts. Here is a degenerationist who in his persona and in the nature of the advice he propounds is exposed as fraudulent. On one level, his espousal of 'proportion' is no more than homespun philosophy masquerading as profundity [...]; he never talks about madness but readily represses it [...]. But on another, his 'proportion' expresses what Forster had Margaret Schlegel [in *Howards End* (1910)] register as truly disproportionate: 'the impertinences that shelter under the name of science.' For Bradshaw wields a formidable Foucauldian 'coercive discourse of power' which Lyndall Gordon rightly identifies behind 'the cant of duty and family ... connecting Harley Street with Westminster' [...]. But it is, I think, clear that Woolf also had in mind the frame of reference of Edwardian race-regeneration with its concern for the health and the fitness of the nation, its distrust of the life of the imagination, its strategies of intervention, containment and separation: it is against this hegemony that Septimus is vainly struggling. (231–2) □

Bradshaw's 'proportion' is directed at 'those troublesome elements of the nation whose reproductive and cultural power must be halted or terminated' (232): Bradshaw secludes England's 'lunatics, forbade childbirth, penalised despair, made it impossible for the unfit to propagate their views, until they, too, shared his sense of proportion' (*MD* 84). As Greenslade comments, the doctors' sense of 'normality' and 'proportion' is 'not an authoritative but an arbitrary notion', and their confidence in it is sustained by 'the prestige of early twentieth-century medical science' (232).

Unlike the critics who trace their descent from phenomenology, via Poole and Hussey, Greenslade is not interested in attempting to recover subjective experience. His focus is principally on discourse and the ways it is used by those in authority. He makes use of Woolf's biographical experience, and suggests that the viciousness of her satire on the doctors derives from it, but he is interested in her biography primarily as a route to finding concrete examples of medical and eugenical discourse in the writings of her doctors, not as a way of tracing links between the real Woolf and her writings.

Lesbianism Historicized

Emily Jensen's 1983 account of lesbianism in *Mrs Dalloway* focused sharply on the text and its intricate interweavings, and was alive to its echoes within the literary tradition, but had nothing to say about its cultural context. By the time of Eileen Barrett's 'Unmasking Lesbian Passion: The Inverted World of *Mrs Dalloway*' (1997), historicism had become a much more mainstream critical practice; to this extent, Barrett's essay overlaps with the work examined in the next chapter.

Barrett was by no means the first to examine Woolf this way. In a conference paper delivered in 1991, Patricia Cramer placed Woolf within a particular tradition of lesbian writing, one whose central preoccupation was 'defining a lesbian or woman-centred identity and eroticism'.[11] Lesbianism is understood as necessarily political: the 'homoerotic self' is a centre 'from which to oppose patriarchal values and to reimagine self and community' (177). Cramer situates *Mrs Dalloway* biographically, in the early years of Woolf's love affair with Vita Sackville-West: Woolf and Sackville-West had met in 1922, and Woolf had begun to feel attracted to her during 1924, at the time she was writing *Mrs Dalloway*. In an important move, Cramer relates the emotional tone of the novel to Woolf's experience of coming out: 'Coming out may happen with [a lesbian's] first sexual experience with a woman, or simply be that moment when she accepts her sexual and emotional preference for women' (179). In Cramer's account, Clarissa is a persona through which Woolf 'reevaluate[d] her own heterosexual history' in the light of her coming out (179). Cramer also locates Woolf's text in a specifically lesbian tradition. The flower imagery – notably the crocus (*MD* 27) – 'rewrites men's conventional associations of women as fragile and vulnerable flowers by using flowers instead as images of female sexual power' (184). The novel's imagery of things wrapped up and unfolding, particularly Sally's present to Clarissa (*MD* 30), is read by Cramer not only as erotic, but as specifically female genital imagery.

Barrett's 'Unmasking Lesbian Passion' begins autobiographically with her own experience of lesbian feminism in the 1970s, a movement in which lesbianism was a political identity as well as a sexual one, and identifies that movement with the political optimism that surrounded suffragism between 1906 and 1911.[12] Those years also saw political analyses of marriage and of the way that young women's education was orientated towards it (146–7). (Barrett cites Woolf's *Three Guineas*, but the crucial pre-war text on this topic is Cicely Hamilton's *Marriage as a Trade* [1909], which, as Sowon Park has suggested, anticipates many of the arguments of Woolf's later book-length essays.)[13] In Barrett's account, *Mrs Dalloway* is a novel that critiques heterosexual marriage as an institution, and that is aware of the ways that lesbianism and male homosexuality were constructed through the discourses of medical science, particularly the new science of 'sexology'.

As the historical context for *Mrs Dalloway*, Barrett notes both later nineteenth-century anxiety about homosexuality, embodied legally in the 1885 Criminal Law Amendment Act, and more sympathetic approaches in works by writers such as Havelock Ellis (*Studies in the Psychology of Sex* [1892–1928]), John Addington Symonds and Edward Carpenter. Carpenter was a direct influence on E. M. Forster's 'overtly homosexual' novel *Maurice* (written 1910–13, published 1971), which Woolf may have read in manuscript. Barrett notes that the sexologists, even when they were hostile to same-sex relationships, 'enabled lesbian self-definition' (150). As a biographical context for *Mrs Dalloway*, Barrett notes Virginia's love for Madge Vaughan, daughter of Symonds. In 1921, Woolf recalled her excitement on realising that Madge was in her home at Hyde Park Gate (therefore no later than 1904), and thinking, 'At this moment she is actually under this roof' (*D2* 122). Those words are echoed in Clarissa's recollected feelings about Sally Seton (*MD* 29). More important for Barrett than any real-life identification is Sally's political radicalism: in the 'passionate friendship' of Sally and Clarissa, 'Woolf captures the intermingling of the intellectual and the erotic, the personal and the political that she experienced in her own feminist friendships' (151).

The view of marriage that young Sally and Clarissa share ('they spoke of marriage always as a catastrophe', *MD* 29) is something that Woolf explores throughout the novel, in Evelyn Whitbread's unnamed ailment, in Lady Bradshaw's 'sinking' into her husband's will (*MD* 85) and in Septimus's marriage to Rezia. Barrett contextualizes Septimus as being like many of the 'conflicted homosexuals' described by the sexologists.

Even a relatively sympathetic sexologist like Havelock Ellis associated lesbian sexuality with criminality and tried 'to demarcate the boundaries' between female friendship and what was known as female 'inversion' (155). Sexologists advised women to sublimate and 'spiritualize' their sexual feelings, and many women lived together as 'companions'. Barrett detects several such characters in *Mrs Dalloway*. At Clarissa's party, Ellie Henderson 'makes mental notes of everything to tell her companion, Edith' (156). Barrett also suggests that the relationship between Lady Bruton and Milly Brush is one that Ellis would have placed 'on the borderland of true sexual inversion' (Ellis, quoted 156). Barrett is particularly interested in the description of Lady Bruton's avocation for emigration: 'this object round which the essence of her soul is daily secreted becomes inevitably prismatic, lustrous, half looking-glass, half precious stone; now carefully hidden in case people should sneer at it; now proudly displayed' (*MD* 92). Woolf's imagery, comments Barrett, 'mirrors that which she associates with Clarissa's lesbian identity, her "infinitely precious" "diamond" [*MD* 30], the privacy of her soul' (156). Contextualizing Lady Bruton's obsession, Barrett notes the irony that emigration was 'one among many solutions of the period devised to rid England of sexual inverts' (156–7).

Barrett suggests that Clarissa too practices the kind of sublimation and self-control recommended by the sexologists. Unlike Septimus, who 'sees his homosexuality as a crime against nature', Clarissa feels her resentment of sex as something 'sent by Nature (who is invariably wise)' (*MD* 27). 'These beliefs allow Clarissa to withdraw into a chaste, impenetrable, nun-like existence where she feels "blessed and purified" (*MD* 25), with "a virginity preserved through childbirth" (*MD* 27)' (158). Barrett argues that in purifying her lesbianism, Clarissa draws on the 'trapped soul theory of same-sex love' (158): Goldsworthy Lowes Dickinson understood his attraction towards men in terms of having 'a woman's soul shut up in a man's body' (Dickinson, quoted 149). 'Whereas Dickinson acknowledges his woman's soul, Clarissa associates her lesbianism with the privacy of the soul, the place where she can feel what men felt, where she can recognize women as the source of the central, erotic feelings that permeate' her being (158). The 'crocus' passage Barrett sees as a moment that, along with the memory of Sally's kiss, 'define[s] the privacy of Clarissa's soul' (159).

In confronting the problem of Miss Kilman, Barrett follows earlier critics in seeing her as Clarissa's alter ego. She suggests that Kilman's 'German origin associates her with the early German sexologists, and her name reflects the popular belief that all lesbians were man haters' (159). Yet there is an admirable side to Miss Kilman, in her encouragement of Elizabeth's aspiration to professional employment (*MD* 115), and in her own achievement as a graduate and 'a woman who had made her way in the world' (*MD* 112). Barrett finds signs of Miss Kilman's attempts to sublimate her desires in her eating and in her religious devotion (160). Such sublimation becomes another version of the 'conversion' that the narrator warns us about after the 'proportion' passage (*MD* 85), and Miss Kilman's attempts at conversion fail.

Barrett attributes the negativity of the portrayal of Miss Kilman to Clarissa's uneasy sexuality:

■ Confronted with the intensity and public display of Doris's lesbian passion, Clarissa loses her sense of proportion. To contain her own sexuality within acceptable private boundaries, she constructs the other, just as the sexologists do. Doris Kilman as lesbian thus becomes the object of her disdain. [...] To preserve the purity, integrity, and privacy of her sapphic moments, Clarissa categorises Doris Kilman, the 'prehistoric monster' *(MD* 106), with her public passion, as lesbian, as deviant, as other. For Clarissa, Doris Kilman embodies the sexologists' perversion of lesbian passion and desire. (161) □

However, Woolf allows Clarissa enough self-awareness for us to see this process of othering for what it is: 'it was not her one hated but the idea of her, which undoubtedly had gathered itself into a great deal that was not Miss Kilman' (*MD* 10). In Barrett's reading, the 'brutal monster' (*MD* 10) that disturbs Clarissa is the 'lesbian within' (161).

Like many readings, Barrett's ends by considering the significance of Septimus's suicide; unusually, it also reintroduces Miss Kilman. 'Suppose he had had that passion?' speculates Clarissa about Septimus (*MD* 157). Barrett argues that Clarissa believes Septimus preferred to die rather than reveal his sexuality, and that '[o]n some level, Clarissa perceives Septimus's failure to speak out as protecting her private lesbian passion' (162). Septimus's preservation of Clarissa's privacy is placed in direct contrast to Miss Kilman, who threatens to 'unmask her' (*MD* 106). But although she detests Miss Kilman, Clarissa

> ■ longs for someone to unmask her secret lesbian passions. [...]. At the height of her party, she sees its 'hollowness' (*MD* 148) and thinks instead of Doris Kilman [...]. Indeed, the reality of Doris's lesbian existence enables Clarissa to release the lesbian within her soul. Doris inspires Clarissa to name – at least to herself – her lesbian desires, and to recognize as positive and satisfying the lesbianism of other women. (162) □

Without denying the negativity with which the novel surrounds Miss Kilman, Barrett finds a place for her, and in a sense, places her in a closer parallel to Septimus than any critic before her: on this reading, there are two haunting presences at Clarissa Dalloway's party, Septimus Warren Smith and Doris Kilman.

While early critics in the area of lesbianism and the body had to overcome a prejudice that Woolf was an asexual being, later critics have been able to assume a more receptive attitude in their readers, and raise questions of historical context; they are able to engage not only in close readings of the text, but in interpretations of its relations to surrounding texts. In this regard, essays like Eileen Barrett's form part of the larger historicist movement to be considered in the next chapter.

CHAPTER SEVEN

Historicist Approaches

The History of the Bloomsbury Group (1953–1981)

As Woolf's cultural moment has receded from our own, it has been increasingly necessary to return her works to their historical context in order to understand them, whether that understanding takes the form of resolving ambiguities or restoring them. Of course it may be a mistake to speak of 'our' own as if present-day readers stood in a singular relation to Woolf: readers in her own time separated by class culture or national culture may already have found some elements of her work difficult to decipher.

The first explicit signs of difference and of contextualization may be found immediately after the Second World War. In *Virginia Woolf and Bloomsbury* (1953), Finnish critic Irma Rantavaara describes the genesis of the book in a British Council summer school in 1947 at which there was a lack of consensus among the tutors about what 'Bloomsbury' was. Rantavaara answers the question by finding a shared philosophy in the work of G. E. Moore, J. McTaggart and Goldsworthy Lowes Dickinson. The centrality of Moore's work to early accounts of 'Bloomsbury' and hence to Woolf's fiction, derived from John Maynard Keynes's 'My Early Beliefs', a memoir written in 1938 for the private Memoir Club of Woolf and her circle, and published in 1949. A contextual account of Woolf that places her in a narrow circle of friends has the merits of specificity, but lacks a sense of the breadth and contradictoriness of the culture she lived in. Moreover, when Rantavaara comes to *Mrs Dalloway* itself, the Bloomsbury context bears little fruit. The main argument positions Woolf as an atheist whose fear of death created a 'craving for a kind of metaphysical thinking':

> ■ She was far from being a full-fledged rationalist or a true sceptic who adamantly refuses to believe in theories which are not watertight when intellectual criticism is applied to them. There is a strong resemblance – stronger

than she would have liked to admit – between her metaphysical thought and that of McTaggart and Lowes Dickinson. (107) ☐

Rantavaara then equates Clarissa with her author, and sees Clarissa's 'transcendental theory' (*MD* 129) as an expression of her author's position.

Rantavaara's study was followed by J. K. Johnstone's *The Bloomsbury Group* (1954), and Michael Holroyd's *Lytton Strachey* (1967). Johnstone saw Forster, Strachey and Woolf as being united by 'a common respect for the things of the spirit' and the inner life, and by 'an admiration for the individual and for the virtues of courage, tolerance, and honesty' (375). Moore's philosophy was important to these attitudes, but so too were a less sharply defined 'Cambridge humanism', deriving from the works of Lowes Dickinson, McTaggart and Leslie Stephen; and, as regards aesthetics, the works of Roger Fry. While Johnstone's definition of a Bloomsbury attitude or attitudes has the virtues of plurality, it is not always easy to relate it to specific qualities of Woolf's novels, and again it leaves out much of her contemporary culture. Holroyd's biography further revived interest in Bloomsbury, aligning its rebellion against Victorianism with the 1960s counter-culture; but, as we have seen in Chapter Two, it did so at the cost of presenting an almost caricatural version of Woolf as anaemic and apolitical. It was soon followed by Quentin Bell's *Bloomsbury* (1968), and for a period in the 1970s and early 1980s, the inclusion of 'Bloomsbury' in a book's title served to increase its appeal to the market. The scholarly work of S. P. Rosenbaum was the most valuable to emerge, as it made available many previously unpublished texts: his edition *The Bloomsbury Group: A Collection of Memoirs, Commentary and Criticism* (1975) was particularly valuable; *The Bloomsbury Group Memoir Club* (2014), published posthumously, has yet to make its mark. Richard Shone's *Bloomsbury Portraits: Vanessa Bell, Duncan Grant, and their Circle* (1976) revalued the visual culture of Woolf's sister and her circle.

In 1981 Rosenbaum reflected on what a literary history of the Bloomsbury Group might look like, and noted that the term 'text' was liberating, while the term 'work' tended to embody older limitations on criticism: 'Much modernist literary theory stil holds that there is a crucial disjunction between works of poetry, fiction, and drama on the one side, and on the other what is lumped together and defined merely negatively as nonfiction' (334). Such a separation obscured the proper understanding of Bloomsbury's literary achievement. Rosenbaum noted the polymorphous genre of Woolf's *A Room of One's Own* (1929), and suggested that literary history needed to take its motto from E. M. Forster: 'Only connect.'

The creation of such connections was facilitated by the publication of Woolf's letters and diaries, but those diaries also point to the limitations of 'Bloomsbury': while they provide fuller accounts of the men and women known as Bloomsbury, they also make reference to a range of people who could be included in 'Bloomsbury' only by the most generous and unscrupulous expansion of the term: for example, the writers Katherine Mansfield and Vita Sackville-West, the composer and suffragist Ethel Smyth, the poet and critic T. S. Eliot. Moreover, the recovery of Woolf's politics by feminist critics of the 1970s broadened the scope of what might count as a context: it no longer needed to be limited to works of literature, philosophy and art, but could include politics, the built environment and everyday activities.

'Reality' and 'the Social System'

To historicize Woolf's works by reference to a context derived from 'Bloomsbury' is to underestimate the breadth of her political interests. Beginning in the late 1970s, critics began to range more widely. They built on the recovery of Woolf's politics begun in the 1960s and early 1970s, and to that extent there is no clear dividing line between the two critical movements. However, historicizing critics were interested in politics and power relations as they manifested themselves in a particular society in a particular place and time; they were interested in specific social practices and in the symbolic means through which power operated.

Alex Zwerdling's '*Mrs Dalloway* and the Social System' (1977) was a pivotal article: it emphasized social class to an extent never seen before in Woolf criticism, and tentatively noted the historical context of Woolf's novel.[1] Zwerdling takes as his starting point Woolf's remark that, in *Mrs Dalloway*, she wanted 'to criticize the social system, and to show it at work, at its most intense' (*D2* 248). It was, at this date, still necessary to argue against a construction of Woolf as an apolitical writer: the remark, argues Zwerdling, had been ignored, because 'it highlights an aspect of her work very different from the traditional picture of the "poetic" novelist interested in states of reverie and vision' (69).[2] He acknowledges that Woolf intensely disliked 'propaganda in art' (69), but proposes that, '[a]s a moralist, Woolf works by indirection, subterraneously undermining the officially accepted code, mocking, suggesting, calling into question, rather than asserting, advocating, bearing witness' (70). Zwerdling remarks that, unlike *The Waves*, '*Mrs Dalloway* has a precise historical setting', in June 1923, and reminds us that there are 'a number of topical references' in the novel which its original readers would have understood, but which may have been lost (70). These observations suggested a new direction for later critics, and, because of their work, Zwerdling's account of the topical references now seems relatively thin. Taking his cue from Peter Walsh's remarks about the changes wrought by the years 1918–1923 (*MD* 61), Zwerdling notes the eclipse of the Liberal party by Labour, and the decline of what Peter Walsh characterizes as 'the public-spirited, British Empire, tariff-reform, governing-class spirit' (*MD* 65). Zwerdling glosses Lady Bruton's remark about 'the news from India' (*MD* 94) by quoting a number of headlines from *The Times* from June 1923 (71).

The substance of the article lies less in its use of historical detail than in Zwerdling's tracing of the emotional consequences of this particular social moment for the threatened class: its insecure suppression of 'alien or threatening forces', its attachment to routine and ritual, and its seemingly stoical repression of emotion. The repression of emotion includes an indifference or hostility to literature, and is achieved, in part, by 'translat[ing] individual human beings into manageable social categories'; Septimus becomes merely 'a case' (74). The 'elegance and composure' of the governing classes is sustained, however, only by the below-stairs activity of their servants. Mental and emotional repression has social exclusion as its correlate. Zwerdling notes that 'Clarissa's party is strictly class-demarcated. No Septimus, no Rezia, no Doris Kilman could conceivably set foot in it' (73).

Zwerdling incorporated his 1977 article into his later study, *Virginia Woolf and the Real World* (1986). However, by 1986, the influence of continental literary theory was being felt in Woolf studies, as was that of cultural history and the New Historicism. The anthology *New French Feminisms* appeared in 1981; the collection of historical essays *The Invention of Tradition*, edited by Eric Hobsbawm and Terence Ranger, appeared in 1983, as did Benedict Anderson's work on nationalism, *Imagined Communities*; Stephen Greenblatt's New Historicist *Renaissance Self-Fashioning* appeared in 1980. The existence of 'the real world' could no longer be taken for granted: it was invented, imagined and constructed by those in positions of power. Reviewing Zwerdling's book, Richard Pearce praised it for establishing Woolf's achievement in the world of 'facts' as well as that of 'vision.' But he also remarked that it demonstrated the limits of 'traditional scholarship':

■ 'The real world' suggests a material place out there, the historical record of which can be grasped by a careful and fair-minded observer, where characters are not only people but unified and stable, where the forces acting on them may be illuminated by sensitive readings of the texts – but where the epistemological and ideological assumptions about history, character, text, and one's approach to them are not questioned.[3] □

Later critics had grown more aware of the textual medium, not only in literary texts, but in historical and cultural evidence.

Jeremy Tambling's 'Repression in *Mrs Dalloway*' (1989) shows the influence of French theory, explicitly citing Julia Kristeva from *New French Feminisms*, and elsewhere deploying the characteristic vocabulary of post-structuralist theory.[4] Tambling also draws on the more conservative critical tradition of scholarly annotation, and makes far more use of topical references than did Zwerdling. Though a misprint in the opening sentence places Clarissa's birth in '1881' – Tambling surely means 1871 – the article was, for its time, unusually preoccupied with factual details, and productive in its use of them. *Mrs Dalloway*, Tambling argues, 'incarnates a critique of Empire and the war, taking the state as the embodiment of patriarchal power, and the upholder of what even Richard Dalloway calls "our detestable social system"' (*MD* 98) (138). Tambling notes how Big Ben had come to stand metonymically for both Parliament and the nation; the broadcasting of its chimes in December 1923 provided 'an apparent, though imaginary, national unity' (139). Time, which earlier critics had treated as an 'existential enemy', is rather 'part of the language of state-power' (139).

Tambling also treats the London of the novel not as neutral backdrop, but as a text to be interpreted. Names such as 'Victoria Street' and the 'Army and Navy Stores' (*MD* 4, 108) have significant histories behind them. Throughout Europe, in the era of 'unification, imperialism, and nationalism', there had been a significant investment in 'uniforms, regalia, monarchy, national anthems, processions and attempts in public buildings to create a sense of a weighty, considerable past, of an extensive history' (140). The London of official statues 'helps to form those who live within its environment': in a phrase that owes something to Marxist critics in the tradition of Louis Althusser (1918–1990), Tambling remarks that character is not 'innate', 'but produced from without, from the lived practices (which must include the ideology) of a society' (144). (Althusser, in 'Ideology and Ideological State Apparatuses' [1970], had argued that ideologies became material when they were inserted into what he referred to as 'rituals' and 'practices'.)[5]

Tambling follows the lead of Michel Foucault in arguing that concepts of madness are not natural, but are produced by 'medical discourse'. While there is certainly a biographical aspect to the characterization of Sir William Bradshaw, Tambling is more interested in the larger historical frame, 'involving the medicalisation of society, the readiness to label people as mentally ill, and the absorbed attention given to nerves and mental instability' (146). Though Tambling does not so explicitly historicize the concept of 'homosexuality', he argues that the novel hints that the prevalent neurosis is due to 'a brutalising and destructive sexual politics' (148). Patriarchy as an ideology is not an abstraction or something 'simply inherent in a family structure': it is, rather, created by 'specific practices' within this society (153). Those practices include Bradshaw declaring whether his patients are 'ill' or not, and popular deference to power, seen in responses to the mysterious grey car near the opening of the novel (*MD* 12–17). Like many following Foucault, Tambling emphasizes the all-encompassing nature of power; he is less able to indicate how a literary work might disrupt the language of power. *Mrs Dalloway*, he says, uses medical discourse to build characters, but it cannot, as a novel, 'criticise' the medical 'model of knowledge' (148). The novel 'can imagine no alternative to the rule of patriarchy' (154). (It is notable, and characteristic of this critical approach, that in both sentences Tambling makes the novel the agent: Woolf as author is relatively powerless over her discourse.) It is instructive to contrast Zwerdling. Though he shared Tambling's pessimism to some extent, feeling it 'improbable' that the outer life of Peter or Clarissa would change, and believing that Woolf 'was too convinced of the fundamental inertia in human nature and institutions to imagine a radical transformation of either', Zwerdling also argued that, by capturing a moment of transformation, when 'the ideal of rigid self-control' began to seem oppressive, Woolf was 'contributing indirectly' to the replacement of that ideal 'by one less hostile to the buried life of feeling in every human being' (81).

Militarism and War

Given the prominence of a shell-shocked soldier in *Mrs Dalloway*, it is difficult to avoid war as a theme: as long ago as 1949 Bernard Blackstone had declared that the 'total motif' of the novel was 'deferred war-shock'.[6] Over the years, awareness of war has broadened, and the critical emphasis has moved away from the 1914–18 war as an event and on to militarism as an ideology. Insofar as militarism realizes itself through historically specific practices, historical research can illuminate the operations of that ideology. Another strand of investigation has questioned the dominant focus on soldiers, and has considered the indirect victims of war.

Septimus Warren Smith has been at the centre of many investigations. The simplest form of historicization seeks real-life precedents for him. His hallucination of a sparrow singing in Greek (*MD* 21) led many early critics to identify his experiences with those of his author, as detailed by Leonard Woolf and retold by Quentin Bell.[7] However, it has also been suggested that the war poems of Siegfried Sassoon and Wilfred Owen might have provided Woolf with source material.[8] Leonard Woolf's brother Philip may also have provided a model.[9] David

Bradshaw has noted a passage in Woolf's notebooks where she asks whether Septimus is 'founded on R', and goes on to ask, 'Why not have something of G.B. in him?'[10] Bradshaw identifies 'R' as Ralph Partridge (1894–1960), and G.B. as Gerald Brenan (1894–1987), both members of Woolf's circle. Partridge had, like Septimus, served in Italy and had been awarded 'crosses' (*MD* 75); Brenan was attached to him in a way that suggests Septimus's attachment to Evans. Rather than identify either man with either character, Bradshaw argues that elements of both, and of their relationship, enter into the depiction of Septimus and Evans.

'Shell-shock' was a relatively new concept in 1923; though the concept drew on existing ideas of mental illness, the term itself is first recorded in the *British Medical Journal* in 1915. Sue Thomas's 'Virginia Woolf's Septimus Smith and Contemporary Perceptions of Shell Shock' (1987) explores the rich seam of documentation that lies behind it. Like many historicist critics, Thomas places her critical project in contrast to biographical readings: she suggests that the novel's anger may derive not only from Woolf's feelings about the rest cures prescribed for her in 1913 and 1915, but also from her anger at the *Report of the War Office Committee of Enquiry into 'Shell-shock'* presented to Parliament in August 1922, and widely publicized in newspapers in that year. Thomas notes that, both in the official documents and in Woolf's novel, 'shell-shock' is not simply a medical matter: how it is conceptualized has ideological roots and political consequences; in Thomas's words, the medical advice is 'tainted by Proportion and Conversion'.[11] Thomas's evidence that Woolf knew of the *Report* or of its coverage in the newspapers is entirely circumstantial: she notes Leonard Woolf's political interests, and Woolf's habitual reading of the *Times*. This is undoubtedly a weak point in the argument, but, setting aside this problem, the *Report* offers valuable insights into contemporary concepts of illness and gender. Thomas notes particularly how the report was interpreted through ideals of manly self-control: the *Times* argued that men could be trained 'to despise danger and to seek the ways of courage' (52). One of those giving evidence to the Commission acknowledged that soldiers experienced a conflict between 'the self-preservation instinct' and 'a group of forces compounded of self-respect, duty, discipline, patriotism, and so forth'; however, he believed that in the trained soldier, the latter would triumph (55). Thomas contrasts this ideal of training with Woolf's presentation of the marching cadets, 'drugged into a stiff yet staring corpse by discipline' (*MD* 44).

The *Report* also bears witness to contemporary methods of prevention and treatment. Thomas quotes the *Report* on the way that the medical officer must persuade the patient to overcome his disability, 'appealing to the patient's social self-esteem to make him co-operate and put forth a real effort of will' (quoted 53–4). She juxtaposes this with Dr

Holmes's implicitly patriotic attempts to persuade Septimus that he should not give his wife 'a very odd idea of English husbands' (*MD* 72). Holmes's reference to Septimus's illness as 'a funk' (*MD* 72) had suggested to at least one critic that Holmes does not believe in mental illness, but Thomas uses her evidence to argue that '[e]very aspect' of his treatment 'is in accord with contemporary medical practices in relation to shell shock' (54).[12]

Thomas treats the Report as the *source* of Woolf's knowledge, rather than as a substantial *example* of official medical discourse. Her work needs to be supplemented with Stephen Trombley's historical research into Woolf's doctors and their writings: there were many relevant routes by which Woolf might have gained knowledge of contemporary medical practice. Nevertheless, the comparisons and contrasts which the report enables Thomas to draw are illuminating of *Mrs Dalloway*'s place in contemporary culture. And although Thomas is not explicit about her theoretical basis, her practice is to treat the novel not as an aesthetic artefact aloof from contemporary discourse, but as a text that is open to intertextual connections with all other forms of writing.

Karen Levenback's essay 'Virginia Woolf and Returning Soldiers' (1996) notes an additional psychological pressure on Septimus. In emphasizing the sacrifice of those who had died in the war, and in being less than generous with pension payments to survivors, particularly to those who had no visible physical injuries, the government 'invalidated' many army veterans. Levenback quotes from the drafts of the novel: 'Death, death – in the service of the Nation. That was the only creditable gift for a man with a wife' (quoted 75). She comments: 'Living in the postwar world, a combatant such as Septimus, who lacked a visible wound, was expected to "get on with it", unobtrusively and discreetly. In *Mrs Dalloway*, Woolf was clearly showing the burden placed upon such "unsung heroes"' (76).

David Bradshaw's '"Vanished, Like Leaves"' (2002) locates the novel's treatment of war in literary and political contexts. The novel's many references to leaves, and particularly the comparison of the sound of marching cadets to 'the patter of leaves' (*MD* 43), suggest that Woolf is employing a literary topos of fallen or falling leaves; she thereby 'encourages the reader to conceive of her book as an elegy'.[13] Bradshaw argues that, although Woolf was sceptical about the state's official war memorials and their tendency to legitimize militarism, the novel nevertheless memorializes the dead.

Bradshaw also considers the significance of the cadets marching from Finsbury Pavement. The allusion 'is not a mere geographical filler, an area of London picked at random from a gazetteer, but yet another signpost which alerts the reader to the all-encompassing nature of the novel's critique of war and militarism' (112). Finsbury Pavement was home to the Territorial Army: Lord Haldane, who had created the organization, was inspired by the kind of nationalism derived from the thought of the German philosopher G. W. F. Hegel (1770–1831) and a vision of 'an entire Nation in Arms'.[14] Like Thomas, Bradshaw focuses on the passage describing the marching cadets, but for him the crucial detail is the 'one will' that co-ordinates their movements (*MD* 44): they have been drugged with a sense of patriotic duty and national purpose.

Masami Usui's 'The Female Victims of War in *Mrs Dalloway*' (1991) turns attention away from Septimus, towards Lucrezia and Miss Kilman.[15] Usui treats Maisie Johnson's feeling that Lucrezia seemed 'foreign' (*MD* 22) as a sign of a more widespread xenophobia, officially enshrined in the 1914 and 1919 Aliens Restrictions Acts. Lucrezia has come to Britain at the worst possible time. Yet she is, in Usui's reading, a war bride, 'a symbol of male triumph, power, egotism, and romanticism' (151). The evidence for this reading is relatively thin, but we have Septimus's confession that he 'had married his wife without loving her' (*MD* 77), and we have evidence of his love for Evans. Usui suggests that, like many wounded soldiers, Septimus treats Lucrezia as a Florence Nightingale figure, 'a nurse who would take care of him unselfishly, patiently, and compassionately' (156). Women become the antidote to the appalling conditions at the Front, and in doing so, lose their independence. Miss Kilman's status as an indirect victim of war is more directly attested in the text: Usui's argument here fills in details of anti-German rioting during the war, and directs attention to the irony that Miss Kilman has worked with the Society of Friends (the Quakers), one of the foremost pacifist organizations.

Historian Jessica Meyer has also briefly considered *Mrs Dalloway*, as the conclusion to an article on the wives of disabled war veterans.[16] Using evidence from the National Archives, Meyer shows how the Ministry of Pensions treated the war wounded and their wives; her evidence lends support to Levenback's case about the invalidation of those who had not died. The passages which reveal Lucrezia's feelings about Septimus (*MD* 13, 19–20) are used by Meyer only to illustrate the 'awful predicament' facing the wives of disabled veterans; her reading adds little to our understanding of the text. However, when considering the small detail of Lucrezia's loose wedding ring (*MD* 20), Meyer brings her primary research to bear with some force: the ring is not only the index of the physical stress of being married to Septimus, but also symbolizes the indirect effects of the war in the form of marital breakdown.

Empire and the International Dimension

Zwerdling mentioned in 1977 that the British Empire of *Mrs Dalloway* was 'crumbling', and noted the passage on the imperial work of 'Proportion' and 'Conversion', but his article gave little attention to the international dimensions of the novel. In 1989 Tambling, as we have seen, gave the Empire greater prominence, and read *Mrs Dalloway* as a coded critique of imperialism. In the 1980s, under the general heading of postcolonialism, and under the stimulus of Edward Said's *Orientalism* (1978), the literary manifestations of British imperialism attracted increasing critical attention.

Trudi Tate's '*Mrs Dalloway* and the Armenian Question' (1994) focuses on Clarissa's uncertainty about whether Richard's committee is concerned with the Armenians or the Albanians, and her subsequent self-indulgence in her roses (*MD* 101–2).[17] The novel's original readers would have known about the genocide of Christian Armenians carried out by the Muslim Turks; over one million were killed or died as the result of starvation. Though Tate does not labour the point, the rhetoric which Clarissa recalls Richard using to describe their suffering echoes that of reports in *The Times*.

The persecution of the Armenians, which lasted from 1915 to 1920, raises the question of whether the war was ever really 'over', a question raised in the novel by the figure of Lady Bexborough (*MD* 4) and, on a larger scale, by Septimus. In 1923, according to Tate, it also raised 'vital issues about human rights and Britain's quasi-imperial responsibilities' (472). *Mrs Dalloway* may be set in London, but it makes reference to a much wider geographical span.

Tate sees *Mrs Dalloway* as a troubling text for feminist critics, because of its ambiguous attitude towards its central female character. Her article tries to avoid sidestepping or falsely resolving the novel's complexity. The novel takes a 'complex view of the relationship between gender, power, and the war'. Its portrait of Clarissa 'is simultaneously sympathetic and satiric'. This complexity 'is what makes the work so unsettling' and it is 'crucial to the book's politics' (470). Tate views *Mrs Dalloway* as 'a political attack on those who managed the social and economic aspects of the war and kept its victims under control afterwards' (470). Though power is concentrated in the hands of men such as Richard, they are supported by women. By contrast to critics who had treated Clarissa favourably, Tate is unsparing: 'Women's ignorance, too, is part of the cultural structure which took Britain to war and continued to oppress its victims' (470). Clarissa's confusion of Armenians and Albanians and her indulgence in her roses is 'her most childish moment in the entire book' (471). Tate is particularly exercised by Clarissa's belief that she could not bridge the 'gulf' between herself and her husband – for example, by understanding his work – without losing her 'independence' (*MD* 101):

■ Clarissa's refusal to engage with the suffering of European refugees – also victims of the war – is masked with proto-feminist statements about marriage. Two quite separate arguments are elided. It is one thing to refuse to live vicariously through Richard, and quite another to ignore a political problem simply because he happens to be engaged with it. Her use of feminist ideas has proved attractive to later feminist readers, yet we need to be cautious about accepting them at face value. Here they are cynically employed as an excuse for refusing adult responsibility. Progressive rhetoric screens an absolute conservatism, which refuses even to think about the sufferings of refugees, much less act on them. (471) □

Tate goes on to argue that 'Clarissa's refusal to think about the Armenian problem [...] provides us with ways of thinking about the structural relationship between Clarissa and Septimus', and about questions of responsibility in the novel. She considers the party scene: whereas Minow-Pinkney had taken the idea of there being 'an embrace in death' (*MD* 156) to imply a reuniting of Septimus with the maternal (see Chapter Five), Tate is reluctant to accept the false consolation of such psychoanalytic readings. She focuses on Clarissa's belief that it was 'her punishment to see sink and disappear here a man, there a woman, in this profound darkness [...]' (*MD* 157). Tate is unsparing of Clarissa's self-dramatizing tendencies: no one is forcing Clarissa to stand alone in her finery: 'It is a childish sulk; another example of Clarissa refusing to take responsibility for her own actions' (480). However, Tate does not specify which actions she means, and in conclusion pulls back slightly, noting that it would be all too easy to see Clarissa as 'purely satiric', as 'a ruling-class woman who thinks "it was very, very dangerous to live even one day"' (481). The passage quoted (*MD* 7) has a critical history going back to Wyndham Lewis in 1934.[18] Tate, unlike Lewis, does not equate Clarissa with her author. However, in attempting to correct the over-sympathetic readings of some critics, she runs the risk of repeating the condemnations of earlier critics, and her reminder that the portrait is simultaneously satiric and sympathetic offers a small corrective. Such a combination yields no easy answers, and Tate ends by presenting the novel as interrogative. Clarissa's ignorance raises questions about women's suffrage:

> ■ Will women's participation in democracy transform politics; or will it transform women? Would readers want Clarissa, who cannot tell the difference between Armenians, Albanians, and Turks, to be making decisions about these people's fates? Obviously not, yet would her decisions be any worse than those made by the men she supports? Would she be different if she had direct responsibility? (481) □

Tate's article is significant both for its thorough historical investigations, which recognize that small textual details can lead to a significant hinterland of historical information, and for its refusal to simplify the complexity of the text's attitudes.

Kathy Phillips's *Virginia Woolf Against Empire* (1994) was the first book-length study of Woolf's attitude to imperialism, and, as such, is frequently cited and included on lists of further reading. However, as the title suggests, Phillips's readings do not always acknowledge the complexity of Woolf's position.[19] Phillips praises Woolf's eye for small detail, and her readings often fruitfully develop seemingly insignificant details: she writes interestingly about the prime minister's vacated chair (*MD* 156). However, the rhetoric with which she presents her arguments does not respect the novel's subtlety: for example, in addressing Zwerdling's argument that Clarissa's reaction to Septimus's death is not typical of her social set, Phillips responds that the novel's satire 'demolishes' Clarissa and the rest of her set (3); elsewhere Woolf's novels 'expose' gender roles and 'powerfully indict' a system of dominance (1). The verbs suggest that Woolf was writing campaigning journalism, not a complex modernist novel. Phillips notes Zwerdling's conclusion that *Mrs Dalloway* cannot be called 'an indictment' of Clarissa, because it views her from within; however, her reading never really engages with the problem of how free indirect discourse relates to satire. Moreover, she tends to treat the characters as if they were the representative figures of classic realist fiction, each individual standing for a particular social class (5). While *Mrs Dalloway* does share something with the classic realist fiction of the Victorian era, such an approach is in practice often reductive.

Like many critics, Phillips considers the skywriting aeroplane:

■ the British kingdom would like its own piece of sky to extend into a worldwide Empire: 'the clouds to which the letters E, G, or L had attached themselves moved freely, as if destined to cross from West to East on a mission of the greatest importance which would never be revealed, and yet certainly so it was – a mission of the greatest importance' [*MD* 18]. The 'destined' imperial 'mission' from West to East, of which Peter's assignment in India is representative, remains, however, an embarrassing blank or, worse, a dangerously garbled directive accepted by uncritical, babyish, sleepwalking citizens. (4) □

That the message is an advertisement, says Phillips, 'reveals, moreover, the basis of the state in commerce' (4). Her argument here reflects her use of Leonard Woolf's *Empire and Commerce in Africa* (1920) as a background text, and she reminds us that, if the aeroplane is indeed advertising toffee, the sugar from which it was manufactured was grown in imperial territories. However, the inclusion of a reference to commerce within the novel does not necessarily 'reveal' anything about the state;

the looseness of the novel's construction, and the absence for long sections of an interpreting narratorial voice, mean that its component parts may be placed in many different relationships. Philips goes on to say that '*Mrs Dalloway* mocks both the commercialism and imperialism in the skywriting scene, by reducing the West-East "mission of the greatest importance" to a nonsense word, "Glaxo"' (4–5). 'Glaxo' was in fact not a nonsense word but the name of a formula milk product.[20] While this information might be used to bolster Phillips's argument, the fact that the same word can be read both as nonsense and as significant indicates further the caution that one must exercise in interpreting this passage. It is, indeed, a passage about the plurality of interpretations that can be produced from a single text.

London

Woolf's evocation of London in *Mrs Dalloway* was praised by many early reviewers, but the dominance of questions of form and style led to the importance of the city being neglected for many years. Though Dorothy Brewster considered London in 1959, her book was restricted to the 'general impression' of London produced by Woolf's novels. In 1979 David Daiches and John Flower's 'Virginia Woolf's London' noted the growth in the city's population between Woolf's birth and 1901, provided a map of *Mrs Dalloway*'s London setting – there were, in 1979, no annotated editions containing such documentation – and identified several unnamed locations in the novel. Their chapter, while useful to readers unfamiliar with the city, does not consider the history of the streets in detail.[21] In the 1970s the city was given a central role in several influential studies of modernity, modernism and modernist writers. Raymond Williams's *The Country and the City* (1973) examined the ways that the two terms were understood relationally; Monroe K. Spears's *Dionysus and the City* (1970) placed urban experience at the centre of modernism, as did Malcolm Bradbury's 'The Cities of Modernism', in the collection *Modernism 1890–1930* (1976). However, Susan Merrill Squier's *Virginia Woolf and London* (1985) is the first study to consider the London of *Mrs Dalloway* in depth.

Squier argues that urban scenes were of particular value in Woolf's attempt to understand patriarchy because they held both personal and cultural significance.

> ■ City scenes can be 'read' in two directions: in to the personal and psychic life of their creator, which they express symbolically and by which they are to some degree shaped, and out to the culture they symbolize and reflect, and by which they are also influenced. (9) □

Squier's approach is, as this would suggest, partly biographical, and draws on the then-new editions of Woolf's letters and diaries. At times the biographical framework can sound reductive, as in Squier's argument that Woolf initially associated the city with 'the male tradition' (3) and, because of her childhood holidays at Talland House, the country with the female. However, Squier argues that Woolf's associations grew more complex with time. Whereas in *Night and Day*, Woolf had seen 'retreat from the city' as the only way for a woman to resolve the conflict between her intellectual and social duties, in *Mrs Dalloway*, Woolf approaches 'the relationship between work and social life from a new angle' (91). In Squier's account, Woolf saw 'social life' – party-going and party-giving – as womanly activities; Woolf had described her attraction to the social life of London as 'a piece of jewellery I inherit from my mother' (*D*2: 250). However, the gendered polarization was not straightforward: after contact with friends, Woolf felt that 'ideas leap in me' (*D*2: 250).

Squier examines the place of the city in *Mrs Dalloway* by focusing on three street scenes: Clarissa's walk to buy the flowers (*MD* 3–12); Peter Walsh's walk from Clarissa's house to Regent's Park (*MD* 41–8); and Septimus's 'hallucinatory ramble' (95) from Bond Street to Regent's Park (*MD* 12–19). All three 'are defined by the streets through which they pass' (95). Clarissa thinks of herself 'as part of the background' (95), merging with her social and physical surroundings. In Squier's reading, Clarissa's walk is primarily revealing of her character; she 'is the classic female product of a patriarchal culture, with the strengths and weaknesses of that position' (98). Squier's interpretation is most attentive to the historical and local-geographical distinctions at work in Woolf's text when examining differences between characters. The difference between Clarissa and her daughter

> ■ is echoed by the different districts of London through which they travel: Clarissa walks through Westminster and up Bond Street, traditionally haunts of male political and female social power, while her daughter takes an omnibus up the Strand, a newly booming center of male and female commercial and professional life. (102) □

Peter Walsh's walk 'through the haunts of masculine imperial and sexual power' reveals his self-conception as 'an active, even daring figure' (104), though this self-conception is self-deception: Squier takes Peter's 'desire for dominance over women' as psychological compensation for his 'lack of success as a colonial administrator' (105). Squier remarks on 'the geographical and historical specificity of Woolf's street iconography' – for example, the statues of the great military and imperial heroes, Nelson, Gordon and Havelock – and its ability to produce 'an acute psychological and political portrait' (106). In considering Septimus's case, Squier makes less of the historical specifics: as 'the city relentlessly mirrors his pain and confusion', he sees around him 'only more evidence of his agonizing sense of turmoil, confusion, and emotional suffocation: lines of lunatics humiliatingly on public display; placards telling of men buried and women burned alive; dead men walking and dogs metamorphosing into men' (112).

Squier makes reference to the diary phrase about the 'social system', but is interested more in Woolf's polarized opposites, 'life & death, sanity & insanity' (*D2* 248). Careful study of the novel, argues Squier, shows that Woolf wanted not simply to show these things 'side by side' (*D2* 207), but 'to transcend the very habit of thinking in dualities, and to criticize a society based upon such habitual polarization' (93). By using street scenes to juxtapose three diverse characters, Woolf forces the reader to consider 'their interrelatedness', and to connect 'what would otherwise remain disconnected: private and public, female and male society' (120). Squier is persuasive on this point, but, although she praises Woolf's geographical and historical specificity, Squier's own study delivers a fairly generalized portrait of London. For example, in considering Elizabeth's journey down the Strand, she does not explain why it was a newly booming centre, nor the place of women in the employment it offered.

Mrs Dalloway opens with a reference to shopping, and shops are a significant part of the spectacle of London that it presents. Reginald Abbott's 'What Miss Kilman's Petticoat Means' (1992) makes the connection between the public and the private, between geography and psychology, by reference to ideas about advertising, display and consumption. His essay is influenced indirectly by Guy Debord's *La société du spectacle* (1967), mediated through Thomas Richards's *The Commodity Culture of Victorian England* (1990) and other cultural histories of shopping and consumption. The Great Exhibition of 1851 had inaugurated a new culture of display, and by the early twentieth century there existed a 'commodity culture': 'a loud, blatant, raucous universe of commodities and their signs whose gravitational pull is irresistible and whose intrusion in all lives is, for better or worse, inevitable' (196). Woolf's essay 'Oxford Street Tide' (part of *The London Scene* essays from 1931–32) and Woolf's diaries provide Abbott with particular insights into Woolf's view of consumerism. Abbott notes the opening of five major department stores in London from 1872 to 1909. However, Clarissa does her shopping in an older, more leisurely manner: that there is 'no splash; no glitter' in Bond Street reminds the well-informed reader that it is defined by contrast to the newer world of department stores; the shop where Clarissa's father had bought his suits for fifty years still survives (*MD* 9). Abbott surveys the attitudes to shopping seen in Richard Dalloway, Hugh Whitbread,

Rezia Warren Smith and Miss Kilman. Hugh Whitbread emerges as the novel's clearest-sighted critic of the commodity spectacle: aware, in particular, that Rigby and Lowndes's clock, displaying the time 'ratified by Greenwich', is designed to create gratitude which will later take the form, 'naturally', of buying socks or shoes from them (*MD* 87). Miss Kilman's purchase of a petticoat from the Army and Navy Stores places her socially. Though the Army and Navy Stores (founded 1872) had originally had a quiet, club-like atmosphere, by 1923 it had become a conventional department store. Miss Kilman's petticoat is mass-produced, and this places her socially: as an historian of shopping has remarked '*ladies* never wore machine-stitched underclothes' (205).[22]

To conclude his discussion of *Mrs Dalloway*, Abbott suggests that the spectacular nature of commodity culture needs to be understood alongside that of exclusively 'aristocratic' spectacles: 'the season, parties, country living, court ritual' (208). Abbott blurs the lines between Woolf and Clarissa, suggesting that Clarissa's 'aristocratic' background was 'home ground' to Woolf, and 'completely in line with the realities of her own life' (209). He argues that the lack of consumption in the novel, the lack of 'direct commodity discourse', serves to keep the novel 'securely on its course to its own "spectacular" conclusion: Clarissa's party' (210). Abbott fails to distinguish between Clarissa's plans for a spectacular conclusion to the day and Woolf's plans for a conclusion to the novel. It is questionable whether *spectacle* is necessary to the latter; what the conclusion needs is a contrast between the life of the party and the death of Septimus; the life of the party does not necessarily consist of spectacle. However, although Abbott's conclusion is unconvincing, the article makes a significant contribution, placing consumerism historically, and suggesting more broadly that many kinds of cultural history might inform our understanding of the novel.

Leena Kore Schröder's '*Mrs Dalloway* and the Female Vagrant' (1995) considers the ways in which London dissolves conventional identities and social hierarchies.[23] Rather than focusing on the major characters, Clarissa and Septimus, the article considers vagrants and foreigners such as Miss Kilman. In thinking about the ways that vagrants escape classification and structure, the article draws lightly and implicitly on post-structuralist thinking: vagrants might be classed as 'the real', in the Lacanian sense of the word; as Kore Schröder writes, the 'manysidedness of the vagrant population has always helped it both to evade identification through official census statistics, and to threaten those same implements of stability and social order' (334). More explicitly, the essay draws on the ideas of the carnivalesque disruption of social convention and the dialogic construction of the truth developed by the Russian theorist Mikhail Bakhtin (1895–1975). While the article could be fruitfully compared to the post-structuralist examinations of subjectivity, its treatment of identity is grounded in historical detail: like Zwerdling, Kore Schröder uses *The Times* from June 1923 to note, as background to the pistol-like sound of the backfiring car, 'revolutionary shots fired in the streets of Russia and Bulgaria' (328), and to counterpoint them to the social world of the upper middle classes and the aristocracy: including 'debutantes at Court, cricket at Lord's and polo at Ranelagh [...]' (329). She places homelessness in the context of Lloyd George's failed 'Homes Fit for Heroes' campaign of 1918, a building programme that was drastically scaled down in 1921 and that ended entirely in 1922. She considers the statistics for homelessness, and for female vagrancy, as well as social attitudes towards vagrants. Methodologically, the article is particularly interesting, as it demonstrates that historicism need not imply a rejection of literary theory, and that New Historicism was not the only possible way of reconciling the two.

Woolf's essay 'Street Haunting' (1927) provides the lens through which Kore Schröder examines the novel's scattered references to vagrants. In Woolf's essay, she writes, 'the fixed boundaries of identity dissolve into a multitude of shattered selves', and 'the private house' no longer protects against what Woolf called 'that vast republican army of anonymous trampers' (324). In 'Street Haunting', Woolf is aware of the grotesque contrast between the world of street-sleepers and the conspicuous displays of luxury in the shop windows. While *Mrs Dalloway* does not highlight the contrast quite so sharply, it is also a novel in which the consumption of luxuries sits alongside abject poverty. Many politicians were concerned that the homeless might become socially disruptive: Lloyd George explicitly presented his housing programme as 'insurance against Bolshevism and Revolution' (quoted 334). The backfiring car, as well as reminding contemporary readers of the assassination of Archduke Ferdinand in Sarajevo in 1914, prefigures future revolutions.

The stories that the English upper middle classes would like to tell about themselves are, however, faltering. Kore Schröder notes how 'the centrality of imperial London' is threatened by 'a primeval counter-history' (330). Bond Street becomes 'a grass-grown path' (*MD* 14) and Regent's Park 'reverts to its ancient shape' (*MD* 21). Alluding to the title of an early twentieth-century children's history of England, Kore Schröder argues that the primeval counter-history 'de-stabilises the constructions of nationalism and Empire that comprise Our Island Story' (331). Kore Schröder reads the contemporaneous essay 'Thunder at Wembley' as a similarly apocalyptic decentring of the imperialist narrative, and she takes one of the novel's 'key ideological statements' to be voiced by Miss Kilman: 'After all, there were people who did not think the English invariably right. [...] There were other points of view' (*MD* 110). London, in Kore Schröder's reading, may be the expression of imperial power, but it is plural enough for us to read it against the grain, and *Mrs Dalloway* embodies this plurality.

Thinking about the urban space of *Mrs Dalloway* and Woolf's other London novels has developed through extensive dialogue with the writings of Walter Benjamin (1892–1940). Parts of Benjamin's *Charles Baudelaire: A Lyric Poet in the Era of High Capitalism* appeared in translation in 1968, the remainder in 1973. Benjamin focuses particularly on the figure of the *flâneur*, a privileged man of leisure, a detached observer of city life who enjoys the anonymity of the crowd. The role or subject-position of *flâneur* had arisen, for men, in the boulevards of nineteenth-century Paris. The crucial poem in Baudelaire's oeuvre, 'Á une passante', concerns the *flâneur*'s projection of romantic fantasies on to a passing woman on the boulevard. As the *flâneur* became important in debates about modernity and modernism, feminist critics questioned its universality; in an influential article, Janet Wolff asked whether a (female) *flâneuse* might exist.[24] Such questions overlap with the questions posed by the work of geographical and sociological theorists such as Henri Lefebvre (1901–1991), Michel de Certeau (1925–86) and Doreen Massey (b. 1944). If, as the 'new geography' has argued, space is constructed through social practices and institutions, and if social expectations about men's and women's relation to space differ, the *flâneur* does not represent a genderless, universal subject position.

Rachel Bowlby's 'Walking, Women, and Writing' (1992) builds on Janet Wolff's article; much of it is concerned with 'Street Haunting', but Bowlby also considers the passage in which Peter Walsh follows the young woman from Trafalgar Square to Oxford Street; in Bowlby's account it is a satirical account of Peter as a *flâneur*.[25] Although Peter believes that the woman is shedding 'veil after veil' to be revealed as 'the very woman he had always had in mind' (*MD* 45), Bowlby argues that

■ With its alternation of clichéd attributes of a certain version of ideal femininity, the 'shedding of veil after veil' to reveal not so much uniqueness as indistinctness, or rather uniqueness *as* indistinctness, a fantasy 'everywoman', the passage is already bordering on parodic literary stereotype. (204) □

Shopping is important in Bowlby's account too; it has been a continuing theme in her critical work. She looks in particular at the passage where Peter's quarry is reflected in the shop windows. Peter distinguishes himself from the 'yellow dressing gowns, pipes, fishing-rods' in the shop windows. But the woman merges:

■ On and on she went, across Piccadilly, and up Regent Street, ahead of him, her cloak, her gloves, her shoulders combining with the fringes and the laces and the feather boas which dwindled out of the shops on to the pavement. (*MD* 46) □

Bowlby comments:

■ Whereas Peter's buccaneering identity is defined by its difference from the accoutrements of masculinity on show, the desirability of his quarry is seen precisely as an extension of the fetishistically feminine bits and pieces visible as they pass. Peter's proud display of himself as distinct from other men and their 'damned proprieties' is parodied in his pursuit of a femininity as predictable as the dull masculinity he is consciously refusing. (205) □

The woman's final evasion of Peter, when she enters (it seems) her flat, is, notes Bowlby, 'the parody of the amorous clinch or climax that might have been expected' (205–6). She highlights particularly the phrase 'and now, and now, the great moment was approaching, for now she slackened, opened her bag, and with one look in his direction...' (*MD* 46), commenting that 'The *passante* narrative... still stands, as the dominant street story, but knowingly fictionalised: "for it was half made up, as he knew very well; invented, this escapade..."' (206, quoting *MD* 46). The inclusion of the woman's point of view (her look is not intended for Peter) 'has produced a parody of a scene whose conventions are clearly understood by both parties, transforming it into a gentle power game where she comes out with the victory' (206). Bowlby concludes by suggesting that the novel might be readjusting the dominant narratives of the street, 'moving the *passante* out of focus to make way for something like a female *flânerie*': Clarissa, after all, exclaims how she loves walking in London (*MD* 5); her surname itself suggests that she is a woman who likes 'to dally along the way, the *flâneuse* herself' (206).

Back to Bloomsbury

Bloomsbury has returned in recent articles placing Woolf's intellectual and ideological position in its historical context. Brian Shaffer's 'Civilization in Bloomsbury' (1994) places *Mrs Dalloway* alongside two texts by Clive Bell, *On British Freedom* (1923) and *Civilization* (1928).[26] Shaffer argues that the novel

■ invokes and critiques, absorbs and parodies Bell's 'much read and much criticized' theory of civilization not only because of its currency at the time, but because Woolf herself remained deeply skeptical about many of its ramifications. (74)[27] □

'Civilization' appears in the novel as one of the words that Clarissa feels she owes to Peter Walsh (*MD* 31), and, in an ironic frame, in Peter's reflections on the ambulance that carries away Septimus's body: 'one of the triumphs of civilization' (*MD* 128), he thinks. Shaffer notes that, in several respects, Peter Walsh resembles Clive Bell, but the argument is based primarily on ideas rather than personalities. One difficulty for Shaffer is that he wishes to argue that *Mrs Dalloway* 'appropriates and transforms' *Civilization* in various ways (74), even though Bell's text was unpublished while she wrote her novel. Bell's preface acknowledges the long gestation period of the work, and it is certain that Woolf had access to Bell's ideas long before she had access to the text; but Shaffer does not adequately distinguish the two.

Shaffer is on safer ground dealing with *On British Freedom*. He notes Bell's condemnation of the 'various "enemies of liberty"' who seek to legislate and to censor the cultural fare consumed by the public. Foremost among them were doctors and moralists, and Shaffer identifies the Holmes and Bradshaw with Bell's sketch of the oppressive doctor, and Miss Kilman with his sketch of the moralistic religious fanatic (79–81). When it comes to *Civilization*, Shaffer argues that Woolf disagrees with Bell. Whereas Bell had argued that 'class stratification [was] necessary for the maintenance of civilization' (83), because servants were necessary to leisure, Woolf's account of Lady Bruton seems to contradict him. Lady Bruton is 'decidedly uncivilized by Bell's standards': she does not read poetry (*MD* 89), and has never read Shakespeare (*MD* 153). As Shaffer puts it, she is 'deadened by leisure', cut off from civilization by the 'grey tide of service' (*MD* 91) that surrounds her. Shaffer begins his article with a quotation from Bakhtin, in which Bakhtin distinguishes 'the text' from 'the work': the latter 'includes its necessary extratextual context' (quoted 73). In the case of *Mrs Dalloway*, Bell's texts are that context; to invoke them as part of 'the work' does not require Woolf to agree with them; rather, she shaped her text through dialogue with them.

Elyse Graham and Pericles Lewis also take Bloomsbury as their starting point in 'Private Religion, Public Mourning, and *Mrs Dalloway*' (2013).[28] Their article also responds to Christine Froula's article on mourning (discussed in Chapter Five), but does so in a register that entirely breaks from psychoanalytic assumptions. They note that many critics have seen Septimus's death as some kind of redemptive sacrifice like that of Jesus, and, while conceding that the language of sacrifice is present in the text, question whether Woolf and the novel really subscribe to it. Woolf's personal atheism is well known. What Graham and Lewis bring to the discussion is the question of the public place of religion in the 1920s. Beginning with the scene of a 'seedy-looking nondescript man' in front of St Paul's Cathedral (*MD* 24), they say that in *Mrs Dalloway*, 'The traditional consolations that the church seems to promise have ceased to inspire the city's inhabitants' (88–9). The historical evidence is somewhat mixed, however. By some measures, membership of churches rose: in 1927, baptisms in the Church of England reached their highest ever percentage (89). In 1926, the weekly news magazine and literary review the *Nation and Athenaeum* undertook a survey of religious attitudes among its readers (largely drawn from the university-educated middle classes of a liberal or 'progressive' political persuasion) and among the readers of the mass-circulation *Daily News*. The *Nation and Athenaeum* had particularly close links to Bloomsbury, having been taken over in 1923 by a consortium led by the economist John Maynard Keynes; Leonard Woolf was its literary editor, and the survey was prompted by Leonard's having claimed that 'liberal scepticism, atheism, or agnosticism' were the characteristic positions of 'educated moderns' (L. Woolf, quoted 90). The survey's results were somewhat contradictory: a majority of the 'educated moderns' 'believed in either Christianity or some sort of "Life Force"' (90), but people were reluctant to subscribe to traditional dogmas such as personal immortality or the divinity of Christ (90–1). The best explanation is that private religious feeling had survived while public dogma had not.

Graham and Lewis claim that *Mrs Dalloway* 'recognizes the historical importance of religious institutions in giving shape and coherence to community life and the search for meaning'; it is aware of the 'dangers and problems of religion', but simultaneously aware that many contemporaries 'covet religious experience', especially where it helps them make sense of the war. The tension is captured in the contrast between Clarissa's 'disdain for the old myths' and Septimus's 'demand for their return' and his plans for a new religion (91).

In engaging with Froula's article, Graham and Lewis accept her contention that *Mrs Dalloway* is a deliberate adaptation of the classical elegiac tradition to 'postwar London's post-theological cosmos' (Froula, quoted 94), but they argue that it is important to distinguish between private and public mourning: 'The novel draws on and critiques a series of public, communal traditions and narratives of mourning, complicating and at times undermining our sense of what it means to participate in them' (94). Where they part company with Froula is with regard to the 'old narratives of sacrifice' which, if accepted, lead to 'incautiously messianic readings of Septimus Smith'. (Woolf's remark about the 'sane truth' and the 'insane truth' has led many critics to seek a kind of truth in Septimus's vision of the world.)

■ Froula follows the familiar reading that makes Septimus a figure of prophetic sanity. In this view, his madness is no true madness but rather a vision too clear to withstand: [...]. Our view is that the translation of death into heroic sacrifice is precisely the kind of sentiment that Woolf strives to resist. Woolf indulges that sentiment because she wants us to feel its history and its power, but ultimately she presents a picture of its ugliness. (95) ☐

Central to Graham and Lewis's argument about elegy and the modern world is a passage not considered by Froula in which Septimus runs through 'the full round of pastoral elegy: the piping of shepherds, the story of loss (drowning, as in *Lycidas*), the death and rebirth of a vegetation god, the multiplication of voices, and the return to the world' (96). They notice in particular that the shepherd boy's anthem in Septimus's vision 'made its exquisite plaint while the traffic passed beneath' (*MD* 58), and its echo in Miss Kilman's later thought: 'In the midst of traffic there stood the habitation of God' (*MD* 113). They find a tension in the novel, particularly its first half, between the knowledge that in modernity, the old elegiac narrative cannot end in consolation, and the 'constant, mysterious, half-articulated suggestions that something is about to happen' (97).

'Mrs Dalloway in Bond Street' also provides important evidence in their argument. The Clarissa of the short story no longer believes in God, but pretends to believe, 'for the sake of the shopgirl selling the gloves and for the "thousands of young men [who] had died that things might go on"' (98–9, quoting *CSF* 158–9). They remark that although Woolf did not believe in the 'celebration of the war dead as a patriotic duty', the passage is filled with a recognition of the responsibility of the living towards the dead, one that, as Clarissa 'exchanges nothings with the shopgirl', 'fills the interaction with electricity' (99). The Clarissa of the novel has never believed in God, and her 'transcendental theory' and belief that 'somehow ... she survived' (*MD* 129, 8) is of interest to Graham and Lewis because of the tension it involves between indifference to death and a hope for some sort of afterlife; they suggest she is 'straining to say that the soul lives on, even though she knows it does not' (101).

In this account, Septimus, as a newcomer to London, is 'vulnerable to the appeal of large institutions', and Graham and Lewis imply that his later messianic fantasy has its roots in his going to church as part of his pre-war 'program of self-improvement' (102). They acknowledge that Septimus sees himself as a scapegoat, but note that he also sees himself as Lazarus, John the Baptist and the Angel of the Annunciation:

> ■ The very eclecticism of these visions, which rapidly build and demolish huge structures of myth, conveys not only the disorganization of madness but also the sense of desperation involved in throwing answers at a problem too large for any known resource to handle. (102) ☐

In *Mrs Dalloway*, Woolf 'seeks to undermine' the validity of 'narratives of loss and redemption.' If Woolf is seeking to reinvent mourning 'as a movement toward provisional and earthbound responses to the problem of loss', then Septimus represents the lingering power of older narratives (103). It is true Clarissa imagines Septimus's death with 'uncanny accuracy', such that the reader may detect a 'mystical possibility'; but it is a possibility that the novel leaves unresolved (104). Like many critics, Graham and Lewis consider Clarissa's reflections in which she feels that she resembles Septimus, and they comment that it is 'hard to know what to do' with it. They suggest that Clarissa's trajectory from shock and sympathy to a moment of triumph is something that strains readers' sympathies with her; and if our sympathies are strained, then we may be sceptical of the idea that Clarissa's party is some form of Eucharist.

> ■ Although Woolf leaves open the possibility of Septimus's death as redemptive, perhaps the novel suggests in the final accounting that, in fact, there is nothing redemptive about it, and we are just prone to telling ourselves stories that will make us feel that there is. (106) □

Woolf, in their view, has identified the danger of turning deaths into myths.

Graham and Lewis's mode of historicization is less reliant on documentation and less concerned with the textuality of history than many articles from the moment when New Historicism was at its peak. Though the *Nation and Athenaeum* survey is important to establishing the tension surrounding religion in the 1920s, having established the historical background, the article concentrates on *Mrs Dalloway* and the critical tradition surrounding it.

'Historicism' covers a wide range of critical practices: historical critics can focus on the histories of ideas, of emotions, of places; they can emphasize the personal connections, drawing on Woolf's diaries and letters and other documents unavailable to the 1925 reader, or a public dimension drawing on historical documents. The agendas set by critics in this chapter continue to be relevant. War and militarism continue to be significant elements in the interpretation of the novel; it seems unlikely that Septimus's part of the story will ever again be treated as mere episode. In relation to the city, Son has given the most explicitly theorized account of the novel, drawing on the work of Lefebvre and de Certeau; Snaith and Whitworth have drawn attention to the intertextual dimensions to Woolf's construction of London, noting similarities with H. G. Wells's *Ann Veronica* (1909); while Raphaël Ingelbien has argued that Woolf's account of Septimus in the city drew on T. S. Eliot's *The Waste Land* (1922); Flint, Frattarola and Rounds have drawn on phenomenology to consider the embodied experience of living in London.[29] And although ideas about the Bloomsbury Group continue to change, both in terms of who was a member and which members mattered most to Woolf, it seems that her immediate circle of acquaintance will continue to inform readings of the novel.

There is, however, another way of thinking about context, one which directs attention not to the context in which Woolf's novels were written, but the context in which they are read. Many readers come to Woolf already acquainted with later writers who were influenced by her, and so some of what seemed strange to her contemporaries now seems familiar. The next chapter considers one aspect of the contemporary reading context, the difference made to *Mrs Dalloway* by creative adaptations, in particular Michael Cunningham's *The Hours* (198).

CHAPTER EIGHT

Mrs Dalloway and *The Hours*

At the end of the 1990s there appeared three creative responses to *Mrs Dalloway*: Marleen Gorris's film adaptation (1997); Michael Cunningham's *The Hours* (1998), a novel which takes Woolf's as its starting point; and Robin Lippincott's *Mr Dalloway* (1999), a sequel. Cunningham's novel was itself adapted into a film by Stephen Daldry, with a screenplay by British playwright David Hare, released at the end of 2002. Responses such as these are creative works, but they are also acts of criticism. They have the power to refocus attention on parts of the original text previously neglected; remediations such as film adaptations can focus attention on what the original medium was uniquely capable of, while adaptations such as Cunningham's can focus attention on the distinctive qualities of Woolf's narrative method. However, as they are acts of criticism not written in the conventional language of criticism, careful attention is required to clarify what they have said.

Of the four works, *The Hours* has been the most valuable stimulus to Woolf criticism. It draws on a late twentieth-century form that reworks canonical works of literature from an unusual perspective: the first texts in this tradition are Jean Rhys's *Wide Sargasso Sea* (1966) and Tom Stoppard's *Rosencrantz and Guildenstern are Dead* (first performed 1966). It also has something in common with other novels that create parallels between events in disparate time periods, such as Peter Ackroyd's *Hawksmoor* (1985) or A. S. Byatt's *Possession* (1990). Cunningham's novel has three strands. One, 'Mrs Dalloway', is set in 1990s New York, and reworks Clarissa Dalloway as Clarissa Vaughan, living with a woman named Sally. In it, Septimus becomes her gay friend Richard Brown; the First World War is replaced by the AIDS epidemic. The second strand, 'Mrs Brown', is set in 1950s suburban America, and concerns Laura Brown, a housewife oppressed by the demands of her social role. The third, 'Mrs Woolf', is set in 1920s England and turns Virginia Woolf into a fictional character, writing her novel.

In James Schiff's 'Rewriting *Mrs Dalloway*: Homage, Sexual Identity, and the Single-Day Novel by Cunningham, Lippincott, and Lanchester'

(2004), the rewritings stimulate questions about why *Mrs Dalloway* should be the chosen text.[1] (Though John Lanchester's *Mr Philips* (2000) is undeniably set on a single day, Schiff is not persuasive about its having a relation to Woolf's novel.) First, he notes 'it is concerned with the ambiguity of sexual identity and desire, a subject that has even greater currency within a contemporary world actively and openly exploring gender construction'. Secondly, *Mrs Dalloway* is 'unique among city novels' for the way it takes 'the complexities of urban life' and, by establishing a network of connections between its characters, makes the city feel 'almost pastoral'. Finally, the novel is about 'what it feels like to be alive – to be a self passing through the moments and hours of a day' (364). To answer these questions, however, is not to explain why novelists should wish to '*explicitly* retell' *Mrs Dalloway*, rather than have it as an invisible framework. Schiff notes that retellings usually revise stories that are 'familiar and prominent within a given culture', such as those of Cinderella, Odysseus, Hamlet, or Hester Prynne. That *Mrs Dalloway* has been rewritten suggests that it is beginning to have mythic status, perhaps because of Woolf's 'handling of gender and sexual identity and her depiction of the fluidity of character' (365). Schiff also notes that Cunningham's and Lippincott's novels are a kind of homage. He asks whether such retellings are not 'simply a convenient way for a contemporary writer to enlarge his or her currency', and more generously asks whether interacting with a 'precursive genius' might not help a writer achieve greater things (366). (The latter case may be true, but would not necessitate the end-product displaying its origins so deliberately.)

Drawing on an interview with Cunningham, Schiff suggests that *The Hours* is 'an attempt [...] to explore and play with "what if" questions posed by Woolf's novel', particularly as regards the constraints on sexuality placed on someone like Clarissa Dalloway in 1920s England. The implied judgement about *Mrs Dalloway*, which Schiff does not tease out, is that it stimulates us to think about the extent to which its characters' actions are determined by their social environment, and that it encourages us to create counter-factual narratives. Such a response begins most obviously in Clarissa's musings over how a marriage to Peter Walsh would have been, but also emerges in small moments such as Clarissa's thinking she 'would have liked to help' Miss Kilman (*MD* 107). Why did she not? the reader might ask; what if she had?

Seymour Chatman's '*Mrs Dalloway*'s Progeny: *The Hours* as Second-degree Narrative' (2005) takes a narratological approach to Cunningham's novel, but pursues the larger implications of its formalist findings.[2] Chatman summarizes the principal features of Cunningham's pastiche of Woolf's style: exclamations; 'interruptions of the flow of thought – marked by commas, parentheses, or dashes – as each Clarissa tries to recover a memory, searches for a word, feels uncertain'; repetitions; frequent '"near" deixis through words like "here," "now," "this"', which serves to emphasize the immediacy of the characters' presence on the scene (274–5). The principal difference concerns the moments when Cunningham presents an external view of his Clarissa. Woolf was critical of the external narration that she associated with novelists like Arnold Bennett. When she presents Clarissa Dalloway externally, she does so through 'the consciousness of another character, often a walk-on, a personage who, despite his or her irrelevance to the plot, could function as a "chorus"' (275). Chatman notes that Cunningham's sentences 'more regularly feature Clarissa as the subject of a visualizable predicate, and hence the narrator as interpreter of the spectacle' (276). His examples include: 'Clarissa ... runs out' (*Hours* 9); 'She delays for a moment the plunge' (*Hours* 9); 'As Clarissa steps down from the vestibule her shoe makes gritty contact with the red-brown, mica-studded stone of the first stair' (*Hours* 10). Such sentences 'presuppose a narrator who moves Clarissa from place to place, instead of letting her thoughts simply flow along, without much concern for her whereabouts' (276).

A related stylistic detail concerns each novelist's preferences as regards verbal tense:

> ■ Woolf often prefers –ing verb forms – both present participles and gerunds – to completed predicates. These emphasize the continuing flow of experience and the co-occurrence of events inside and outside the mind, the to-and-fro of memory, opinion, perception (fittingly, as we learn, since Clarissa Dalloway has a life-and-death interest in continuation). (276) □

Cunningham, on the other hand, 'favors a verb form we don't find in *Mrs Dalloway* – the historic present tense', of which one of his examples is 'Clarissa crosses Eighth Street' (*Hours* 13). 'Whether the historic present suggests a greater immediacy than the simple preterite is debatable, but its use is clearly less evocative of the eddying dynamics of the protagonist's inner life than Woolf's present participles' (277). These observations lead to a large one about the two novels' treatment of time. The clock chimes in *Mrs Dalloway* provide 'a detached real-life chronological armature for the multiplicity of consciousness'; they 'facilitate daringly unpredictable shifts from one consciousness to another' (277). Chatman suggests that there is a larger purpose: 'Woolf is concerned with the whole life of London and beyond it, the British Empire. Her city is more than just background' (277). (Of particular relevance here, though unmentioned by Chatman, is the reference to Greenwich, home of the global meridian line (*MD* 24).) *The Hours*, on the other hand, uses the 'hour' as a 'thematic leitmotif' (277), for example in the contrast between Richard's despair and Clarissa's optimism: 'there will be ecstatic hours and darker hours, but still we cherish the city, the morning' (*Hours* 225).

Returning to his point about 'walk-on' or choric characters, Chatman notes the fluidity with which Woolf's narrative focus moves from one mind to another, and this brings him to his larger contrast:

■ In *Mrs Dalloway*, shifting mental filters through chance proximity has important political as well as aesthetic implications. The technique emphasizes the democracy of the city street (in the face of England's official class rigidity), a place where everyone, even the youngest or most modest denizen, enjoys the dignity of a name and even a partial view of the scene. (278) □

Each of these minor characters has an independent life: 'the technique democratically reminds us that there is more to the vibrant world of London than Clarissa's party and Septimus's death' (278). *The Hours*, by contrast, covers a much narrower scope. In particular, 'it attenuates the number and abruptness of shifts among consciousnesses' (278). In consequence, and despite the chronological range of Cunningham's novel (the 1920s, the 1950s, the 1990s), he 'does not achieve the broad cultural sweep of *Mrs Dalloway*'. Although Cunningham's Greenwich Village has been compared to Bloomsbury, '*Mrs Dalloway* is not set in Bloomsbury; it is not concerned with a colony of artists and intellectuals; its purview is the whole of London's population, indeed the whole of a British empire in decline' (280). Cunningham's novel, Chatman says witheringly, is limited to 'a group of professionals in the entertainment industry living in Greenwich Village' (280). While this is not true, or true only of the 'Mrs Dalloway' strand of *The Hours*, it serves as a reminder of the broader scope of Woolf's novel.

My own account (also from 2005) is relevant here. In its concern with the 'social system', *Mrs Dalloway* owes something to the nineteenth-century 'condition-of-England' novel such as Elizabeth Gaskell's *North and South* or Charles Dickens's *Bleak House* (1852–53).

■ Though largely set in London, it is concerned with the geographically wider effects of British imperialism. *The Hours* does not claim to be a novel about 'America' or about America's quasi-imperial tendencies. [...] Cunningham's recontextualizing implies that Woolf is a novelist concerned primarily with sexuality and personal relations, and that her interest in national and international politics is unimportant.[3] □

While the decision to make Richard a man with AIDS rather than a veteran of a recent American war (Vietnam, or the Gulf War of 1991) is a sign of Cunningham's willingness to break with Woolf's text, it also reduces the scope of his novel.

Clarissa and Sally Seton's kiss at Bourton is one of the crucial details that Cunningham reworks from *Mrs Dalloway*. As Schiff says, somewhat disdainfully, 'Cunningham essentially mass-produces the kiss, including one in nearly every major scene.'[4] Cunningham's reworking is one of the starting points for Kate Haffey's investigation in 'Exquisite Moments and the Temporality of the Kiss in *Mrs Dalloway* and *The Hours*' (2010); her other starting point is the work of theorists on Queer Temporality.[5] Haffey notes that the kiss 'seems to upset or rupture the forward flow of time' in the narrative, existing outside its 'cause and effect logic' (138). Haffey builds her argument in opposition to Elizabeth Abel's 'Narrative Structure(s) and Female Development' (1983) (see Chapter Five). Abel's account typifies a heterosexual narrative of development in which all subjects are moving towards heterosexual marriage and reproduction. Such a scheme can accommodate same-sex desire as an immature 'phase': such a view is inscribed within *Mrs Dalloway* in Richard's explanation of Elizabeth's attraction to Miss Kilman as possibly being 'only a phase [...] such as all girls go through' (*MD* 10). Clarissa's feelings for Sally are 'often constructed [by critics] as representing a period of girlhood innocence' (139). A reading such as Abel's

> ■ normalizes Clarissa's experience into a universal (read: heterosexual) narrative of female experience. Because she sees Clarissa's life in terms of the development from one life stage to the next, Abel is unable to read the intricacies of the plot as anything more than the progression from girlhood to mature adulthood. (139) □

Clarissa's memories of her love for Sally present an obstacle to Abel's reading, but also allow her to construct the moment of hearing about Septimus's suicide as the moment where Clarissa breaks free of the past and is able to 'embrace the imperfect pleasures of adulthood more completely' (Abel, quoted 140).

Haffey's counter-argument begins with the texture of past and present in *Mrs Dalloway*: she argues that they 'are not as easily separated' as Abel would like them to be. In the opening scene, for example, it is impossible to decide whether the squeak belongs to London now or Bourton in the past.

> ■ The interpenetration of past and present also occurs when Clarissa calls forth her memories of Sally. Thus to focus on Clarissa's feelings for Sally as located only in the past [...] is to ignore the ways in which this moment returns again and again to affect Clarissa's present. (141) □

Haffey draws on critical work which distinguishes between narrative and lyric time, and suggests that there are at least elements of lyric time in *Mrs Dalloway*. Narrative time represents 'a sequence of events that move dynamically in time and space' (Friedman, quoted 142) while lyric time is a simultaneity. The 'lyric moment' in *Mrs Dalloway* is something the characters cannot move past; it is not simply 'a moment that begins then ends or that momentarily interrupts narrative' (142). (Although Haffey does not draw the analogy, there are similarities between such moments and traumatic memories in trauma theory: both resist integration into narrative.) The moment in *Mrs Dalloway* resembles what Eve Sedgwick has called the 'queer moment', and Haffey draws out in particular the implications of Sedgwick's description of such moments as 'eddying': queer moments 'represent whirlpools within the flow of time'; as the *American Heritage Dictionary* would have it, they move 'contrary to the direction of the main current' (143).

Sedgwick's introduction to her collection of essays *Tendencies* (1992) begins by suggesting that everyone working in gay and lesbian studies 'is haunted by the suicides of adolescents'; when she looks at her adult friends working in the field, she feels 'the survival of each one is a miracle' (quoted 143). The temporality of haunting creates an 'intense connection' between 'adolescent and adult selves' (143). Haffey finds just such a temporality in *Mrs Dalloway*, and suggests that we should read the moments between Clarissa and Sally as queer moments that 'disrupt the common distinctions between adolescence and adulthood' (144). Because the adult and the child exist simultaneously in Clarissa's mind, it becomes difficult to subscribe to Abel's developmental reading of the novel.

In developing this argument, Haffey turns to a sentence that has been almost entirely neglected in studies of the novel. It comes as Clarissa reflects, alone, on Septimus's suicide:

■ No pleasure could equal, she thought, straightening the chairs, pushing in one book on the shelf, this having done with the triumphs of youth, lost herself in the process of living, to find it, with a shock of delight, as the sun rose, as the day sank. (*MD* 157) □

Haffey comments:

■ This sentence is often read as establishing that 'no pleasure could equal ... this having done with the triumphs of youth' – that Clarissa takes the greatest pleasure in knowing that here youth is over with. While this reading seems to account for the first half of the sentence, it doesn't seem to deal with the second half. The second half of the sentence is perhaps more complex than the first. In particular, the phrase 'to find it' seems difficult to connect to the rest of the sentence. What exactly does the 'it' refer to? The 'pleasure'? 'The process'? A particular form of happiness? Does it repeat the 'it' of 'it was due to Richard'? Or perhaps there is no clear antecedent to 'it' in this passage. (148)

She goes on to suggest that 'it' might refer back to 'youth': 'Clarissa's pleasure, then, stems from the process of living in which she goes from feeling at one moment that she is done with the triumphs of youth to suddenly and unexpectedly finding her youth in the next moment' (148). She further goes on to suggest that 'it' might be identical to 'the thing' that Septimus had preserved through his suicide, his 'treasure' (*MD* 156). *Mrs Dalloway*, Haffey concludes, is 'not a text about moving from the past into the future, but rather one about the preservation of the past in the present' (149).

The Hours is important because Haffey sees it as 'the most detailed analysis' of the kiss, one offering three 'readings' of it (138); Haffey's language implies that Cunningham's novel can be read as a critical work. She argues that it 'spotlights the earlier novel's focus on moments and takes it in a new direction' (149). She notes the ambiguity of the term 'the hours' in his novel: sometimes it represents an oppressive sense of clock time (derived from a Bergsonian reading of *Mrs Dalloway*'s clocks), but other times the term seems 'synonymous with moments' (150), and is on this aspect that Haffey concentrates.

For Haffey, each of Cunningham's variations on the Clarissa–Sally kiss is 'a reading' that considers its temporality (150). While in *Mrs Dalloway* the kiss and its recurrences 'are able to disrupt developmental narratives', in *The Hours* Cunningham 'examines the way in which these moments represent a particular and perhaps peculiar relation to futurity' (150). In the 'Mrs Brown' strand of The Hours, Laura Brown unexpectedly kisses her friend Kitty on the lips. The kiss breaks their impersonations of conventional heterosexual housewives, taking them 'outside of the narratives that script their actions on a daily basis' (151). The novel also shows the women attempting to explain the kiss, recuperating it into a conventional narrative. In the 'Mrs Dalloway' strand of the novel, Clarissa Vaughan is, like her Woolfian namesake, haunted by a kiss in her past, but it was one with Richard, her gay friend:

> ■ For Clarissa, it is this kiss that is transgressive and not her relationship with Sally. By switching the gender of these characters, Cunningham is able to more clearly delineate the significance of the kiss. These moments hold such power not because they are same-sex kisses (indeed, one is not) but because they exist outside an imaginable, scripted future. (152) □

A novel can perform analytical work on another novel, Haffey implies, by altering variables in the original story in order to see – or at least to ask – what difference they would make.

The third reworking of the kiss comes in the 'Mrs Woolf' strand of the novel, when Virginia kisses her sister Vanessa. Haffey focuses particularly on the language of innocence that surrounds it: 'It is an innocent kiss, innocent enough, but just now in this kitchen, behind Nelly's back, it feels like the most delicious and forbidden of pleasures' (*Hours* 154); later Virginia thinks of it as 'not quite innocent' (*Hours* 210). By associating the kiss both with childhood innocence and with its other, Cunningham creates 'a strange temporality that crosses the division between childhood and adulthood' (156). More importantly for Haffey, Cunningham also 'highlights the difference between moments and narratives. The kiss is not about anything else but what it is like to experience a moment' (156). Like the other kisses in *The Hours*, this one

■ partakes of the feeling that 'anything might happen' [*Hours* 210]. It allows Virginia to experience a moment, to not know what the future holds, to step out of narrative and its conventions. It does not move the plot forward towards closure, climax or conclusion but allows for the pleasure of a pause in action. (157) □

In Cunningham's imagining of the composition of *Mrs Dalloway*, Woolf 'preserves this moment in a different kind of narrative, one that keeps alive the connection between past and present and allows this queer moment to continue' (158).

Haffey concludes by considering Arnold Bennett's criticism of *Mrs Dalloway*: that although it contained 'brief passages' which were 'so exquisitely done that nothing could be done better', the real test of quality in a novel was 'sustained power' (Bennett, quoted 158). Haffey presents Bennett as an advocate of traditional narrative temporality, and Woolf and Cunningham as innovators. The reason Woolf and Cunningham focus on the kiss is that, in conventional romantic narrative,

■ The moment of the kiss is the moment in which a relationship takes a sexual turn. It is a beginning of something that is yet unknown. Within the framework of presumptive heterosexuality, this future is often pre-imagined: courtship, marriage, reproduction, etc. (159) □

But in *Mrs Dalloway* and *The Hours*, 'the kiss is explored as a kiss rather than as a stop along the way to sex' (159).

Haffey's analysis of *Mrs Dalloway* is insightful and original, but one might ask whether Cunningham's novel is essential to it. Unlike more sceptical readers of Cunningham, Haffey is more interested in the qualities of *Mrs Dalloway* that are revealed by *The Hours* and its implicit analysis than in the qualities that are revealed by the differences between the two novels. Although Schiff's remark about 'mass-produced' kisses is a crude criticism, it is worth asking whether the multiplication of kisses in *The Hours*, the very thing that enables Cunningham's narrative to be treated as an analysis, also diminishes the effect that Woolf creates from the singularity of Clarissa and Sally's moment.

Although critical interest to date has largely focused on *The Hours*, Schiff's suggestion that *Mrs Dalloway* has achieved the same degree of familiarity and prominence as *Hamlet* or *The Odyssey* implies that it is open to other reworkings which will in turns illuminate the particular qualities of the original. Monica Latham has discussed Rachel Cusk's *Arlington Park* (2006) in relation to *Mrs Dalloway*, and Jem Poster has more briefly called attention to similarities between Woolf's novel and Gail Jones's *Five Bells* (2011), a novel set in contemporary Sydney.[6] At the time of writing there have been no sustained explorations of the connection between *Five Bells* and *Mrs Dalloway*, but the questions for the critic interested in *Mrs Dalloway* are similar to those in this chapter: in what ways does the novel (and criticism about it) offer *critical* insights into its source text? In what ways does the novel *differ* from the source, and what does that tell us about Woolf's themes, her mode of writing, and its relation to her context?

CONCLUSION

In the ninety years since it was published, critical conceptions of how to approach *Mrs Dalloway* have been in constant flux. Many factors have coincided to bring about change. The broadest change, from an interest in Woolf as an experimental novelist aloof from worldly concerns to an interest in her as a politically motivated writer engaged with the immediately contemporary, partly parallels a wider change in the self-conception of literary criticism, as it moved from the formalist outlook of the New Criticism and similar schools to the politically aware outlooks of Marxism, feminism and post-colonialism. Within that broad change there have been other currents and counter-currents: for example, questions about how far the critic should make use of biographical and autobiographical materials; or about how far the critic should make use of non-literary texts when discussing context, and what might count as 'literary' or 'non-literary'. Some of the changes may be traced to the changing demographics of the university student body: around 1950, literary criticism very often silently embodied the assumptions and outlook of a white male middle-class group; the rising representation of women in higher education – at first, mostly white middle-class women – foregrounded questions of gender. Others, such as the emergence of sexuality as an area of critical discourse, derive from changing social attitudes.

Other changes are due to factors more specifically related to Woolf studies. In 1960, though modernist literature had become academically respectable, it was understood along lines that placed T. S. Eliot as critic and poet at the centre of the canon, with James Joyce's *Ulysses* understood as one of the major texts. Woolf and her works were accepted in so far as they conformed to those standards. Part of the struggle to win acceptance for Virginia Woolf and her works was a struggle to change the terms on which the modernist canon was understood. The rise of feminist literary criticism made that change possible.

Perceptions and critical agendas have also changed with the publication of biographies and autobiographical materials. The publication of *A Writer's Diary* (1953) provided some autobiographical materials, but these were mostly focused on Woolf's life as a writer. More material appeared in Leonard Woolf's autobiography (1964–69) and Quentin Bell's biography of Virginia Woolf (1972), but the situation changed more fundamentally with the publication of Woolf's letters, diaries and memoirs. As we have seen at several points in the present work, these primary texts enabled critics to challenge the accounts in Leonard's autobiography and Bell's biography, and enabled a deeper understanding of Woolf and of *Mrs Dalloway* from a phenomenological point of view (notably in Poole's and Hussey's work) and a range of psychoanalytic perspectives. The diaries and letters indirectly contributed to historicist work, by providing solid evidence of Woolf's awareness of contemporary events. The rise of historicist criticism has altered ideas of what the editor of an annotated edition might validly comment on.

Although it is possible that new information about Woolf's life may emerge in the future, or that new texts may be unearthed, it is unlikely that anything on the scale of the published diaries, letters and memoirs will appear. Recent years have seen the discovery of a small group of unpublished essays (*Carlyle's House and Other Sketches* [2003], ed. David Bradshaw), the editing and publication of the juvenile *Hyde Park Gate News* (2005), written by Woolf and her siblings, and the publication of Woolf's photographs (*Snapshots of Bloomsbury* [2006], ed. Maggie Humm); S. P. Rosenbaum edited what survives of the Bloomsbury Memoir Club papers, supplementing and contextualizing the already-published papers by Woolf (2014). Most recently, Clara Jones has discovered an unpublished sketch by Woolf of a cook (2014). The *Virginia Woolf Bulletin* has published previously unknown letters by Woolf in every issue since its inception in 1999. But these works are drops in the ocean compared to the materials that appeared between 1975 (when the first volume of letters appeared) and 1984 (when the last volume of diaries was published). Practically speaking, the most major advance in documentation has come with the appearance of the final two volumes of the *Essays of Virginia Woolf*, edited by Stuart N. Clarke (2009 and 2011), making available some previously unpublished material, and gathering other essays conveniently together.

Future directions in relation to *Mrs Dalloway* seem likely to come from new critical agendas within the field of literary criticism. The most obvious comes with the further development of post-colonial criticism and the emergence of critical interests in modernism as a transnational phenomenon.[1] Valerie Reed Hickman has recently considered what the transnational paradigm means for Woolf studies and for feminism, using *Mrs Dalloway* as her focus.[2] Transnational criticism of modernism is often comparativist, juxtaposing canonical European modernist texts with texts written outside Europe in what Susan Stanford Friedman has called 'cultural parataxis';[3] exactly what might happen to *Mrs Dalloway* will depend on which comparisons gain critical traction. On a different spatial scale, as noted at the end of Chapter Seven, urban space continues to be a productive area of study in relation to *Mrs Dalloway*. There has been growing interest in Woolf and the non-human, within the frames both of ecocriticism and animal studies. Christina Alt's *Virginia Woolf and the Study of Nature* (2010) is relevant here, while Bonnie Kime Scott's *In the Hollow of the Wave* (2012) is more directly ecocritical in conception; articles have appeared on the non-human in *Between the Acts* and in Woolf's shorter fiction.[4] Approaches to *Mrs Dalloway* from ecocritical and animal-studies perspectives have been made by Vicki Tromanhauser, Sara Dunlap and Justyna Kostkowska.[5]

The concern for the otherness of the non-human found in ecocriticism is echoed in ethical approaches to Woolf's work, part of a larger 'ethical turn' in criticism. The origins of the ethical turn in Woolf studies could be traced to the special Woolf issue of *Modern Fiction Studies* in 2004: Laura Doyle, in her Introduction, framed the contents as having an ethical focus, and Jessica Berman's article explicitly theorized the ethical with reference to French theorists Emmanuel Levinas (1906–1995) and Gilles Deleuze (1925–1995).[6] However, Lorraine Sim, in her critical survey, notes a range of other influences, including discussions that seek to relate Woolf's ethics to work of G. E. Moore.[7]

The juxtapositional practices of transnational criticism suggest another means by which perceptions of *Mrs Dalloway* might change in time. Elizabeth Covington's 2013 article on Storm Jameson's *A Day Off* (1933) as class-conscious critique of Woolf's novel suggests that if the canon were altered, readers might begin to foreground different aspects of *Mrs Dalloway*.[8] Another single-day novel, Mulk Raj Anand's *Untouchable* (1935), is frequently mentioned as an interlocutor.[9] Similarly, our understanding of *Mrs Dalloway* could be transformed by new creative adaptations and remediations. As I have argued elsewhere, Marleen Gorris's film of the novel is formally conservative, and fails to find any filmic equivalent for the novel's free indirect discourse or its rapid transitions of point of view.[10] A new adaptation by a more adventurous director (and studio) might foreground elements of the text that had previously been neglected. More probably, we may learn more about *Mrs Dalloway* from further literary adaptations.

Woolf recognized that innovative works of literature often appeared to lay the emphasis 'on such unexpected places' that they appeared to have no emphasis at all (*E3* 35). As literary cultures have assimilated *Mrs Dalloway* and the modernist novel, some of the 'shapes of things' in its crepuscular space have become familiar and recognizable. But it is a sign of its richness as a text that interpretations have not become fixed or settled. The shapes continue to shift; there are always new themes, new ideas and new emotions to emphasize.

Notes

INTRODUCTION

1. For a full history of the composition and publication of the novel, see A. E. Fernald, 'Introduction', in *Mrs. Dalloway*, ed. A. E. Fernald (Cambridge: Cambridge University Press, 2015), pp. xli–lxxxi.
2. T. S. Eliot, *The Use of Poetry and the Use of Criticism* (London: Faber, 1933), p. 130.
3. J. Bennett, *Virginia Woolf: Her Art as a Novelist* (1945; Cambridge: Cambridge University Press, 1964), p. 99.
4. F. W. Bradbrook, 'Virginia Woolf: The Theory and Practice of Fiction', in *The Modern Age*, ed. B. Ford (London: Pelican, 1961), p. 265.

1 EARLY RESPONSES

1. Anon., 'A Long, Long Chapter', in *Virginia Woolf: Critical Assessments*, ed. E. McNees, 4 vols (Mountfield: Helm Information, 1994), vol. 3, p. 265.
2. S. Lynd, 'Town and Country', *Time and Tide*, 6.20 (15 May 1925), p. 472.
3. S. Lynd, 'Town and Country', p. 472. For Leonard Bast's reference to Stevenson, see E. M. Forster, *Howards End* (1910), ch. 14.
4. R. Hughes, 'A Day in London Life', in *Virginia Woolf: The Critical Heritage*, ed. R. Majumdar and A. McLaurin (London: Routledge & Kegan Paul, 1975), pp. 159–60.
5. Anon., 'A Novelist's Experiment', in *Critical Heritage*, p. 162. The *TLS* review was published anonymously, but the authorship may be determined with reference to the online *Times Centenary Archive*.
6. P. C. Kennedy, 'New Novels', in *Critical Heritage*, p. 166.
7. J. W. Krutch, 'The Stream of Consciousness', in *Critical Assessments*, vol. 3, p. 273.
8. N. Royde-Smith, 'Mrs Woolf's New Novel', in *Critical Assessments*, vol. 3, p. 271.
9. N. Royde-Smith, 'Mrs Woolf's New Novel', p. 272.
10. G. Raverat, letter to V. Woolf, 22 April 1925, *Virginia Woolf & the Raverats: A Different Sort of Friendship*, ed. W. Pryor (Bath: Clear Books, 2003), p. 174.
11. H. McAfee, 'Some Novelists in Mid-Stream', *Yale Review*, 15.2 (January 1926), p. 340.
12. P. C. Kennedy, 'New Novels', in *Critical Heritage*, p. 165. I have corrected 'in' to 'is'.
13. R. Hughes, 'A Day in London Life', in *Critical Heritage*, p. 159.
14. Anon, 'A Novelist's Experiment', in *Critical Heritage*, p. 160.
15. H. Bergson, *Creative Evolution*, trans. A. Mitchell (London: Macmillan, 1911), p. 54.
16. J. W. Krutch, 'The Stream of Consciousness', in *Critical Assessments*, p. 274.
17. M. Sinclair, 'The Novels of Dorothy Richardson', *The Egoist* 5 (April 1918), p. 59.
18. G. M. Turnell, 'The Novels of Virginia Woolf', *Cambridge Review*, 50 (19 October 1928), p. 29.
19. Ibid., p. 30.
20. A. Bennett, 'Is the Novel Decaying?', *Critical Heritage*, p. 113.
21. M. Turnell, *The Novel in France* (London: Hamish Hamilton, 1950), p. 324.
22. Woolf, quoted by W. Lewis, *Men Without Art* (1934; Santa Rosa, CA: Black Sparrow, 1987), p. 136.
23. W. Lewis, *Men Without Art*, p. 137.

24. W. Lewis, *Men Without Art*, p. 138.
25. W. Lewis, *Men Without Art*, p. 139.
26. W. Lewis, *Men Without Art*, p. 139.
27. For fuller accounts of Leavis and *Scrutiny*, see R. Storer, *F. R. Leavis* (Abingdon: Routledge, 2009) and C. Hilliard, *English as a Vocation: The Scrutiny Movement* (Oxford: Oxford University Press, 2012).
28. M. C. Bradbrook, 'Notes on the Style of Mrs Woolf', *Scrutiny* 1.1 (May 1932), p. 33.
29. D. Lodge, 'Lawrence, Dostoevsky, Bakhtin: D. H. Lawrence and Dialogic Fiction', *Renaissance and Modern Studies* 29 (1985), pp. 16–32, has been particularly influential.
30. M. C. Bradbrook, 'Notes', pp. 33–4.
31. M. C. Bradbrook, 'Notes', p. 34.
32. W. H. Mellers, 'Mrs Woolf and Life', *Scrutiny* 7.1 (June 1937), p. 71.
33. W. H. Mellers, 'Mrs Woolf and Life', p. 71.
34. F. R. Leavis, 'After *To the Lighthouse*', *Scrutiny* 10.3 (January 1942), p. 297.
35. F. R. Leavis, 'After *To the Lighthouse*', p. 297.
36. Ibid.
37. F. R. Leavis, 'After *To the Lighthouse*', p. 298.
38. Q. D. Leavis, 'Caterpillars of the Commonwealth Unite!' *Scrutiny* 7 (September 1938), pp. 203–14.
39. W. Holtby, *Virginia Woolf* (London: Wishart, 1932), p. 140.
40. W. Holtby, *Virginia Woolf*, p. 143.
41. W. Holtby, *Virginia Woolf*, p. 153.
42. F. Delattre, *Le Roman psychologique de Virginia Woolf* (Paris: Librairie Philosophique J. Vrin, 1932).
43. R. Gruber, *Virginia Woolf: A Study* (Leipzig: Bernhard Tauchnitz, 1935), p. 1. A later edition of the book, *Virginia Woolf: The Will to Create as a Woman* (New York: Carroll & Graf, 2005), comes with an extensive introduction telling the story of how Gruber came to write the thesis, and of her subsequent meeting with Woolf; the 2005 edition preserves the pagination of the 1935 text.
44. J. Bennett, *Virginia Woolf* (Cambridge: Cambridge University Press, 1945), p. vii.
45. G. E. Moore, *Principia Ethica* (Cambridge: Cambridge University Press, 1903), p. 188.
46. Bennett quotes Woolf's 'The Novels of George Meredith', *E*5, p. 550.
47. B. Blackstone, *Virginia Woolf: A Commentary* (London: Hogarth, 1949).
48. J. Guiguet, *Virginia Woolf and Her Works*, trans. J. Stewart (London: Hogarth, 1965), p. 21.
49. W. K. Wimsatt and M. C. Beardsley, 'The Intentional Fallacy', *Sewanee Review* 54.3 (1946), pp. 468–88.
50. R. Brower, *The Fields of Light: An Experiment in Critical Reading* (New York: Oxford University Press, 1951).
51. W. K. Wimsatt and M. Beardsley, 'The Affective Fallacy', *Sewanee Review* 57. 1 (1949), pp. 31–55.
52. A. Fleishman, *Virginia Woolf: A Critical Reading* (Baltimore, MD: Johns Hopkins University Press, 1975).
53. M. Eliade, *The Myth of the Eternal Return*, trans. W. R. Trask (New York: Pantheon, 1954); M. L. Lord, 'Withdrawal and Return: An Epic Story Pattern in the Homeric Hymn to Demeter and in the Homeric Poems', *Classical Journal* 62.6 (1967), pp. 241–8.

2 RECOVERING WOOLF: CRITICISM IN THE ERA OF SECOND-WAVE FEMINISM

1. M. Holroyd, *Lytton Strachey* (London: Heinemann, 1967), pp. 399–400.
2. E. M. Forster, *Virginia Woolf* (Cambridge: Cambridge University Press, 1941).
3. M. Holroyd, *Lytton Strachey*, pp. 400–1, p. 403.

4. L. Woolf, *Downhill All the Way: An Autobiography of the Years 1919–1939* (London: Hogarth, 1967), p. 27.
5. Q. Bell, *Virginia Woolf*, 2 vols (London: Hogarth, 1972), vol. ii, p. 161.
6. Q. Bell, *Virginia Woolf*, vol. ii, p. 187.
7. Q. Bell, *Virginia Woolf*, vol. ii, p. 186.
8. Q. Bell, *Virginia Woolf*, vol. ii, p. 186.
9. P. Parrinder, 'The Strange Necessity', in *James Joyce: New Perspectives*, ed. C. MacCabe (Brighton: Harvester, 1982), p. 160.
10. H. Kenner, *A Sinking Island* (London : Barrie & Jenkins, 1988), p. 176.
11. J. Marcus, 'Lycanthropy: Woolf Studies Now', *Tulsa Studies in Women's Literature* 8.1 (1989), p. 102.
12. C. Heilbrun, *Hamlet's Mother and Other Women* (New York: Columbia University Press, 1990), pp. 58–77; see S. M. Gilbert, 'Woman's Sentence, Man's Sentencing', in *Virginia Woolf and Bloomsbury*, ed. J. Marcus (Basingstoke: Macmillan, 1987), pp. 208–24.
13. H. Richter, 'The *Ulysses* Connection: Clarissa Dalloway's Bloomsday', *Studies in the Novel* 21.3 (1989), pp. 305–19.
14. Condensed from H. Richter, 'The *Ulysses* Connection', p. 307.
15. Though the phrase has an obvious precedent in Forster's *Howards End*, it does not appear in *Mrs Dalloway*.
16. The text in *A Writer's Diary* differs in small details.
17. R. Samuelson, 'The Theme of Mrs Dalloway', *Chicago Review* 11.4 (1958), pp. 57–76.
18. H. Marder, *Feminism and Art: A Study of Virginia Woolf* (Chicago and London: University of Chicago Press, 1968).
19. The term 'second-wave' dates from 1968: see N. A. Hewitt, Introduction, in *No Permanent Waves: Recasting Histories of U. S. Feminism*, ed. N. A. Hewitt (New Brunswick, NJ: Rutgers University Press, 2010), p. 1.
20. B. R. Silver, 'The Authority of Anger: "Three Guineas" as Case Study', *Signs* 16 (1991), pp. 340–70 (pp. 356–7).
21. V. Woolf, *The Voyage Out* (1915), ed. Lorna Sage (Oxford: Oxford University Press, 1992), p. 291.
22. J. Marcus, *Art and Anger: Reading Like a Woman* (Columbus: Ohio State University Press, 1988).
23. L. R. Edwards, 'War and Roses: The Politics of *Mrs Dalloway*', in *The Authority of Experience: Essays in Feminist Criticism*, ed. A. Diamond and L. R. Edwards (Amherst: University of Massachusetts Press, 1977), pp. 160–77.
24. J. O. Love, *Worlds in Consciousness: Mythopoetic Thought in the Novels of Virginia Woolf* (Berkeley: University of California Press,1970), p. 151.
25. A. Fleishman, *Virginia Woolf* (1975), p. 80.
26. See, e.g., M. Rosenthal, *Virginia Woolf* (London : Routledge & Kegan Paul, 1979), p. 36.

3 WOOLF AND PHILOSOPHY

1. E. M. Forster, in *Virginia Woolf: The Critical Heritage*, ed. R. Majumdar and A. McLaurin (1975), p. 69.
2. P. C. Kennedy, 'New Novels', in *Critical Heritage*, p. 166.
3. G. Bullett, in *Critical Heritage*, p. 164.
4. R. Hughes, in *Critical Heritage*, p. 159.
5. Garnett, in *Critical Heritage*, p. 384.
6. Garnett, in *Critical Heritage*, p. 384.
7. B. G. Brooks, in *Critical Heritage*, p. 453.
8. J. H. Roberts, '"Vision and Design" in Virginia Woolf', *PMLA* 61 (1946), pp. 835–47.
9. A. Benjamin, 'Towards an Understanding of the Meaning of Virginia Woolf's *Mrs Dalloway*', *Wisconsin Studies in Contemporary Literature* 6.2 (1965), pp. 214–27.

10. A. N. Whitehead, *Science and the Modern World* (1925; Cambridge: Cambridge University Press, 1926), pp. 61–5.
11. H. Richter, *Virginia Woolf: The Inward Voyage* (Princeton, NJ: Princeton University Press, 1970), p. xi.
12. In making these claims, Richter cites J.K. Johnstone, *The Bloomsbury Group* (1954), pp. 32–8, 54–9 and L. Woolf's *Sowing: An Autobiography of the Years 1880 to 1904* (1960), pp. 146–7.
13. S. K. Kumar, *Bergson and the Stream of Consciousness Novel* (London and Glasgow: Blackie, 1962), pp. 74–6.
14. Kumar gives a fuller account, pp. 64–7, and in his notes on p. 153.
15. M. A. Gillies, *Henri Bergson and British Modernism* (Montreal: McGill-Queen's University Press, 1996).
16. M. Inwood, *Heidegger* (Oxford : Oxford University Press 1997), p. 62.
17. S. K. Kent, *Making Peace: The Reconstruction of Gender in Interwar Britain* (Princeton: Princeton University Press, 1993).
18. L. Ruotolo, *Six Existential Heroes: The Politics of Faith* (Cambridge, MA: Harvard University Press, 1973).
19. M. Heidegger, *Existence and Being* (London: Vision, 1949) pp. 365–6.
20. J. Naremore, *The World Without a Self: Virginia Woolf and the Novel* (New Haven, CT: Yale University Press, 1973).
21. R. Poole, *The Unknown Virginia Woolf* (Cambridge: Cambridge University Press, 1978); M. Hussey, *The Singing of the Real World: The Philosophy of Virginia Woolf's Fiction* (Columbus: Ohio State University Press, 1986).
22. By my count 'he could not feel' occurs six times (*MD* 74–5); 'he did not feel' follows shortly afterwards (*MD* 77).
23. F. Kermode, *The Uses of Error* (London: HarperCollins, 1991), pp. 280– 2; M. Spilka, 'New Life in the Works: Some Recent Woolf Studies', *NOVEL: A Forum on Fiction*, 12.2 (1979), pp. 169–84; H. Lee [review of Poole], *Review of English Studies*, ns 31, (1980), pp. 103–6.

4 STRUCTURALISM AND POST-STRUCTURALISM

1. J. Culler, *Literary Theory: A Very Short Introduction* (Oxford: Oxford University Press, 1997), pp. 63–4.
2. The pioneering English-language work is J. D. Culler's *Structuralist Poetics: Structuralism, Linguistics and the Study of Literature* (London: Routledge & Kegan Paul, 1975). For a fuller introduction, see R. D. Parker, *How to Interpret Literature*, 3rd edn (Oxford: Oxford University Press, 2014), ch. 3.
3. The classic work is Vladimir Propp's *Morphology of the Folktale* (1928; translated 1968).
4. R. Jakobson, 'Two Aspects of Language and Two Types of Aphasic Disturbances', in *Fundamentals of Language* by R. Jakobson and M. Halle (1956).
5. D. Lodge, *The Modes of Modern Writing : Metaphor, Metonymy, and the Typology of Modern Literature* (London : Edward Arnold, 1977).
6. Lodge's quotation comes from C. Woodring, *Virginia Woolf* (New York: Columbia University Press, 1966), p. 19.
7. N. Armstrong, 'A Language of One's Own: Communication-Modeling Systems in *Mrs Dalloway*', *Language and Style: An International Journal* 16.3 (1983), pp. 343–60.
8. Armstrong transliterates Lotman's first name as 'Jurij'.
9. T. L. Ebert, 'Metaphor, Metonymy, and Ideology: Language and Perception in *Mrs Dalloway*', *Language and Style: An International Journal* 18.2 (1985), pp. 152–64.
10. E. Bishop, 'Writing, Speech, and Silence in *Mrs Dalloway*', *English Studies in Canada* 12.4 (1986), pp. 397–423.
11. J. Derrida, 'Interview: Jacques Derrida', with G. Scarpetta and J.L. Houdebine, *Diacritics* 2.4 (1972), p. 38.

12. H. Marder, 'Split Perspective: Types of Incongruity in *Mrs Dalloway*', *Papers on Language and Literature* 22.1 (1986), pp. 51–69.
13. P. L. Caughie, *Virginia Woolf and Postmodernism: Literature in Quest and Question of Itself* (Urbana and Chicago: University of Illinois Press, 1991).
14. G. Doherty, 'Life Styles and Death Sentences: The Dying Art of *Mrs Dalloway*', in *Afterwords*, ed. Nicholas Royle (Tampere: Outside Books, 1992), pp. 134–59.
15. E. Dalgarno, *Virginia Woolf and the Visible World* (Cambridge: Cambridge University Press, 2001), p. 71.

5 WOOLF AND PSYCHOANALYSIS

1. E. R. Steinberg, 'Freudian Symbolism and Communication', *Literature and Psychology* 3.2 (1953), pp. 2–5; F. Wyatt, 'Some Comments on the Use of Symbols in the Novel', *Literature and Psychology* 4.2 (1954), pp. 15–23; Steinberg, 'Note on a Novelist too Quickly Freudened', *Literature and Psychology* 4.2 (1954), pp. 23–6; Steinberg, 'Note on a Note', *Literature and Psychology* 4.4 (1954), pp. 64–5.
2. V. Woolf, letter dated 7 December 1931, quoted by R. Hoops, *Der Einfluß der Psychoanalyse auf die englische Literatur* (Anglistische Forschungen, Heft 77) (Heidelberg, 1934), p. 147, n. 2; L. Woolf, quoted by Steinberg, 'Note on a Note', p. 64.
3. K. Hollingsworth, 'Freud and the Riddle of *Mrs Dalloway*', in *Studies in Honor of John Wilcox*, ed. A. D. Wallace and W. O. Ross (Detroit: Wayne State University Press, 1958), pp. 239–50; A. Page, 'A Dangerous Day: Mrs Dalloway Discovers Her Double', *Modern Fiction Studies* 7 (1961), pp. 115–24.
4. B. A. Schlack, 'A Freudian Look at *Mrs Dalloway*', *Literature and Psychology* 23 (1973), pp. 49–58.
5. M. Spilka, *Virginia Woolf's Quarrel with Grieving* (Lincoln: University of Nebraska Press, 1980).
6. S. Henke, 'Virginia Woolf's Septimus Smith: An Analysis of "Paraphrenic" and the Schizophrenic Use of Language', *Literature and Psychology* 31.4 (1981), pp. 13–23.
7. See, e.g., E. M. Forster, *Maurice* (written c.1913, published 1971), ch. 41.
8. T. Moi, *Sexual/Textual Politics: Feminist Literary Theory* (London: Methuen, 1985), p. 162.
9. E. Abel, 'Narrative Structure(s) and Female Development: The Case of *Mrs Dalloway*', in *The Voyage In: Fictions of Female Development*, ed. E. Abel, M. Hirsch and E. Langland (Hanover, NH and London: University Press of New England, 1983), pp. 161–85.
10. For 'companionship' Abel has 'comradeship'.
11. J. Wyatt, 'Avoiding Self-Definition: In Defense of Women's Right to Merge (Julia Kristeva and *Mrs Dalloway*)', *Women's Studies* 13.1–2 (1986), pp. 115–26.
12. M. Minow-Pinkney, *Virginia Woolf and the Problem of the Subject* (Brighton: Harvester, 1987).
13. J. Little, *The Experimental Self* (Carbondale: Southern Illinois University Press, 1996), pp. 47–8.
14. T. Tate, '*Mrs Dalloway* and the Armenian Question', *Textual Practice* 8.3 (1994), pp. 479–80.
15. V. Woolf, *Moments of Being*, ed. J. Schulkind (London: Pimlico, 2002), p. 93.
16. J. Mepham, 'Mourning and Modernism', in *Virginia Woolf: New Critical Essays*, ed. P. Clements and I. Grundy (London: Vision, 1983), pp. 137–56.
17. S. B. Smith, 'Reinventing Grief Work: Virginia Woolf's Feminist Representations of Mourning in *Mrs Dalloway* and *To The Lighthouse*', *Twentieth Century Literature* 41.4 (1995), pp. 310–27.
18. C. Froula, '*Mrs Dalloway*'s Postwar Elegy: Women, War, and the Art of Mourning', *Modernism/Modernity* 9.1 (2002), pp. 125–63.
19. On unanimism, see A. McLaurin 'Virginia Woolf and Unanimism', *Journal of Modern Literature* 9.1 (1981–2), pp. 115–22, and 'Consciousness and Group Consciousness in

Virginia Woolf', in *Virginia Woolf: A Centenary Perspective*, ed. E. Warner (Basingstoke: Macmillan, 1984), pp. 28–40.
20. D. Eberly and S. Henke, 'Introduction', in *Virginia Woolf and Trauma: Embodied Texts*, ed. S. Henke and D. Eberly (New York: Pace University Press, 2007), p. 5.
21. M. Briggs, 'Veterans and Civilians: Traumatic Knowledge and Cultural Appropriation in *Mrs Dalloway*', in *Virginia Woolf and Communities: Selected Papers from the Eighth Annual Conference on Virginia Woolf*, ed. J. McVicker and L. Davis (New York: Pace University Press, 1999), pp. 43–9.
22. K. DeMeester, 'Trauma and Recovery in Virginia Woolf's *Mrs Dalloway*', *MFS: Modern Fiction Studies* 44.3 (1998), pp. 649–73.

6 SEXUALITY AND THE BODY

1. A. Lorde, 'The Erotic as Power' (paper delivered in 1978, published 1979), in *The Audre Lorde Compendium* (London: Pandora, 1996), pp. 106–12; B. W. Cook, '"Women Alone Stir My Imagination": Lesbianism and the Cultural Tradition', *Signs* 4 (1979), pp. 718–39.
2. A. Rich, 'Compulsory Heterosexuality and Lesbian Existence', *Signs* 5.4 (1980), pp. 631–60.
3. E. H. Rogat, 'The Virgin in the Bell Biography', *Twentieth Century Literature* 20 (1974), pp. 96–113; J. Marcus, 'Quentin's Bogey', *Critical Inquiry* 2.3 (1985), pp. 486–97.
4. E. Jensen, 'Clarissa Dalloway's Respectable Suicide', in *Virginia Woolf: A Feminist Slant*, ed. J. Marcus (Lincoln: University of Nebraska Press, 1983), pp. 162–79.
5. S. Henke, '*Mrs Dalloway*: The Communion of Saints', in *New Feminist Essays on Virginia Woolf*, ed. J. Marcus (Lincoln: University of Nebraska Press, 1981), p. 136.
6. S. Henke, '*Mrs Dalloway*: The Communion of Saints', p. 137.
7. Jensen, p. 174.
8. G. E. Lyon, 'Virginia Woolf and the Problem of the Body', in *Virginia Woolf: Centennial Essays*, ed. E. K. Ginsberg and L. M. Gottlieb (Troy, NY: Whitston, 1983), pp. 111–25.
9. T. Fulker, 'Virginia Woolf's Daily Drama of the Body', *Woolf Studies Annual* 1 (1995), pp. 3–25.
10. W. Greenslade, *Degeneration, Culture and the Novel, 1880–1940* (Cambridge: Cambridge University Press, 1994).
11. P. Cramer, 'Notes from Underground: Lesbian Ritual in the Writings of Virginia Woolf', in *Virginia Woolf Miscellanies: Proceedings of the First Annual Conference on Virginia Woolf*, ed. M. Hussey and V. Neverow-Turk (New York: Pace University, 1992), pp. 177–88 (p. 177).
12. E. Barrett, 'Unmasking Lesbian Passion: The Inverted World of *Mrs Dalloway*', *Virginia Woolf: Lesbian Readings*, ed. E. Barrett and P. Cramer (New York: New York University Press, 1997), pp. 146–64.
13. S. S. Park, '"Doing Justice to the Real Girl": The Women Writers' Suffrage League', in *A Suffrage Reader: Charting Directions in British Suffrage History*, ed. C. Eustace, J. Ryan and L. Ugolini (London: Leicester University Press, 2000), pp. 90–104.

7 HISTORICIST APPROACHES

1. A. Zwerdling, '*Mrs Dalloway* and the Social System', *PMLA* 92 (1977), pp. 69–82.
2. Zwerdling notes that the remark about 'the social system' had been discussed by Samuelson in 'The Theme of *Mrs Dalloway*' and by A. D. Moody in 'The Unmasking of Clarissa Dalloway', *Review of English Literature* 3.1 (1962), pp. 67–79, but he had not encountered the work of Blanchard and Rachman: M. Blanchard, 'Socialization in *Mrs Dalloway*', *College English* 34.2 (1972), pp. 287–305; S. Rachman, 'Clarissa's Attic: Virginia Woolf's *Mrs. Dalloway* Reconsidered', *Twentieth Century Literature: A Scholarly and Critical Journal* 18.1 (1972), pp. 3–18.
3. R. Pearce, 'Virginia Woolf's Reality', *Novel: A Forum on Fiction* 21 (1987), p. 93.

4. J. Tambling, 'Repression in *Mrs Dalloway*', *Essays in Criticism* 39 (1989), pp. 137–55.
5. L. Althusser, 'Ideology and Ideological State Apparatuses', in *Lenin and Philosophy, and Other Essays*, trans. B. Brewster (London: New Left Books, 1971), p. 158.
6. B. Blackstone, *Virginia Woolf* (London: Hogarth, 1949), p. 98.
7. L. Woolf, *Beginning Again*, pp. 77, 164; Q. Bell, *Virginia Woolf*, vol. i, p. 90. H. Lee reviews this evidence in *Virginia Woolf* (1996), pp. 195–6.
8. M. C. Burroughs, 'Septimus Smith: A Man of Many Words', *University of Windsor Review* 22.1 (1989), pp. 70– 8.
9. K. L. Levenback, 'Virginia Woolf and Returning Soldiers: The Great War and the Reality of Survival in Mrs. Dalloway and The Years', *Woolf Studies Annual* 2 (1996), pp. 71–88. An expanded version of the article, with fuller historical documentation, appears in Levenback's *Virginia Woolf and the Great War* (1999).
10. Woolf, quoted by D. Bradshaw, '"Vanished, Like Leaves": The Military, Elegy and Italy in Mrs. Dalloway', *Woolf Studies Annual* 8 (2002), pp. 107–25 (p. 121).
11. S. Thomas, 'Virginia Woolf's Septimus Smith and Contemporary Perceptions of Shell Shock', *English Language Notes* 25.2 (December 1987), pp. 49–57 (p. 50).
12. Thomas contrasts L. Gordon's *Virginia Woolf: A Writer's Life* (Oxford: Oxford University Press, 1984), p. 65.
13. Bradshaw, 'Vanished, Like Leaves', p. 107.
14. Bradshaw, p. 110, quoting M. E. Howard, *Lord Haldane and the Territorial Army* (1967).
15. M. Usui, 'The Female Victims of the War in *Mrs Dalloway*', in *Virginia Woolf and War: Fiction, Reality, and Myth*, ed. M. Hussey (Syracuse, NY: Syracuse University Press, 1991), pp. 151–63.
16. J. Meyer, '"Not Septimus Now": Wives of Disabled Veterans and Cultural Memory of the First World War in Britain', *Women's History Review* 13.1 (2004), pp. 117–38.
17. T. Tate, '*Mrs Dalloway* and the Armenian Question', *Textual Practice* 8.3 (Winter 1994), pp. 467–86. Another version of the essay appears in Tate's *Modernism, History and the First World War* (Manchester: Manchester University Press, 1998), pp. 147–70.
18. W. Lewis, *Men Without Art*, ed. S. Cooney (Santa Ros, CA: Black Sparrow, 1987), p. 139.
19. Similar criticisms have been made by E. B. Rosenman in *Modern Fiction Studies* 41 (1996), pp. 176–7.
20. The referent of 'Glaxo' was noted by R. Abbott, 'What Miss Kilman's Petticoat Means: Virginia Woolf, Shopping, and Spectacle', *Modern Fiction Studies* 38.1 (1992), p. 202; D. Bradshaw gives more detail in his annotated edition (*MD* 172).
21. D. Brewster, *Virginia Woolf's London* (London: George Allen & Unwin, 1959), p. 11; David Daiches and John Flower, *Literary Landscapes of the British Isles* (New York: Paddington Press, 1979).
22. Abbott, quoting A. Adburgham, *Shopping in Style* (London: Thames & Hudson, 1979), p. 176.
23. L. K. Schröder, '*Mrs Dalloway* and the Female Vagrant', *Essays in Criticism* 45 (1995), pp. 324–46.
24. J. Wolff, 'The Invisible Flâneuse: Women and the Literature of Modernity' (1985), in *The Problems of Modernity: Adorno and Benjamin*, ed. A. Benjamin (London: Routledge, 1989), pp. 141–56; E. Wilson, 'The Invisible *Flâneur*', *New Left Review* 191 (January–February 1992), pp. 90– 110.
25. R. Bowlby, 'Walking, Women, and Writing' (1992), in *Feminist Destinations and Further Essays on Virginia Woolf* (Edinburgh: Edinburgh University Press, 1997), pp. 191–219.
26. B. W. Shaffer, 'Civilization in Bloomsbury: Woolf's *Mrs Dalloway* and Bell's "Theory of Civilization"', *Journal of Modern Literature* 19.1 (1994), pp. 73–87.
27. Shaffer quotes Leon Edel, *Bloomsbury: A House of Lions* (London: Hogarth, 1979), p. 253.
28. E. Graham and P. Lewis, 'Private Religion, Public Mourning, and *Mrs Dalloway*', *Modern Philology* 111.1 (2013), pp. 88–106.

29. Y. Son, *Here and Now: The Politics of Social Space in D.H. Lawrence and Virginia Woolf* (Abingdon: Routledge, 2006), pp. 180– 92; A. Snaith and M. H. Whitworth, 'Introduction: Approaches to Space and Place in Woolf', in *Locating Woolf: The Politics of Space and Place*, ed. A. Snaith and M. H. Whitworth (Basingstoke: Palgrave Macmillan, 2007), pp. 19–23; R. Ingelbien, 'They Saw One They Knew: Baudelaire and the Ghosts of London Modernism', *English Studies: A Journal of English Language and Literature* 88.1 (2007), pp. 43–58; K. Flint, 'Sounds of the City: Virginia Woolf and Modern Noise', in *Literature, Science, Psychoanalysis, 1830– 1970*, ed. H. Small and T. Tate (Oxford: Oxford University Press, 2003), pp. 181–94; A. Frattarola, 'Listening for "Found Sound" Samples in the Novels of Virginia Woolf', *Woolf Studies Annual* 11 (2005), pp. 133–59; A. L. Rounds, 'Dissolves in *Mrs Dalloway*: The Soundscape of a Novel', *Literary Imagination* 13.1 (2011), pp. 58–70.

8 MRS DALLOWAY AND THE HOURS

1. J. Schiff, 'Rewriting Woolf's *Mrs Dalloway*: Homage, Sexual Identity, and the Single-day Novel by Cunningham, Lippincott, and Lanchester', *Critique: Studies in Contemporary Fiction* 45.4 (2004), pp. 363–82.
2. S. Chatman, '*Mrs Dalloway*'s Progeny: *The Hours* as Second-Degree Narrative', in *A Companion to Narrative Theory*, ed. J. Phelan and P. J. Rabinowitz (Malden, MA: Blackwell, 2005), pp. 269–81.
3. M. H. Whitworth, *Virginia Woolf* (Oxford: Oxford University Press, 2005), p. 223.
4. J. Schiff, 'Rewriting Woolf's *Mrs Dalloway*', p. 370.
5. K. Haffey, 'Exquisite Moments and the Temporality of the Kiss in *Mrs Dalloway* and *The Hours*', *Narrative* 18.2 (2010), pp. 137–62.
6. M. Latham, 'Variations on *Mrs. Dalloway*: Rachel Cusk's *Arlington Park*', *Woolf Studies Annual* 19 (2013), pp. 195–213; J. Poster, '*Five Bells* by Gail Jones', *Guardian* (19 March 2011).

CONCLUSION

1. M. Cuddy-Keane, 'Modernism, Geopolitics, Globalization', *Modernism/ Modernity* 10.3 (2003), pp. 539–58; L. Doyle and L. Winkiel, eds, *Geomodernisms* (Bloomington and Indianapolis: Indiana University Press, 2005); S. S. Friedman, 'Periodizing Modernism: Postcolonial Modernities and the Space/Time Borders of Modernist Studies', *Modernism/ Modernity* 13.3 (2006), pp. 425–43; M. A. Wollaeger and M. Eatough, eds, *The Oxford Handbook of Global Modernisms* (New York: Oxford University Press, 2012).
2. V. R. Hickman, 'Clarissa and the Coolies' Wives: *Mrs Dalloway* Figuring Transnational Feminism', *MFS: Modern Fiction Studies* 60.1 (2014), pp. 52–77.
3. J. Berman, *Modernist Fiction, Cosmopolitanism and the Politics of Community* (Cambridge: Cambridge University Press, 2001), p. 4.
4. C. Alt, *Virginia Woolf and the Study of Nature* (Cambridge: Cambridge University Press, 2010); B. K. Scott, *In the Hollow of the Wave: Virginia Woolf and Modernist Uses of Nature* (Charlottesville: University of Virginia Press, 2012); V. Westling, 'Virginia Woolf and the Flesh of the World', *New Literary History* 30.4 (1999), pp. 855–75; D. L. Swanson, 'Woolf's Copernican Shift: Nonhuman Nature in Virginia Woolf's Short Fiction', *Woolf Studies Annual* 18 (2012), pp. 53–74. Scott provides a fuller critical survey.
5. V. Tromanhauser, '*Mrs Dalloway*'s Animals and the Humanist Laboratory', *Twentieth Century Literature* 58.2 (2012), pp. 187–12; S. Dunlap, '"One Must Be Scientific": Natural History and Ecology in *Mrs Dalloway*', *Interdisciplinary / Multidisciplinary*

Woolf: Selected Papers from the Twenty-Second Annual International Conference on Virginia Woolf, ed. A. Martin and K. Holland (Clemson, SC: Clemson University Digital Press, 2013), pp. 127–31; J. Kostkowska, *Ecocriticism and Women Writers* (New York: Palgrave Macmillan, 2013).
6. L. Doyle, 'Introduction: What's Between Us', *MFS: Modern Fiction Studies* 50.1 (2004), pp. 1–7; J. Berman, 'Ethical Folds: Ethics, Aesthetics, Woolf', *MFS: Modern Fiction Studies* 50.1 (2005), pp. 151–72. See also Berman's *Modernist Commitments: Ethics, Politics, and Transnational Modernism* (New York: Columbia University Press, 2011).
7. L. Sim, *Virginia Woolf: The Patterns of Ordinary Experience* (Farnham: Ashgate, 2010), pp. 175–99.
8. E. Covington, 'Splitting the Husk: The Day Novel and Storm Jameson's *A Day Off*', *Genre: Forms of Discourse and Culture* 46.3 (2013), pp. 265–84.
9. A. Snaith, 'The Hogarth Press and Networks of Anti-Colonialism', in *Leonard and Virginia Woolf, The Hogarth Press and the Networks of Modernism*, ed. Helen Southworth (Edinburgh: Edinburgh University Press, 2010); J. Berman, *Modernist Commitments* (2011); J. Berman, 'Neither Mirror Nor Mimic: Transnational Reading and Indian Narratives in English', in *The Oxford Handbook of Global Modernisms*, ed. Wollaeger and Eatough, pp. 205–27.
10. M. H. Whitworth, *Virginia Woolf* (Oxford: Oxford University Press, 2005), pp. 212–17.

Bibliography

EDITIONS
Bradshaw, D., ed. *Mrs Dalloway*. Oxford: Oxford University Press, 2000.
Fernald, A. E., ed. *Mrs Dalloway*. Cambridge: Cambridge University Press, 2015. This promises to be the standard scholarly edition of the novel.
McNichol, S., ed. *Mrs Dalloway*, with an Introduction and Notes by E. Showalter. Penguin, 1992.
Wussow, H., ed. *Virginia Woolf 'The Hours': The British Museum Manuscript of* Mrs. Dalloway. New York: Pace University Press, 1996.

BIOGRAPHICAL
Briggs, J. *Virginia Woolf: An Inner Life*. London: Penguin, 2005. Focuses on Woolf as a writer and on the genesis of her works.
Kenyon-Jones, C., and A. Snaith. 'Tilting at Universities: Virginia Woolf at King's College London'. *Woolf Studies Annual* 16 (2010), 1–44. Corrects the misapprehension that Woolf never attended a university.
Lee, H. *Virginia Woolf*. London: Chatto & Windus, 1996.
Mepham, J. *Virginia Woolf: A Literary Life*. London: Macmillan, 1991. Focuses on Woolf as a professional writer.
Woolf, V. *The Diary of Virginia Woolf*, ed. A. O. Bell, assisted by A. McNeillie, 5 vols. London: Hogarth, 1977–84.

GENERAL
Beer, G. *Virginia Woolf: The Common Ground*. Edinburgh: Edinburgh University Press, 1996.
Bowlby, R. *Feminist Destinations and Further Essays on Virginia Woolf*. Edinburgh: Edinburgh University Press, 1997.
Kirkpatrick, B.J., and S. N. Clarke. *A Bibliography of Virginia Woolf*. 4th edn. Oxford: Oxford University Press, 1997.
Sellers, S, ed. *The Cambridge Companion to Virginia Woolf*. 2nd edn. Cambridge: Cambridge University Press, 2010.
Snaith, A., ed. *Palgrave Advances in Virginia Woolf Studies*. Basingstoke: Palgrave Macmillan, 2007.

CHAPTER ONE: EARLY RESPONSES
Bennett, J. *Virginia Woolf*. Cambridge: Cambridge University Press, 1945.
Blackstone, B. *Virginia Woolf: A Commentary*. London: Hogarth, 1949.
Bradbrook, M. C. 'Notes on the Style of Mrs Woolf'. *Scrutiny* 1.1 (May 1932), 33–8.
Brower, R. *The Fields of Light: An Experiment in Critical Reading*. New York: Oxford University Press, 1951.
Delattre, F. *Le Roman psychologique de Virginia Woolf*. Paris: Librairie Philosophique J. Vrin, 1932.
Fleishman, A. *Virginia Woolf: A Critical Reading*. Baltimore, MD: Johns Hopkins University Press, 1975.
Gruber, R. *Virginia Woolf: The Will to Create as a Woman*. New York: Carroll & Graf, 2005.
Guiguet, J. *Virginia Woolf and Her Works*, trans. J. Stewart. London: Hogarth, 1965.

Holtby, W. *Virginia Woolf*. London: Wishart, 1932.
Leavis, F. R. 'After *To the Lighthouse*', *Scrutiny* 10.3 (January 1942), 295–8.
Leavis, Q. D. 'Caterpillars of the Commonwealth Unite!' *Scrutiny* 7 (September 1938), 203–14.
Lewis, W. *Men Without Art*. 1934; Santa Rosa, CA: Black Sparrow, 1987.
Majumdar, R., and A. McLaurin, eds. *Virginia Woolf: The Critical Heritage*. London: Routledge & Kegan Paul, 1975.
McAfee, H. 'Some Novelists in Mid-Stream', *Yale Review* 15.2 (January 1926), 336–52.
McNees, E., ed. *Virginia Woolf: Critical Assessments*. Mountfield: Helm Information, 1994.
Mellers, W. 'Mrs Woolf and Life'. *Scrutiny* 7.1 (June 1937), 71–5.
Pryor, W., ed. *Virginia Woolf & the Raverats: A Different Sort of Friendship*. Bath: Clear Books, 2003.
Turnell, G. M. 'The Novels of Virginia Woolf'. *Cambridge Review* 50 (19 October 1928), 29.

CHAPTER TWO: RECOVERING WOOLF: CRITICISM IN THE ERA OF SECOND-WAVE FEMINISM

Bazin, N. T. *Virginia Woolf and the Androgynous Vision*. New Brunswick, NJ: Rutgers University Press, 1973.
Edwards, L. R. 'War and Roses: The Politics of *Mrs Dalloway*'. In *The Authority of Experience: Essays in Feminist Criticism*, ed. A. Diamond and L. R. Edwards. Amherst: University of Massachusetts Press, 1977.
Forster, E. M. *Virginia Woolf*. Cambridge: Cambridge University Press, 1941.
Heilbrun, C. *Hamlet's Mother and Other Women*. New York: Columbia University Press, 1990.
Holroyd, M. *Lytton Strachey*. London: Heinemann, 1967.
Kenner, H. *A Sinking Island*. London: Barrie & Jenkins, 1988.
Love, J. O. *Worlds in Consciousness: Mythopoetic Thought in the Novels of Virginia Woolf*. Berkeley: University of California Press, 1970.
Marder, H. *Feminism and Art: A Study of Virginia Woolf*. Chicago and London: University of Chicago Press, 1968.
Parrinder, P. 'The Strange Necessity'. In *James Joyce: New Perspectives*, ed. C. MacCabe. Brighton: Harvester, 1982.
Richter, H. 'The *Ulysses* Connection: Clarissa Dalloway's Bloomsday'. *Studies in the Novel* 21.3 (1989), 305–19.
Samuelson, R. 'The Theme of Mrs Dalloway'. *Chicago Review* 11.4 (1958), 57–76.

CHAPTER THREE: WOOLF AND PHILOSOPHY

Benjamin, A. 'Towards an Understanding of the Meaning of Virginia Woolf's *Mrs Dalloway*'. *Wisconsin Studies in Contemporary Literature* 6.2 (1965), 214–27.
Gillies, M. A. *Henri Bergson and British Modernism*. Montreal: McGill-Queen's University Press, 1996.
Hussey, M. *The Singing of the Real World: The Philosophy of Virginia Woolf's Fiction*. Columbus: Ohio State University Press, 1986.
Kumar, S. K. *Bergson and the Stream of Consciousness Novel*. London and Glasgow: Blackie, 1962.
Naremore, J. *The World Without a Self: Virginia Woolf and the Novel*. New Haven, CT: Yale University Press, 1973.
Poole, R. *The Unknown Virginia Woolf*. Cambridge: Cambridge University Press, 1978.
Richter, H. *Virginia Woolf: The Inward Voyage*. Princeton, NJ: Princeton University Press, 1970.
Roberts, J. H. '"Vision and Design" in Virginia Woolf'. *PMLA* 61 (1946), 835–47.
Ruotolo, L. *Six Existential Heroes: The Politics of Faith*. Cambridge, MA: Harvard University Press, 1973.

CHAPTER FOUR: STRUCTURALISM AND POST-STRUCTURALISM

Armstrong, N. 'A Language of One's Own: Communication-Modeling Systems in *Mrs Dalloway*'. *Language and Style* 16.3 (1983), 343–60.

Bishop, E. 'Writing, Speech, and Silence in *Mrs Dalloway*'. *English Studies in Canada* 12.4 (1986), 397–423.

Caughie, P. *Virginia Woolf and Postmodernism: Literature in Quest and Question of Itself*. Urbana: University of Illinois Press, 1991.

Doherty, G. 'Life Styles and Death Sentences: The Dying Art of *Mrs Dalloway*'. In *Afterwords*, ed. N. Royle. Tampere, Finland: Outside Books, 1992.

Ebert, T. L. 'Metaphor, Metonymy, and Ideology: Language and Perception in *Mrs Dalloway*'. *Language and Style: An International Journal* 18.2 (1985), 152–64.

Gilbert, S. N. 'Woman's Sentence, Man's Sentencing: Linguistic Fantasies in Woolf and Joyce'. In *Virginia Woolf and Bloomsbury*, ed J. Marcus. Basingstoke: Macmillan, 1987.

Lodge, D. *The Modes of Modern Writing : Metaphor, Metonymy, and the Typology of Modern Literature*. London: Edward Arnold, 1977.

Marder, H. 'Split Perspective: Types of Incongruity in *Mrs Dalloway*'. *Papers on Language and Literature* 22.1 (1986), 51–69.

CHAPTER FIVE: WOOLF AND PSYCHOANALYSIS

Abel, E. 'Narrative Structure(s) and Female Development: The Case of *Mrs Dalloway*'. In *The Voyage In: Fictions of Female Development*, ed. E. Abel, M. Hirsch and E. Langland. Hanover, NH and London: University Press of New England, 1983.

Abel, E. *Virginia Woolf and the Fictions of Psychoanalysis*. Chicago and London : University of Chicago Press, 1989.

Briggs, M. 'Veterans and Civilians: Traumatic Knowledge and Cultural Appropriation in *Mrs Dalloway*'. In *Virginia Woolf and Communities: Selected Papers from the Eighth Annual Conference on Virginia Woolf*, ed. J. McVicker and L. Davis. New York: Pace University Press, 1999.

Dalziell, T. '"Why then grieve?": Virginia Woolf's Mournful Music'. *Modernist Cultures* 8 (2013), 82–99.

DeMeester, K. 'Trauma and Recovery in Virginia Woolf's *Mrs Dalloway*'. *MFS: Modern Fiction Studies* 44.3 (1998), 649–73.

Ferrer, D. *Virginia Woolf and the Madness of Language*, trans. G. Bennington and R. Bowlby. London: Routledge, 1990.

Flint, K. 'Peter Walsh's Pocket-Knife'. *Times Literary Supplement* (6 February 2004), 12–14.

Froula, C. '*Mrs Dalloway*'s Postwar Elegy: Women, War, and the Art of Mourning'. *Modernism/Modernity* 9.1 (2002), 125–63.

Henke, S. 'Virginia Woolf's Septimus Smith: An Analysis of "Paraphrenic" and the Schizophrenic Use of Language'. *Literature and Psychology* 31.4 (1981), 13–23.

Henke, S. 'Virginia Woolf and Post-Traumatic Subjectivity'. In *Virginia Woolf: Turning the Centuries*, ed. A. Ardis and B. K. Scott. New York: Pace University Press, 2000.

Henke, S., and D. Eberly, eds. *Virginia Woolf and Trauma: Embodied Texts*. New York: Pace University Press, 2007.

Little, J. *The Experimental Self*. Carbondale: Southern Illinois University Press, 1996.

Mepham, J. 'Mourning and Modernism'. In *Virginia Woolf : New Critical Essays*, ed. P. Clements and I. Grundy. London: Vision, 1983.

Minow-Pinkney, M. *Virginia Woolf and the Problem of the Subject*. Brighton: Harvester, 1987.

Schlack, B. A. 'A Freudian Look at *Mrs Dalloway*'. *Literature and Psychology* 23 (1973), 49–58.

Smith, S. B. 'Reinventing Grief Work: Virginia Woolf's Feminist Representations of Mourning in *Mrs Dalloway* and *To The Lighthouse*'. *Twentieth Century Literature: A Scholarly and Critical Journal* 41.4 (1995), 310–27.

Spilka, M. *Virginia Woolf's Quarrel with Grieving.* Lincoln: University of Nebraska Press, 1980.
Waugh, P. *Feminine Fictions: Revisiting the Postmodern.* London: Routledge, 1989.
Wyatt, J. 'Avoiding Self-Definition: In Defense of Women's Right to Merge (Julia Kristeva and *Mrs Dalloway*)'. *Women's Studies* 13 (1986), 115–26.

CHAPTER SIX: SEXUALITY AND THE BODY

Barrett, E. 'Unmasking Lesbian Passion: The Inverted World of *Mrs Dalloway*'. In *Virginia Woolf: Lesbian Readings*, ed. E. Barrett and P. Cramer. New York: New York University Press, 1997.
Brimstone, L. 'Towards a new Cartography: Radclyffe Hall, Virginia Woolf and the Working of Common Land'. In *What Lesbians Do in Books*, ed. E. Hobby and C. White. London: Women's Press, 1991.
Cook, B. W. 'Women Alone Stir My Imagination'. *Signs* 4 (1979), 718–39.
Cramer, P. 'Notes from Underground: Lesbian Ritual in the Writings of Virginia Woolf'. In *Virginia Woolf Miscellanies: Proceedings of the First Annual Conference on Virginia Woolf*, ed. M. Hussey and V. Neverow-Turk. New York: Pace University Press, 1992.
Fulker, T. 'Virginia Woolf's Daily Drama of the Body'. *Woolf Studies Annual* 1 (1995), 3–25.
Greenslade, W. *Degeneration, Culture and the Novel, 1880–1940.* Cambridge: Cambridge University Press, 1994.
Henke, S. '*Mrs Dalloway*: The Communion of Saints'. In *New Feminist Essays on Virginia Woolf*, ed. J. Marcus. Lincoln: University of Nebraska Press, 1981.
Jensen, E. 'Clarissa Dalloway's Respectable Suicide'. In *Virginia Woolf: A Feminist Slant*, ed. J. Marcus. Lincoln: University of Nebraska Press, 1983.
Lorde, A. 'The Erotic as Power'. In *The Audre Lorde Compendium: Essays, Speeches and Journals.* London: Pandora, 1996.
Lyon, G. E. 'Virginia Woolf and the Problem of the Body'. In *Virginia Woolf: Centennial Essays*, ed. E. K. Ginsberg and L. M. Gottlieb. Troy, NY: Whitston, 1983.
Marcus, J. 'Quentin's Bogey'. *Critical Inquiry* 2.3 (1985), 486–97.
Moran, Pat. *Word of Mouth: Body Language in Katherine Mansfield and Virginia Woolf.* Charlottesville and London: University Press of Virginia, 1996.
Rich, A. 'Compulsory Heterosexuality and Lesbian Existence'. *Signs* 5.4 (1980), 631–60.
Rogat, E. H. 'The Virgin in the Bell Biography'. *Twentieth Century Literature* 20 (1974), 96–113.
Roof, J. 'The Match in the Crocus'. In *Discontented Discourses: Feminism/Textual Intervention/Psychoanalysis*, ed. M. S. Barr and R. Feldstein. Urbana: University of Illinois Press, 1989.
Simpson, K. '"Queer Fish": Woolf's Writing of Desire between Women in *The Voyage Out* and *Mrs Dalloway*'. *Woolf Studies Annual* 9 (2003), 55–82.
Smith, P. J. *Lesbian Panic: Homoeroticism in Modern British Women's Fiction.* New York: Columbia University Press, 1997.
Taylor, N. 'Erasure of Definition: Androgyny in *Mrs Dalloway*'. *Women's Studies: An Interdisciplinary Journal* 18.4 (1991), 367–77.

CHAPTER SEVEN: HISTORICIST APPROACHES

Abbott, R. 'What Miss Kilman's Petticoat Means: Virginia Woolf, Shopping, and Spectacle'. *Modern Fiction Studies* 38.1 (1992), 193–214.
Blanchard, M. 'Socialization in *Mrs Dalloway*'. *College English* 34.2 (1972), 287–305.
Bowlby, R. 'Walking, Women, and Writing'. In *Feminist Destinations and Further Essays on Virginia Woolf.* Edinburgh: Edinburgh University Press, 1997.
Bradshaw, D. 'Introduction'. In *Mrs Dalloway*, ed. D. Bradshaw. Oxford: Oxford University Press, 2000.
Bradshaw, D. '"Vanished, Like Leaves": The Military, Elegy and Italy in *Mrs Dalloway*'. *Woolf Studies Annual* 8 (2002), 107–25.
Cohen, S. 'The Empire from the Street: Virginia Woolf, Wembley, and Imperial Monuments'. *MFS: Modern Fiction Studies* 50.1 (2004), 85–109.

Flint, K. 'Sounds of the City: Virginia Woolf and Modern Noise'. In *Literature, Science, Psychoanalysis, 1830–1970*, ed. H. Small and T. Tate. Oxford: Oxford University Press, 2003.

Frattarola, A. 'Listening for "Found Sound" Samples in the Novels of Virginia Woolf'. *Woolf Studies Annual* 11 (2005), 133–59.

Graham, E., and P. Lewis. 'Private Religion, Public Mourning, and *Mrs Dalloway*', *Modern Philology* 111.1 (2013), 88–106.

Hankins, L. K. 'Virginia Woolf and Walter Benjamin: Selling Out(Siders)'. In *Virginia Woolf in the Age of Mechanical Reproduction*, ed. P. Caughie. New York: Garland, 2000.

Ingelbien, R. 'They Saw One They Knew: Baudelaire and the Ghosts of London Modernism'. *English Studies: A Journal of English Language and Literature* 88.1 (2007), 43–58.

Levenback, K. L. 'Virginia Woolf and Returning Soldiers: The Great War and the Reality of Survival in *Mrs Dalloway* and *The Years*'. *Woolf Studies Annual* 2 (1996), 71–88.

Meyer, J. '"Not Septimus Now": Wives of Disabled Veterans and Cultural Memory of the First World War in Britain'. *Women's History Review* 13.1 (2004), 117–38.

Peach, L. *Virginia Woolf*. Basingstoke: Palgrave Macmillan, 2000.

Randall, B, and J. Goldman, eds. *Virginia Woolf in Context*. Cambridge: Cambridge University Press, 2011.

Rounds, A. L. 'Dissolves in *Mrs Dalloway*: The Soundscape of a Novel'. *Literary Imagination* 13.1 (2011), 58–70.

Schröder, L. K. '*Mrs Dalloway* and the Female Vagrant'. *Essays in Criticism* 45 (1995), 324–46.

Shaffer, B. W. 'Civilization in Bloomsbury: Woolf's *Mrs Dalloway* and Bell's "Theory of Civilization"'. *Journal of Modern Literature* 19.1 (1994), 73–87.

Snaith, A., and M. H. Whitworth, eds. *Locating Woolf: The Politics of Space and Place*. Basingstoke: Palgrave Macmillan, 2007.

Son, Y. *Here and Now: The Politics of Social Space in D.H. Lawrence and Virginia Woolf*. Abingdon: Routledge, 2006.

Squier, S. M. *Virginia Woolf and London*. Chapel Hill: University of North Carolina Press, 1985.

Tambling, J. 'Repression in *Mrs Dalloway*'. *Essays in Criticism* 39 (1989), 137–55.

Tate, T. '*Mrs Dalloway* and the Armenian Question'. *Textual Practice* 8.3 (1994), 467–86.

Thomas, S. 'Virginia Woolf's Septimus Smith and Contemporary Perceptions of Shell Shock'. *English Language Notes* 25.2 (1987), 49–5.

Usui, M. 'The Female Victims of the War in *Mrs Dalloway*'. In *Virginia Woolf and War: Fiction, Reality, and Myth*, ed. M. Hussey. Syracuse, NY: Syracuse University Press, 1991.

Whitworth, M. H. *Virginia Woolf*. Oxford: Oxford University Press, 2005.

Wicke, J. '*Mrs. Dalloway* Goes to Market: Woolf, Keynes, and Modern Markets'. *NOVEL: A Forum on Fiction* 28.1 (1994), 5–23.

Zwerdling, A. '*Mrs Dalloway* and the Social System'. *PMLA* 92 (1977), 69–82.

Zwerdling, A. *Virginia Woolf and the Real World*. Berkeley and London: University of California Press, 1986.

CHAPTER EIGHT: *MRS DALLOWAY* AND *THE HOURS*

Alley, H. '*Mrs Dalloway* and Three of Its Contemporary Children'. *Papers on Language and Literature: A Journal for Scholars and Critics of Language and Literature* 42.4 (2006), 401–19.

Chatman, S. '*Mrs Dalloway*'s Progeny: *The Hours* as Second-Degree Narrative'. In *A Companion to Narrative Theory*, ed. J. Phelan and P. J. Rabinowitz. Malden, MA: Blackwell, 2005.

Haffey, K. 'Exquisite Moments and the Temporality of the Kiss in *Mrs. Dalloway* and *The Hours*'. *Narrative* 18.2 (2010), 137–62.

Hardy, S. B. 'The Unanchored Self in *The Hours* after Dalloway'. *Critique: Studies in Contemporary Fiction* 52.4 (2011), 400–11.

Hughes, M. J. 'Michael Cunningham's *The Hours* and Postmodern Artistic Re-Presentation'. *Critique: Studies in Contemporary Fiction* 45.4 (2004), 349–61.

Latham, M. 'Variations on *Mrs. Dalloway*: Rachel Cusk's *Arlington Park*'. *Woolf Studies Annual* 19 (2013), 195–213.

Leavenworth, M. L. 'A Life as Potent and Dangerous as Literature Itself': Intermediated Moves from *Mrs Dalloway* to *The Hours*'. *Journal of Popular Culture* 43.3 (2010), 503–23.

Poster, J. '*Five Bells* by Gail Jones'. *Guardian* (19 March 2011).

Schiff, J. 'Rewriting Woolf's *Mrs Dalloway*: Homage, Sexual Identity, and the Single-Day Novel by Cunningham, Lippincott, and Lanchester'. *Critique: Studies in Contemporary Fiction* 45.4 (2004), 363–82.

Spengler, B. 'Michael Cunningham Rewriting Virginia Woolf: Pragmatist vs. Modernist Aesthetics'. *Woolf Studies Annual* 10 (2004), 51–79.

CONCLUSION

Alt, C. *Virginia Woolf and the Study of Nature*. Cambridge: Cambridge University Press, 2010.

Berman, J. 'Ethical Folds: Ethics, Aesthetics, Woolf'. *MFS: Modern Fiction Studies* 50.1 (2005), pp. 151–72.

Berman, J. 'Neither Mirror Nor Mimic: Transnational Reading and Indian Narratives in English'. In *The Oxford Handbook of Global Modernisms* ed. M. A. Wollaeger and M. Eatough. Oxford: Oxford University Press, 2012.

Covington, E. 'Splitting the Husk: The Day Novel and Storm Jameson's *A Day Off*. *Genre: Forms of Discourse and Culture* 46.3 (2013), 265–84.

Dunlap, S. '"One Must Be Scientific": Natural History and Ecology in *Mrs Dalloway*', in *Interdisciplinary / Multidisciplinary Woolf: Selected Papers from the Twenty-Second Annual International Conference on Virginia Woolf*, ed. A. Martin and K. Holland. Clemson, SC: Clemson University Digital Press, 2013.

Hickman, V. R. 'Clarissa and the Coolies' Wives: *Mrs Dalloway* Figuring Transnational Feminism'. *MFS: Modern Fiction Studies* 60.1 (2014), 52–77.

Jones, C. 'Virginia Woolf's 1931 "Cook Sketch"'. *Woolf Studies Annual* 20 (2014), 1–24.

Kostkowska, J. *Ecocriticism And Women Writers: Environmentalist Poetics of Virginia Woolf, Jeanette Winterson, and Ali Smith*. New York: Palgrave Macmillan, 2013.

Scott, B. K. *In the Hollow of the Wave: Virginia Woolf and Modernist Uses of Nature*. Charlottesville: University of Virginia Press, 2012.

Sherman, D. 'A Plot Unraveling into Ethics: Woolf, Levinas, and "Time Passes"'. *Woolf Studies Annual* 13 (2007), pp. 159–80.

Sim, L. *Virginia Woolf: The Patterns of Ordinary Experience*. Farnham: Ashgate, 2010.

Swanson, D. L. 'Woolf's Copernican Shift: Nonhuman Nature in Virginia Woolf's Short Fiction'. *Woolf Studies Annual* 18 (2012), 53–74.

Tromanhauser, V. '*Mrs Dalloway*'s Animals and the Humanist Laboratory'. *Twentieth Century Literature* 58.2 (2012), 187–12.

Westling, L. 'Virginia Woolf and the Flesh of the World'. *New Literary History* 30.4 (1999), 855–75.

Index

Abbott, Reginald 138–9
Abel, Elizabeth 91–3, 152
adaptations of *Mrs Dalloway* 148–56, 159
aeroplane 65, 72, 117, 135–6
Alexander, Jean 50
Alt, Christina 159
Althusser, Louis 128
Anand, Mulk Raj 159
androgyny 80–1, 95–6
animal studies 159
Armenian genocide 49, 133
Armstrong, Nancy 76–80, 82
atheism 124
Auerbach, Erich 96

Bakhtin, Mikhail 139, 143
Banfield, Ann 71–3
Barrett, Eileen 120–3
Bast, Leonard 8
Bazin, Nancy 80, 88
beggar woman (character) 98
Bell, Clive 142–3
Bell, Quentin 125; biography of Woolf 34–5, 66, 87, 111
Benjamin, Anna 55
Benjamin, Walter 141
Bennett, Arnold 2, 12, 77, 155
Bennett, Joan 5–6, 18–20
Bentley, Mr (character) 117
Bergson, Henri 11, 16, 58–61
Berman, Jessica 159
Bishop, Edward 82–3
Blackstone, Bernard 20–2, 129
Bloomsbury Group 124–6, 142–7
Bourton 61, 70, 92–3, 112
Bowlby, Rachel 141–2
Bowley, Mr (character) 97
Bradbrook, Frank 6
Bradbrook, Muriel 14
Bradbury, Malcolm 136
Bradshaw, David 130, 131–2, 158

Bradshaw, Sir William (character) 31–2, 45–6, 67, 78–9, 104–5; a 'one-dimensional' portrait 47–8
Brenan, Gerald 130
Brewster, Dorothy 136
Brierly, Professor (character) 78
Briggs, Marlene 106–7
British Council 124
Brower, Reuben 22–6
Brush, Milly (character) 105
Bruton, Lady (character) 121–2
Bullett, Gerald 52

Cambridge 125
Camus, Albert 61
Carpenter, Edward 121
Caruth, Cathy 106
Caughie, Pamela 84–5
caves, beautiful (Woolf, *Diary*) 27, 60
Cézanne, Paul 9, 55
characters, central 5, 46
characters, minor 151; function of 97
Chatman, Seymour 149–51
Chodorow, Nancy 94
cinema 10
city 136–42 *see also* London
civilization 142–3
Clarke, Stuart N. 158
Cixous, Hélène 90
class, social 46–7, 116–17
clocks 58–61
close reading 22
colonialism 79
companions 121
condition-of-England novel 29, 151
consumerism 138–9
Cook, Blanche Wiesen 110
counter-culture 125
Covington, Elizabeth 159
Cramer, Patricia 120
Criminal Law Amendment Act (1885) 121
Cunningham, Michael, *The Hours* 148–56

175

INDEX

Daiches, David, and John Flower 136
Daily News 9
Dalgarno, Emily 85
Dalloway, Clarissa (character) 1, 6, 133–4
   as *flâneuse* 142
   as Gemini 41
   as goddess 49
   as heroine 6, 62–4, 83–4
   as hostess 45, 78
   as object of satire 6, 83–4, 133–5
   as virginal 30
   date of birth 128
   multiple identities 70, 94
   see also lesbianism; transcendental theory
Dalloway, Elizabeth (character) 93
de Beauvoir, Simone 43
De Courtrivon, Isabelle 90, 91
degeneration 118
Delattre, Floris 16
DeMeester, Karen 107–8
Dempster, Carrie (character) 117
Derrida, Jacques 82
DeSalvo, Louise 106
Dickinson, Goldsworthy Lowes 122, 124
Dickinson, Violet 92
doctors 118
Doherty, Gerald 85
Doyle, Laura 159
dread 63–4
Duckworth, George 105
Dunlap, Sara 159

Eberly, David 106
Ebert, Teresa L. 80–1
ecocriticism 159
Edel, Leon 42
Edwardians 77
Edwards, Lee R. 46–9
elegy 102–5, 145
Eliade, Mircea 31
Eliot, T. S. 2
   opinion of Joyce's *Ulysses* 38
Ellis, Havelock 121
embodiment 66–71, 114–16
Empire, British 128, 132–6, 140–1, 150
ethical turn 159
Evans (character) 88
existentialism 61–5

Felman, Shoshana 105
feminism, second-wave 43
film adaptations 159
Finsbury Pavement (London) 131–2
flâneur/flâneuse 141–2
Fleishman, Avrom, 28–32; challenged by Lee R. Edwards 46, 49
Flint, Kate 146–7
form 9, 22; integration of past and present 27
formalism, Russian 97
Forster, E. M. 33
   Howards End 8, 119
   Maurice 121
   on absence of philosophy in Woolf's fiction 51
Foucault, Michel 111, 118–19, 128–9
Frankl, Viktor 108
Frattarola, Angela 146–7
Freud, Sigmund 86–7
   Civilization and its Discontents 94, 102
   Future of an Illusion, The 102
   'On Narcissism' 89
Friedman, Susan Stanford 158
Froula, Christine 102–5; criticisms of 144
Fry, Roger 9, 53, 125
   Transformations 53
   Vision and Design 53
Frye, Northrop 31
Fulker, Teresa 115–17

Galsworthy, John 8
Garnett, David, review of *The Years* 52
Gillies, Mary Ann 60–1
Glaxo 136
Gorris, Marleen, *Mrs Dalloway* (film) 148, 159
Graham, Elyse, and Pericles Lewis 143–6
Graham, J. W. 59–60
Greenslade, William 118–9
Gruber, Ruth 17
Guiguet, Jean, 26–8; criticism of Bernard Blackstone 21

Haffey, Kate 152–6
Hafley, James 59
Haldane, Lord 132
Hamilton, Cicely 120
Harcourt Brace (publishers) 2

INDEX 177

Heidegger, Martin 61, 62
Heilbrun, Carolyn, 38–9
Henke, Suzette 83, 89–90, 106, 113
  DeMeester's criticism of 108
Herman, Judith 106
Hickman, Valerie Reed 158
Hilbery, Mrs (character) 89
Hogarth Press 2
Hollingsworth, Keith 86
Holroyd, Michael 33–4, 125
Holtby, Winifred 16
Hughes, Richard 8, 9, 19, 52
Humm, Maggie 158
Husserl, Edmund 56, 67
Hussey, Mark 68–70, 115
Hutton, Jim (character) 78, 88
Hyslop, T. B. 118

imagery 23
  bird 30
inauthenticity 61–2
India 127
Ingelbien, Raphaël 146
interruption 111–12
Irigaray, Luce 90

Jakobson, Roman 75, 80
James, William 11, 16
Jameson, Storm 159
Jensen, Emily 111–14
Johnstone, J. K. 125
Jones, Clara 158
Jones, Gail, *Five Bells* 156
Joyce, James, *Ulysses* 8–9, 12–13, 18, 35–41, 37, 116

kangaroo 92
Keats, John 87–8
Kenner, Hugh 37
Kermode, Frank 70–1
Keynes, John Maynard 102, 144
  'My Early Beliefs' 124
Kierkegaard, Søren 61
Kilman, Miss (character) 113–14, 117, 122–3
King's College, Cambridge 18
Knox-Shaw, Peter 107
Kore Schröder, Leena 139–41
Kostkowska, Justyna 159

Kristeva, Julia 90, 91, 93–9, 128
Krutch, Joseph Wood 8–9, 11
Kumar, Shiv 59

Labour Party 127
Lacan, Jacques 90–1
Latham, Monica 156
Laub, Dori 105
Lawrence, D. H. 13, 14
  compared to Woolf 53
Leaska, Mitchell 50
Leavis, F. R. 14–15
Lee, Hermione 71
Lehmann, John 111
leitmotif 112
lesbianism 110–14, 120–3
Levenback, Karen 131
Lévi-Strauss, Claude 74
Lewis, Wyndham 12–13, 134
Liberal Party 127
Lippincott, Robin 148
literary theory 127
Literature and Psychology 86
Little, Judy, criticism of Minow-Pinkney 99
Lodge, David 75–6
London 81, 136–42
Lord, Mary Louise 31
Lorde, Audre 110
Lotman, Yuri 77
Lynd, Sylvia 7
Lyon, George Ella 114–15

manliness 47
Mansfield, Katherine 2
Marcus, Jane 111
Marder, Herbert
  Feminism and Art 43–6
  'Split Perspective' 83–4
Marks, Elaine 90, 91
materialist novelists 115
Maxse, Kitty 103–4
McAfee, Helen 9
McDowall, Arthur Sydney 8, 10–11
McNichol, Stella 2
McTaggart, J. 124–5
medicine 118
Mellers, W. H. 14
memory 60–1
menopause 116

178 INDEX

Mepham, John 100
Merleau-Ponty, M. 67
metaphor 75–6, 80–1
metonymy 75–6, 80–1
Meyer, Jessica 132
militarism 129–32
Minow-Pinkney, Makiko 95–9, 134
modernism 35
Moore, G. E. 19, 53, 56, 124, 125, 159
motor-car 46
mourning 99–105, 143–6

Naremore, James 64–5, 84
narratology 149–51
Nation and Athenaeum 144
New Criticism 19, 22, 112
New French Feminisms 90, 91
New Stateman 8, 9–10, 51

Ong, Walter J. 82
orality 82
Owen, Wilfred 129

Page, Alex 86
Page, Norman 83
Park, Sowon 120
Parrinder, Patrick 36–7
Partridge, Ralph 130
pattern 22
Pearce, Richard 127
phenomenological approaches, criticisms of 70–1
phenomenology 56, 66–71
Phillips, Kathy 135–6
philosophy 51–73
  comments in early reviews 51–3
  see also Bergson; existentialism; phenomenology; Russell
Pirandello, Luigi, compared to Woolf 52
poem, *Mrs Dalloway* as 42
Poole, Roger 66–8, 106, 114
Post-Impressionism 53
post-structuralism 82
Poster, Jem 156
Pre-Oedipal 91–3, 96
Proportion 78–9, 84
Proust, Marcel 13
psychoanalysis 86–109

Rantavaara, Irma 124–5
Raverat, Gwen, letter to Woolf 9
reader, ordinary 79–80
realism, psychological 16
reception theory 83
religion 143–6
rhythm 94–5
Rich, Adrienne 110–11, 114
Richardson, Dorothy 9
Richter, Harvena
  'The Ulysses Connection' 39–41
  Virginia Woolf 55–8
Roberts, John Hawley 53–5
Rogat, Ellen Hawkes 111
Rose, Phyllis 84
Rosenbaum, S. P. 125, 158
Rounds, Anne L. 146–7
Royde-Smith, Naomi 9
Ruotolo, Lucio 62–4
Russell, Bertrand 51, 71–2
Rylands, George 18

Sacks, Peter 102
Sackville-West, Vita 111
sacrifice 144–5
Said, Edward 133
Samuelson, Ralph 42–3
Sartre, Jean-Paul 61
Sassoon, Siegfried 129
satire, *Mrs Dalloway* as 6, 9, 83–4, 133–5
Saussure, Ferdinand de 74, 77
Savage, D. S. 42
Savage, George 118
Schiff, James 148–9, 152
Schlack, Beverly Ann 86
Scott, Bonnie Kime 159
Scrutiny 12, 14–15
semiotic, the (Kristeva) 94–5
semiotics, Tartu-Moscow school of 77
sensibility 33
Seton, Sally (character) 121
sexuality 110–14, 120–3; avoidance of 21–2
Shaffer, Brian 142–3
Shakespeare, William 23, 82–3; *Cymbeline*, 20, 23, 52, 88; *Othello*, 20
shell-shock 130
Shelley, Percy Bysshe, *Adonaïs* 87–8, 103, 116; 'Ozymandias' 101

Shone, Richard 125
shopping 138–9, 141
Silver, Brenda, criticism of Herbert Marder. 44
Sim, Lorraine 159
Sinclair, May 9, 11
single-day novel 148–9
Smith, Rezia (Lucrezia) Warren (character) 7, 63, 93, 132
Smith, Septimus Warren (character) 67–8, 89, 98–9, 129–31
   as Clarissa's double 2, 93
   as scapegoat 29–30
   as schizophrenic 57
   scenes, irrelevance of 6, 7
   suicide of 24–5, 63–4, 123
Smith, Susan Bennett 100–2
Smyth, Ethel 111
Snaith, Anna, and Michael H. Whitworth 146
social system (Woolf, *Diary*) 2, 41–2, 126
solitary traveller passage 25, 30, 78
Son, Youngjoo 146
Spears, Monroe K. 136
Spilka, Mark 71, 87–9
Squier, Susan Merrill 136–8
Stephen, Julia 88
   death of 87, 89, 92, 114–15
Stevenson, R. L. 8
Strachey, Lytton 18, 84
structuralist approaches 74–85
structuralist linguistics 74–5
structure 22
style 56–7, 64–5, 94–5
stylistic analysis 96
Sylvia (character) 88, 92–3, 104
symbolism, phallic 86
Symonds, John Addington 121

Tambling, Jeremy 128–9, 133
Tate, Trudi, 133–5
temporality, queer 152
Thomas, Sue 130–1
time 58–61
Time and Tide 7
Times Literary Supplement 8
tragedy, Mrs Dalloway as 9
transcendental theory (Clarissa's) 65, 96, 125, 145
transnational criticism 158
trauma 105–9
Tromanhauser, Vicki 159
Trombley, Stephen 131
tunnelling (Woolf, *Diary*) 27, 60
Turkle, Sherry 90
Turnell, G. M. 12

unanimisme 103
unity 23, 84–5, 97
Usui, Masami 132

vagrants 139–41
values 18
Vaughan, Madge 121
Vietnam War 1

Walsh, Peter (character) 25
war 129–32
Western Mail 7
Whitbread, Hugh (character) 105, 139
Whitworth, Michael H. 151
Williams, Raymond 136
Woolf, Leonard 86, 144
   Autobiography 34
   Empire and Commerce in Africa 135
Woolf, Philip 129
Woolf, Virginia
   biographical accounts of 33–5
   denial of interest in philosophy 59
   doctors 118
   as 'invalid of Bloomsbury' 20, 33–4, 37
   WORKS:
   Carlyle's House and Other Sketches 158
   'Character in Fiction' 13
   The Hours (draft version of *Mrs Dalloway*) 1–2, 42, 102, 105
   'Introduction to *Mrs Dalloway*' 2, 27, 54, 84, 87
   Jacob's Room 12, 27
   'Memories of a Working Women's Guild' 116–17
   'Modern Fiction' 15, 36
   'Modern Novels' 1, 116
   Moments of Being 87
   'Mr Bennett and Mrs Brown' 53, 116
   'Mrs Dalloway in Bond Street' 1, 116, 87, 103–4, 145

Woolf, Virginia (*continued*)
  Mrs Dalloway's Party 2
  Night and Day 89
  'The Novels of George Meredith'
    52–3
  'On Being Ill' 116
  'Sketch of the Past' 60, 84, 114
  'Street Haunting' 140
  Three Guineas 43
  'Thunder at Wembley' 140
  To the Lighthouse 14, 15
  '*Twelfth Night* at the Old Vic' 82–3
  Voyage Out, The 1, 115
  Writer's Diary, A 2, 26, 41, 43, 157–8

Wussow, Helen 2
Wyatt, Jean 93–5

Yale Review 9

Zwerdling, Alex 84, 126–7, 129, 132–3
  criticisms of 127

Printed by Printforce, the Netherlands